This book is a major contribution to the history of analytic philosophy in general and of logical positivism in particular. It provides the first detailed and comprehensive study of Rudolf Carnap, one of the most influential figures in twentieth-century philosophy.

The focus of the book is Carnap's first major work, *Der logische Aufbau der Welt* (The logical structure of the world). It reveals tensions in that work by placing it within the context of German epistemology and philosophy of science in the early twentieth century. Alan Richardson argues that Carnap's move to philosophy of science in the 1930s was largely an attempt to resolve the tension in his early epistemology.

This book fills a significant gap in the literature on the history of twentieth-century philosophy. It will be of particular importance to historians of analytic philosophy, philosophers of science, and historians of science.

Carnap's construction of the world

Carnap's construction of the world

The *Aufbau* and the emergence of logical empiricism

ALAN W. RICHARDSON
University of British Columbia

CAMBRIDGE
UNIVERSITY PRESS

PUBLISHED BY THE PRESS SYNDICATE OF THE UNIVERSITY OF CAMBRIDGE
The Pitt Building, Trumpington Street, Cambridge CB2 1RP, United Kingdom

CAMBRIDGE UNIVERSITY PRESS
The Edinburgh Building, Cambridge CB2 2RU, United Kingdom
40 West 20th Street, New York, NY 10011-4211, USA
10 Stamford Road, Oakleigh, Melbourne 3166, Australia

© Cambridge University Press 1998

This book is in copyright. Subject to statutory exception
and to the provisions of relevant collective licensing agreements,
no reproduction of any part may take place without
the written permission of Cambridge University Press.

First published 1998

Printed in the United States of America

Typeset in Palatino

Library of Congress Cataloging-in-Publication Data
Richardson, Alan W.
Carnap's construction of the world : the 'Aufbau' and the
emergence of logical empiricism / Alan W. Richardson.
p.   cm.
Includes bibliographical references and index.
ISBN 0-521-43008-9 (hardcover)
1. Carnap, Rudolf, 1891–1970. – Logische Aufbau der Welt.
2. Knowledge, Theory of – History – 20th century.   3. Logical
positivism – History – 20th century.   I. Title.
B945.C163L6336   1997
121 – dc21   97-8814
                                           CIP

A catalog record for this book is available from the British Library.

ISBN 0 521 43008 9 hardback

To my mother and father
Elizabeth Catherine Fredricks Richardson
and
Edward Thompson Richardson

Die Gesamtheit und die Stufenfolge der reinen "Reihenformen" liegt im System der Wissenschaften, insbesondere im Aufbau der exakten Wissenschaft, vor uns. Hier findet daher die Theorie ein reiches und fruchtbares Gebiet, das unabhängig von jeder metaphysischen und psychologischen Voraussetzung über das "Wesen" des Begriffs, lediglich seinem logischen Gehalt nach untersucht werden kann. Diese Selbstständigkeit der reinen Logik aber bedeutet keineswegs ihre Isolierung innerhalb des philosophischen Systems. Schon ein flüchtiger Überblick über die Entwicklung der "formalen" Logik konnte uns zeigen, wie hier allmählich die dogmatische Starrheit der traditionellen Formen sich zu lösen beginnt. Und die neue Form, die sich jetzt herauszubilden beginnt, bedeutet zugleich die form für einen neuen Inhalt. Psychologie und Erkenntniskritik, das Problem des *Bewusstseins* wie das Problem der *Wirklichkeit* nehmen an diesem Prozess teil. Denn innerhalb der Grundprobleme gibt es nirgends absolute Trennungen und Grenzscheiden: jede Umgestaltung eines im echten und fruchtbaren Sinne 'formalen' Begriffs zieht hier zugleich eine neue Auffassung des gesamten Gebietes nach sich, das durch ihn beherrscht und geordnet wird.

Ernst Cassirer (1910)

Also es ist kein Zweifel, wir müssen uns in historische Betrachtungen vertiefen, wenn wir uns als Philosophen und das, was in uns als Philosophie werden will, sollen verstehen können . . . Die historische Besinnung, die wir hier im Auge haben müssen, betrifft unsere Existenz als Philosophen und korrelativ die Existenz der Philosophie, die ihrerseits ist aus unserer Existenz.

Edmund Husserl (1954)

Contents

Acknowledgments		*page* ix
Introduction		1
1	Reconstructing the *Aufbau*	5
	Fundamentals of the epistemology of the *Aufbau*	6
	The received view of the *Aufbau*	10
	Russell's external world program	13
	Carnap's *Aufbau* and Russell's external world program	22
	The *Aufbau* in context	28
2	The problem of objectivity: An overview of Carnap's constitutional project	31
	Knowledge versus experience: The problem of subjective origins	32
	Structure and objectivity	35
	Purely structural definite description	47
	Quasi analysis	51
	Goodman's objections to quasi analysis	59
3	An outline of the constitutional projects for objectivity	65
	The lowest levels of the constitutional system	65
	The constitution of the world of physics	70
	The constitution of the intersubjective world	76
	The elimination of Rs	87
	The problem of objectivity	89
4	The background to early Carnap: Themes from Kant	92
	The Kantian problematic	92
	The various notions of the synthetic *a priori*	101
5	The fundamentals of neo-Kantian epistemology	116
	Transcendental and formal logic	117

	Conventionalism and the logic of objective knowledge	124
	Problems for the neo-Kantians	134
	The transition to Carnap	138
6	Carnap's neo-Kantian origins: *Der Raum*	139
	Logic and convention: Mathematical and physical space	140
	Intuition and spatial knowledge	153
7	Critical conventionalism	159
	On the task of physics	159
	The three-dimensionality of space and causality	167
	The temporal determination of space	172
	The general conventionalism of *Physikalische Begriffsbildung*	175
	Critical conventionalism and the *Aufbau*	180
8	Epistemology between logic and science: The essential tension	183
	The unity of science and logical convention	184
	Epistemology as empirical science	187
	Epistemology as formal science	191
	Logical empiricism	197
	The *Aufbau* in the formal mode of speech	198
9	After objectivity: Logical empiricism as philosophy of science	207
	From epistemology to the logic of science	207
	Toward a logical point of view	213
	One dogma of the logic of science	217
	The point of the logic of science	225

Bibliography	230
Index	239

Acknowledgments

In nearly every life, I suspect, there are occurrences of good fortune whose true impact first becomes manifest some years later. For me, professionally, this occurred when, as an undergraduate, I found myself at the University of Pennsylvania during the few years when Thomas Ricketts and Michael Friedman were both in the Department of Philosophy there. I, as a result, came to be philosophically shaped early on by two people of great philosophical creativity and historical sensitivity. It is little wonder, then, that I subsequently sought out Michael Friedman to serve as my dissertation director, when I came to realize that my main interest was in the history of analytic philosophy. This work is a distant descendant of the dissertation that Friedman directed. Most of what I know about how to approach figures in the history of analytic philosophy was learned from Friedman and Ricketts, and I expect to learn a great deal again from the objections that these philosophers will raise to this work.

I have had the good fortune to have traveled widely during my early philosophical career. I have learned much about the history of analytic philosophy, about history and philosophy of science, and about philosophy in general from many friends and colleagues along the way. Among those whose influence on these pages is larger than they might expect or even notice are Jane Camerini, Jonathan Dancy, Gary Ebbs, Arthur Fine, Janet Folina, Peter Galison, Ronald Giere, Geoffrey Gorham, Andy Hamilton, Ernst Hamm, Gary Hatfield, Geoffrey Hellman, Philip Kitcher, Patricia Ross, Thomas A. Ryckman, Steven Shapin, Lawrence Shapiro, Miriam Solomon, David Sullivan, Thomas Uebel, and Bas van Fraassen. I also have the good fortune to be less likely to be traveling quite so much in the near future. For this I would like to thank my colleagues at the University of British Columbia, especially Steven Savitt, Catherine Talmage, Earl Winkler, and Stephen Straker.

The research leading to this work was funded by a postdoctoral

Acknowledgments

fellowship at the University of Pennsylvania and also by a grant from the National Science Foundation (number DIR-9105217), a Leverhulme Postdoctoral Research Fellowship at the University of Keele, and a postdoctoral year at the Science Studies Program at the University of California at San Diego. My research has also been aided by the Archives for Scientific Philosophy in the Twentieth Century at the University of Pittsburgh. Many thanks to Gerald Heverly for his help and also to the University of Pittsburgh for permission to cite and quote unpublished material. This work incorporates, as well, material from essays of mine that have appeared in *Proceedings of the Philosophy of Science Association, Synthese, Grazer Philosophische Studien, Proceedings of the Aristotelian Society,* and *Minnesota Studies for the Philosophy of Science.* In almost every case, the wording, and at times the view put forward, have been substantially altered. I would like to thank the editors of these journals and books for permission to use this material.

Various drafts of this book were my constant companions for (too) many years as I wandered the earth, seeking my place in the world of philosophy. Therefore, it has also been the companion of some other persons for a time. I would like to thank Melanie Morton, Lisa Morin, and Shannon Shea for inspiration, forbearance, food, and fun during various trying times. What more have I to offer you?

Introduction

THIS study examines a particular portion of Rudolf Carnap's philosophical career, from a particular point of view. The period covered is roughly the fifteen years from Carnap's first publication – his 1922 dissertation, *Der Raum* – to the full flowering of his theory of the logical syntax of scientific language in his 1934 book, *Die logische Syntax der Sprache* and his seminal 1936–7 paper, "Testability and Meaning." Although in the final chapter I speak to some central issues in the analyticity debate, I make no claim to deal with the details of Carnap's semantic period, for by the syntax period his general philosophical orientation had already been set, and those details are largely irrelevant for the story I want to tell. That is the story of Carnap's thinking about what it is to have an epistemology of empirical knowledge. The principal text for the story is Carnap's first book, *Der logische Aufbau der Welt* (The logical structure of the world; hereafter *Aufbau*). This was his most detailed and influential statement of a project in general epistemology. It contrasts both with the methodological focus of his earliest essays and with the rejection of epistemology that marks his syntax period.

The account given is somewhat novel. It rejects the easy assimilation of Carnap's epistemological views to those of Bertrand Russell's "external world program." This rejection is guided by contextual and historiographic concerns. The Russellian perspective fails to engage with the text of the *Aufbau* in anything like its own terms. Rather, it imposes on it a philosophical perspective concerning epistemology that stands quite at odds with Carnap's own views of what epistemology is and what it is for. The first principle of the present study is, then, a desire to let Carnap's account of the epistemological problem and its solution take center stage. That account is, of course, one that he himself ultimately rejected when he rejected the entire project of the *Aufbau* in the mid-1930s.

Introduction

Carnap's account of the epistemological problem trades in the distinction between the objective and the subjective. He grants that knowledge begins in subjective streams of experience. This, however, is not the solution to the problem of knowledge but the very problem itself. Carnap's problem is how to account for the objectivity of knowledge despite its subjective origins. The problem itself and the role of formal notions in its solution, combined with indubitable facts about the sort of philosophical education Carnap received in the 1910s in Jena, reorient the story toward a rather different philosophical tradition from Russell's – the tradition of scientific neo-Kantianism that was in full flower in the Marburg and Southwest schools in the first quarter of the twentieth century. The philosophers principally associated with the Marburg school are Hermann Cohen, Paul Natorp, and Ernst Cassirer; those associated with the Southwest school include Heinrich Rickert and Wilhelm Windelband.[1]

Beyond the intrinsic philosophical interest in reading the *Aufbau* in light of the epistemological project with which Carnap himself claimed to be dealing, evaluating the work with an eye toward the distinction between the objective and the subjective raises *the* important interpretative difficulty with the work. Carnap claims to be giving an account of how objectivity in the empirical realm is possible, but in fact he gives *two* such accounts. By reading the *Aufbau* in the context of the stresses and strains inherent in scientific neo-Kantianism, I can make sense of why Carnap is compelled to provide two such accounts. Moreover, these stresses surely are the very ones that Carnap came to find unbearable by the mid-1930s when he argued against the traditional project of epistemology.

The present focus, then, is well within a new tradition in the interpretation of Carnap and some of his fellow logical empiricists, a tradition that finds Kantian and neo-Kantian themes to dominate the early thinking of these authors. I am greatly indebted to the pioneering work done by Susan Haack (1977), Werner Sauer (1985, 1989), and especially Michael Friedman (1983b, 1987, 1991, 1992a, 1996).[2] This research is itself

---

1 Neo-Kantianism never made as large an impact as it might have in the English-speaking world. Interest has been rekindled recently, although again mainly in the German-speaking world. See Köhnke (1986) and Schnädelbach (1983) for general histories of the movement. Recent readers of original materials are Flach and Ollig (1979–80) and Ollig (1982, 1987).
2 A recent dissenting view that urges a continued attractiveness to standard foundationalist views of Carnap's early work can be found in Hudson (1994). I have made no

Introduction

only one branch of a generally more philosophically and historically nuanced understanding of logical empiricism and its origins to be found in the work of a great many authors, including Nancy Cartwright and Jordi Cat (1996), Peter Galison (1990, 1996), Alberto Coffa (1991), Joelle Proust (1986/1989), Don Howard (1994, 1996), Thomas Ryckman (1991, 1992, 1996), Thomas Oberdan (1990, 1993, 1996), Thomas Uebel (1992a, 1992b, 1992c, 1996), Thomas Ricketts (1985, 1986, 1994), Warren Goldfarb (1988, 1996), Goldfarb and Ricketts (1992), Dan Isaacson (1992), Joia Lewis Turner (Lewis 1991, 1996), Richard Creath (1987, 1991b, 1996), and others.[3]

The present study falls into four general divisions. Chapters One through Three present the interpretative puzzle and provide a fairly detailed exegesis of Carnap's "constitutional" project. They concentrate on how this project is meant to fulfill the constraints of Carnap's two accounts of objectivity. Chapters Four and Five provide the historical background to this puzzle, presenting thumbnail sketches of relevant aspects of the Kantian and neo-Kantian understanding of the methodology of the exact sciences. Chapters Six and Seven provide highlights of Carnap's pre-*Aufbau* development, again with an eye toward the puzzle about objectivity. Chapters Eight and Nine, finally, present the reasons for Carnap's two projects for objectivity and argue that his ambivalence is the source of his rejection of epistemology. I shall show that, far from being an old empiricism in new logical clothing, Carnap's "logical empiricism" is a unique philosophical vision with implications for the possibility of a traditional epistemology that have yet to be noted. Indeed, by my account, W. V. Quine emerges as much the more traditional of the two voices in the Carnap–Quine debate on analyticity.

There are two larger arenas within which this study may prove useful. First, the notion of objectivity is increasingly the subject of discussion again these days, finding a place in current debates in fields such as metaphysics, epistemology, and moral theory. Indeed, the concept lends itself to such a wide use, for it seems to cut across cherished conceptual distinctions between, for example, metaphysical questions about reality (objectivity as objecthood) and epistemological questions about knowledge (objectivity as intersubjectivity). The present study is

---

effort to rebut Hudson on a point-by-point basis, preferring to let the story stand on its own; for a rebuttal of Hudson, see Uebel (1996).

3 See also the various papers in volumes such as Bell and Vossenkuhl (1992), Giere and Richardson (1996), Haller (1982), Haller and Stadler (1993), Rescher (1985), Salmon and Wolters (1994), Stadler (1993), and Uebel (1991).

Introduction

one chapter of the history of this vexing but seemingly ineliminable concept.[4] Second, by focusing attention on neo-Kantianism, I hope to invite philosophers to participate in a larger historical undertaking. A great many aspects of nineteenth- and early twentieth-century *wissenschaftliche Philosophie* (scientific philosophy) have scarcely been examined. The neo-Kantians have been disparaged as uninteresting, pedantic, overly professionalized, insulated, and superseded. Their work had, however, important and, in ways neither generally acknowledged nor understood, lasting influence on the subsequent development of analytic as well as Continental philosophy. Analytic philosophy can scarcely afford to continue to avert its eyes from its origins if it is to understand its place in the world of philosophy in general. To this end, nothing would exceed in value a general history of scientific philosophy. In the 1920s, Carnap, Cassirer, Otto Neurath, Edmund Husserl, and Martin Heidegger all thought of themselves as doing "scientific philosophy." This is an extraordinary fact, and one toward which our historical understanding could very usefully be directed.

4 Objectivity is a theme in recent work by Popper (1972), Bloor (1974), Nagel (1979), Williams (1985), Putnam (1990), Longino (1990), and many others. Most of the chapters of the history of objectivity are being written by historians of science; compare Daston (1992) and Daston and Galison (1992).

CHAPTER ONE

Reconstructing the *Aufbau*

THERE is no question that Rudolf Carnap's first major book, *Der logische Aufbau der Welt* (The logical structure of the world; hereafter *Aufbau*), published in 1928, is a central document of analytic philosophy. Its place has been secured by Carnap's general importance in setting the agenda for analytic philosophy from the late 1920s until his death in 1970. The *Aufbau* itself has been seen as perhaps the crucial document in the formation of the project of logical positivism.[1] It is also Carnap's most sustained attempt to provide a general epistemology of empirical knowledge. Because of its historical role in shaping analytic philosophy generally and logical positivism in particular, many of the standard-bearers of analytic philosophy have had occasion to engage in interpretations of this book – often as a way of motivating their own philosophical enquiries. Among them we find Hillary Putnam, David Lewis, and, most importantly, Nelson Goodman and W. V. Quine.[2]

There is no better place to turn for a preliminary account of the epistemology put forward in Carnap's book than to the text itself. To fix certain points of reference, therefore, let us, without further ado, rehearse some of the principal themes of Carnap's epistemological project.

---

1 This view is suggested in the history of the Vienna Circle presented by Otto Neurath et al. (1929). It forms a large part of W. V. Quine's understanding of the project of logical empiricism, as one can see from the way he presents his account of traditional epistemology in "Epistemology Naturalized" (1969) and "In Praise of Observation Sentences" (1993).
2 Compare, for example, Putnam (1981, 1983), Lewis (1969), Goodman (1953, 1963), Quine (1961, 1969, 1993). Quine's (1961) views on the *Aufbau* are perhaps the most famous; Goodman's 1953 study remains the single most detailed examination of any aspect of the project of the *Aufbau*, however.

Reconstructing the Aufbau

FUNDAMENTALS OF THE EPISTEMOLOGY OF THE AUFBAU

Der logische Aufbau der Welt begins with these words (§1): "The aim of the present investigations is the establishment of an epistemo-logical [erkenntnismässig-logischen] system of objects or concepts, the 'constitutional system.'"[3] Two important points are then made. First, "object" is taken "in its widest possible sense, namely, for anything about which a statement can be made" (§1). That is, an object is anything that one can meaningfully say anything at all about. Second, Carnap tells us that he is not merely interested in a taxonomy or classification of objects, but that in his "constitutional" system (§1) "concepts are to be derived, 'constituted,' stepwise from certain basic concepts, so that a family tree of concepts results in which every concept finds a definite place."[4] The two questions we must ask, then, are What is a "constitutional system"? and, What makes the constitutional system of the *Aufbau* epistemologically important?

Carnap tells us somewhat informally, early on, that (§2)

To reduce *a* to *b,c* or to *constitute a* from *b,c* means to produce a general rule that indicates for each individual statement about *a* the way it must be transformed in order to yield a statement about *b,c*. This rule of translation we call a "constitution rule" or a "constitutional definition" (since it has the form of a definition).

---

3   Following Friedman (1992a), I shall, as far as is stylistically feasible, use the word "constitution" and its variant forms for the German term *Konstitution* and its variant forms, and also for the verb *konstruieren*. The English translation of the *Aufbau* by R. George uses the term "construction" for these words. George's translation has stylistic advantages but obscures the difference in meaning between *Konstitution* and *Konstruktion* (and its variant forms), with some important repercussions. For example, my use of "constitution" severs the close linguistic tie that George's translation makes between Russell's "logical constructions" and Carnap's project.

4   It may seem that Carnap is sloppily moving back and forth between the view that objects are constituted and the view that concepts are constituted, in these passages. In a sense, he is doing just that, but he will soon (§5) argue that it is a matter of indifference just how one expresses this point: "Fundamentally, it isn't at all a matter of two different views, rather only of two different interpretative modes of speech." What matters for Carnap is not the domain of constitution, but constitution itself. His primary goal is to demarcate the philosophical difference between what he calls constitution and both realistic and idealistic conceptions of concept formation or object construction. The important difference is that constitution is a purely logical relation. See the remarks in the text later in the present chapter.

Fundamentals of the epistemology of the Aufbau

A constitutional system is, then, a stepwise introduction of new concepts via such constitutional definitions. Since constitution is transitive, the constitutional system will show how to define all of the higher-level concepts from the concepts chosen as the basis of the system.

As becomes clear in his more formal exposition (§§26–45), Carnap takes the logical system in which he is working to be the theory of relations and the simple theory of types outlined by Alfred N. Whitehead and Bertrand Russell in the second edition of Whitehead and Russell's *Principia Mathematica*, 1925, first published in 1910.[5] Similarly, he takes the notion of constitutional definition to be explicit definition – in most instances, "definition in use," as understood by Russell and Whitehead and exhibited in their logicist reduction of mathematics to logic.[6] Indeed, the logicist definition of the concepts of classical mathematics is clearly the paradigm case of a constitutional system for Carnap (§12).

Carnap's constitutional systems have the concepts of the empirical sciences as their domain, however. He claims (§2) that this definitional procedure for the concepts of a science is part of the axiomatization of a theory.[7] This theme is also taken up in his 1927 essay "Eigentliche und

---

5 Carnap is not as forthcoming as he ought to be about the version of the theory of types with which he is working. He is clearly employing an extensionalist (§§40–5) theory of types (§§29–30), however, and he makes no mention of matters such as ramification and reducibility. He explicitly endorses the simple theory of types in his *Abriss der Logistik* (1929), written at the same time as the *Aufbau*, however, and there is no good reason to deny that this is his conception of logic in the latter book. There is, however, ample reason to think that in the *Aufbau*, Carnap has no well worked out views on questions of philosophy of logic that address issues being raised by the mid-1920s about the type theoretic view of logic and its relation to mathematics. He certainly does not address such issues in any systematic way. His pronouncements on the nature of logical truth indicate an inchoate commitment to conventionalism (cf. §§107, 179), on the one hand, and a nod in the direction of Wittgenstein's (1921/1961) notion of tautology (cf. §107 again), on the other. Carnap's conception of logic and its philosophical role will occupy us throughout. We will have opportunity to think about why his views on logic are hard to locate within the context of the types of debates noted.

6 Carnap's claim that definition in use, which is now usually called "contextual definition" and contrasted with explicit definition, is "explicit definition in the wider sense" can be found in §39. It is in this sense that I employ the term "explicit definition" here, since my concern is the distinction between a system of definitions found in a constitutional system and implicit definition of concepts via an axiom system. This is the distinction that drives Carnap's project throughout the *Aufbau*.

7 His target here and elsewhere (e.g., §15) is Hilbertian implicit definition accounts of axiom systems that claim that the concepts mentioned in the axioms are defined by their role in the axioms. Carnap, at this time, clearly thinks that an axiomatization of a

uneigentliche Begriffe" (Proper and improper concepts; hereafter *EUB*), where, in discussing the axiomatic formulation of scientific theories, he writes (pp. 355–6):

> The concepts of any domain, be it geometry or economics, allow themselves to be so ordered that certain concepts are placed undefined at the beginning and the remaining concepts are defined with the help of these *"basic concepts."* . . . Such a *derivation* occurs through an *explicit definition*, i.e., through establishing that a certain new concept word is to be synonymous with an expression that consists of old words, i.e., of such as have already been defined or which designate the basic concepts. If such a derivation for a concept is given, we say of it that it is *"constituted"* on the basis of the basic concepts of the domain. In this way the concepts of any domain allow themselves to be ordered in a "constitutional system."

Thus, a constitutional system for a domain is a system of basic concepts for that domain and explicit definitions of the other concepts in the domain constructed on this basis.

In the *Aufbau*, Carnap is not concerned with constitutional systems for particular special sciences such as economics. Rather, he seeks to give credence to the idea that there are constitutional systems that capture all the concepts of all the sciences. This is one of the points of the theory of constitution: to sketch the way in which the concepts of all the sciences are related. This is the thesis of the unity of science, which Carnap calls (§16) "a basic thesis of constitution theory." He tries to lend plausibility to this thesis in the *Aufbau* by sketching a single constitutional system that indicates how all the various important types of scientific concepts can be constituted. At the same time, Carnap wants to show that the concepts of metaphysics cannot be constituted even within systems that are adequate for the constitution of the whole of unified science. Thus, in such a general constitutional system for science (and I shall follow Carnap's *Aufbau* usage and call only such systems "constitutional systems" henceforth), every concept of the sciences finds a definite place. This, in turn, shows that all the statements of science make determinate, meaningful claims. Moreover, it shows that metaphysics contains only ill-formed, nonconstitutible pseudoconcepts and, hence, that the alleged claims of metaphysics are not claims at all.

  theory is not complete until a constitutional system for the concepts of the relevant science is given.

Fundamentals of the epistemology of the Aufbau

We have a tolerably clear idea of what a constitutional system is at this point. What makes the system for unified science of the *Aufbau* an "epistemo-logical" (§1) system, however? After all, there is no obvious connection between the definitional order of constitution and the order of knowledge. Indeed, if one took the axiomatization view seriously and viewed constitutional systems for the special sciences as taking as their basis the theoretical terms of the axiomatization, it would seem that the definitional and epistemological orders would in general diverge greatly. For example, the basic concepts used in the axiomatization of a branch of physics – say, electromagnetism – are concepts such as 'electromagnetic field' and 'electric potential,' in terms of which we would try to define concepts such as 'light' and 'current.' But, if anything, the latter notions seem much closer to the epistemological starting point of the theory of electromagnetism; they are, so to speak, the terms in which the evidence for electromagnetic theory is cast.

Carnap agrees with this in general, so he must present something more to undergird the claim that the constitutional system of the *Aufbau* is epistemically ordered. To do this he starts with the epistemological point, shared, he alleges (§178), by all epistemological schools, that "the subjective origin of all knowledge lies in the contents of experience and their interweavings [Erlebnisinhalten und ihren Verflechtungen]" (§3). This establishes the basis of the system as subjective experience, the basic items of which Carnap calls "elementary experiences." Carnap then looks to empirical psychology, especially Gestalt psychology (§66), for an account of the structure of this experience in human agents and uses this as the basis from which to start his constitutional system. Thus, the basis of the system turns out to be a single relation, which he terms "the recollection of similarity relation" (Rs) which holds between two elementary experiences if one is similar to the memory of the other.

The constitutional system, then, proceeds in accordance with very general epistemological ordering principles and the more fine-grained methodological order of the introduction of concepts found in "the method of indicators" (§49) in science. That is, Carnap takes it as uncontroversial that our knowledge of the physical world is based on our subjective experience, that our knowledge of the psychological states of others is mediated by their behavior as physical objects, and that the psychological states of others form our evidence for claims to knowledge about cultural objects such as caste systems or capitalist states. This gives the gross structure of the constitutional levels: the "auto-psychological" (one's own psychological states); the physical; the "heteropsychological" (the psychological states of others); and the cultural.

Within each of these levels we inspect the evidentiary claims of the relevant sciences (e.g., botanists identify plants by their foliage, flowers, fruit, shape, etc.) to see the order in which the constitutional definitions are to go if they are to capture the relation of "epistemic primacy" (§54).[8]

THE RECEIVED VIEW OF THE *AUFBAU*

Thus, we are presented with an epistemically ordered constitutional system that is meant to show that all scientific concepts can be constituted from an experiential basis and that no metaphysical concepts can be so constituted. Little wonder, then, that there has arisen a received view of Carnap's book that sees it as the high-water mark of good old-fashioned empiricism. This view, moreover, seems to fit into Carnap's role as the staunch defender of logical empiricism, a role that appears to stem precisely from the *Aufbau*. It is a view Carnap himself endorses in his retrospective "Intellectual Autobiography" (pp. 16–19) and that formed the basis of the *Aufruf* (call to arms) of the Vienna Circle in their monograph *Die wissenschaftliche Weltauffassung* (The scientific conception of the world), jointly authored by Carnap with Otto Neurath and Hans Hahn in 1929.[9]

The primary responsibility for this account of the *Aufbau* must, however, rest with W. V. Quine. Quine has found occasion to discuss the project of the book with some frequency in his career. Indeed, perhaps the two most influential documents of the Quinean reorientation of epistemology, his "Two Dogmas of Empiricism" (1953/1961) and "Epistemology Naturalized" (1969), are motivated in large part by lessons Quine asks us to take from what he regards as the epistemological failure of Carnap's project in the *Aufbau*.[10]

The following two statements from these essays by Quine express the essence of the received view of the *Aufbau* accepted today by most philosophers:

8 Compare the remarks about the nucleus and secondary parts of cognitions in §3b of *Scheinprobleme*.
9 Primary authorship for the Vienna Circle's call to arms is still disputed. Most authorities claim Neurath as the principal author but assert that Hahn and Carnap had veto rights for anything they did not like. The list of historical predecessors for logical empiricism claimed in the work is, I think, misleading. It certainly does not apply in any clear way to Carnap, as we will see.
10 Such an argumentative structure can be found again in a much later work of Quine's, his (1993) "In Praise of Observation Sentences."

The received view of the Aufbau

Radical reductionism, conceived now with statements as units, set itself the task of specifying a sense-datum language and showing how to translate the rest of significant discourse, statement by statement, into it. Carnap embarked on this project in the *Aufbau*.
The language which Carnap adopted as his starting point was not a sense-datum language in the narrowest conceivable sense, for it included also the notations of logic, up through higher set theory . . . Carnap's starting point is very parsimonious, however, in its extralogical or sensory part. In a series of constructions in which he exploits the resources of modern logic with much ingenuity, Carnap succeeds in defining a wide array of important additional sensory concepts which, but for his constructions, one would not have dreamed were definable on so slender a base. He was the first empiricist who, not content with asserting the reducibility of science to terms of immediate experience, took serious steps toward carrying out the reduction. (Quine 1961, p. 39)

To account for the external world as a logical construct of sense-data – such, in Russell's terms was the program [Russell's epistemological program of the 1910s – AR]. It was Carnap, in his *Der logische Aufbau der Welt* of 1928, who came nearest to executing it . . .

What then could have motivated Carnap's heroic efforts on the conceptual side of epistemology, when hope of certainty on the doctrinal side was abandoned? There were two good reasons still. One was that such constructions could be expected to elicit and clarify the sensory evidence for science . . . The other reason was that such constructions would deepen our understanding of our discourse about the world, even apart from questions of evidence; it would make all cognitive discourse as clear as observation terms and logic and, I must regretfully add, set theory. (Quine 1969, pp. 74–5)

Thus, on the received view, Carnap is seen as taking his epistemological inspiration from strict empiricism. We begin with an epistemologically privileged language of sensation and seek to exploit the resources of modern logic to make good on empiricism's long-standing promissory note that this language is conceptually rich enough to capture all of scientific knowledge. The project extends our understanding of the world by simultaneously clarifying what we are saying when we engage in theoretical discourse and indicating what the empirical evidence is or must be for such claims to be true. Russell had announced this updated empiricist project, and Carnap takes it up with energy and ingenuity.

Quine argues, however, that this phenomenalist and constructivist program in the *Aufbau* does not succeed. Not only is it impossible to derive the totality of science from sensory experience; scientific discourse cannot be couched in exclusively observational terms, even with the aid of the logical system of Whitehead and Russell's *Principia Mathe-*

matica (seen by Quine, much to his regret, as set theory). For, as Quine argues in "Two Dogmas," highly theoretical sentences of empirical science do not have sensory import individually. Rather, only large portions of theory have empirical consequences, and, hence, only large segments of theory can be "translated" into observational terms.[11]

This objection Quine raises is not a bolt from the blue, however. Quine sees the objection as implicit in a change of method of definition found in Carnap's book itself. The problem comes right at the crucial moment for the phenomenalist project, when Carnap seeks to move beyond the solipsistic world of phenomena (Carnap's autopsychological realm) to the physical world. At this crucial stage, Quine notes, Carnap drops the project of giving explicit definitions. Rather, he provides methodological principles for the mapping of qualities from the private realm of experience onto physical space-time points. Thus, at the critical moment, Carnap turns his back on the empiricist's only allowable methods. Thus, Quine objects (1953/1961, p. 40),

Statements of the form "Quality q is at point-instant $x;y;z;t$" were, according to [Carnap's] canons, to be apportioned truth values in such a way as to maximize and minimize certain over-all features, and with the growth of experience the truth values were to be progressively revised in the same spirit. I think this is a good schematization (deliberately oversimplified, to be sure) of what science really does; but it provides no indication, not even the sketchiest, of how a statement of the form "Quality q is at $x;y;z;t$" could ever be translated into Carnap's initial language of sense data and logic. The connective "is at" remains an added undefined connective; the canons counsel us in its use but not its elimination.

This feature of the book is unavoidable, on Quine's view, and indicates that there is in fact no way Carnap could have succeeded in the task he set himself. Rather, we must abide by the lessons inherent in Carnap's use of these methodological canons and give up the project of sensory reductionism.

This, then, is the received view of the *Der logische Aufbau der Welt:* It was the most ambitious and successful attempt to use the resources of modern logic to carry out the reduction of all scientific discourse into

---

11 Of course, Quine (1953/1961, p. 79) notes that it is rather absurd to talk of translation in a case where entire paragraphs of theory can be couched in sensory terms but none of the sentences composing the paragraph can be. So, he there proposes that it is more useful to think of the holistic project not as providing a translation of the theory into sensory terms but as providing the empirical import or evidential basis of the theory.

the terms of immediate experience. The principal legacy of the book is that it failed in this reduction – and that it failed not merely in fact but in principle. That is, the important lesson of the *Aufbau* is that Carnap so rigorously formulated the empiricist thesis of reducibility and used the logical resources available to the empiricist with such precision and ingenuity that it became clear that the failure of Carnap's attempt at providing a constructional system is symptomatic of the impossibility of the program as a whole.

This view is not only Quine's. Another prominent statement of this view is found in Hillary Putnam's *Reason, Truth, and History* (1981, p. 181):

The claim that statements about material objects are translatable into statements about actual and possible sensations seems as a matter of fact to be false. Careful logical investigation of this claim, starting with the work of Carnap and the Vienna Circle in the 1930s, convinced the phenomenalists themselves [read: the Carnap of the *Aufbau*] that the claim was unfounded.

Examples could be multiplied here, but the general line is, I trust, both clear and familiar.

This is not, of course, to say that it is correct. The primary business in this chapter is to give a preliminary argument for reexamining the epistemology of the *Aufbau*. I shall do this by looking in some more detail at the project that Russell announces in the "external world program" and raising some interpretative worries about reading this program into Carnap's project in the *Aufbau*. I shall argue that the received view misses the most characteristically Carnapian understanding of the problem of empirical knowledge. As such, it ascribes to Carnap certain goals that he does not in fact have and makes central certain problems that are not central to Carnap's own avowed concerns. It also wholly misses what I take to be the crucial tension in the epistemology of the *Aufbau*, which is evident only when we do take Carnap's own formulation of the problem of epistemology seriously.

RUSSELL'S EXTERNAL WORLD PROGRAM

Early in the second decade of the twentieth century, Bertrand Russell, under the influence of G. E. Moore and Alfred North Whitehead, turned his attention away from the purely logical work that had occupied him from roughly the turn of the century through the writing of *Principia Mathematica* in 1910 and toward epistemological issues in the empirical realm.[12] His epistemology was, of course, greatly influenced by his earlier logical work. Here I can hardly give an adequate account of the details of Russell's epistemological thought during the "external world" period, when his principal project was to answer the idealist's challenge by showing that we do have knowledge of a world external to our minds.[13] For the purposes of our comparison with the *Aufbau*, we shall focus on three aspects of Russell's general point of view in epistemology: first, the importance of logic and logicism for philosophy; second, the role of the theory of descriptions and the distinction between "knowledge by acquaintance" and "knowledge by description"; third, the relation of epistemological to ontological issues in Russell's work.

Russell is, of course, chiefly renowned for his work in logic and, in particular, the project of logicism – the reduction of mathematics to logic. This was extremely important to Russell in his flight from the neo-Hegelian idealism of his youth and from idealistic philosophy, including its Kantian variants, in general.[14] For Russell, logicism with respect to mathematics denied Kant's most plausible case of synthetic *a priori* knowledge, the knowledge of mathematics and geometry. If such knowledge could be founded on logic alone, there would be no need for Kantian pure intuition.[15] Hence, the whole of transcendental idealism would be shaken.[16]

Logicism was based on a new conception of formal logic that Russell developed from the work of Gottlob Frege and Giuseppe Peano. This logic differs in many respects from the traditional logic of Aristotle: it has a function–argument structure; it accepts relations and relational propositions not reducible to subject–predicate form; and it fully ex-

---

12 We will see that Russell's understanding of analysis took an epistemic turn as early as 1905, but he did not concern himself with issues of empirical knowledge until his 1912 *Problems of Philosophy*. On the influence of Whitehead on Russell's external world program, see Russell's (1914) preface to *Our Knowledge of the External World*, where Whitehead is in essence credited with the idea behind the "supreme maxim of scientific philosophizing."
13 A much more systematic treatment is given in Hylton (1990, chap. 8).
14 On Russell's early idealism see Hylton (1990, pt. 1, esp. chap. 3) and Griffin (1991).
15 The extension of logicism to geometry is one of Russell's differences from the founder of logicism and modern logic, Gottlob Frege. As far as I know, no large-scale investigation of this difference between the two champions of logicism has been undertaken. Such a project would illuminate the similarities and differences between their conceptions of mathematics in general.
16 Compare on this point Russell's call to arms against Kant at the conclusion of "Mathematics and the Metaphysicians" (1901/1981c).

ploits variables and the generality they confer. All these features allowed logicians for the first time to have a mathematically interesting field of study. By the time Russell's attention had turned to epistemological issues, his conception of logic had settled on the ramified type theoretic hierarchy of propositional functions found in the first edition of *Principia Mathematica*.

For Russell, there were two distinct parts to logic: formal logic and philosophical logic.[17] Formal logic consisted of the kind of material which formed the business of *Principia Mathematica*: for example, proofs and definitions. In the sense of formal logic, the truths of logic consisted of the most general truths: The logical truths contained only logical constants and variables bound by quantifiers. Formal logic, therefore, lacked a special subject matter of its own; its laws were the most general laws about everything. The philosophical part of logic, on the other hand, did have a subject matter, namely, propositions and their (formal) logical forms. Logic in this sense forms the subject matter of, among other writings, the introduction to *Principia Mathematica;* the whole first part of Russell's first book on logic, *The Principles of Mathematics* (1903); and "On Denoting" (1905/1973). Both parts of logic provide crucial elements to Russell's thinking on the nature of philosophy.

Formal logic, of course, provides the content of the logicist reduction. *Principia Mathematica* is devoted to the derivation of classical mathematics from the new formal logic. Hence, formal logic enables us to go beyond Kant and see all of classical mathematics as purely logical.[18] But it also does more than this. For Russell, the analytic maneuvers he exploits in his attempt to reduce mathematics to logic provide tools that are useful to the philosopher in any area of philosophy. The methods of definition and the patterns of proof exhibited in formal logic, precisely because of their absolute generality, provide templates usable for various philosophical endeavors where reduction of one realm of objects (and facts about those objects) to another realm is deemed desirable.

---

17 See Russell (1914/1981d, pp. 85f.) and Goldfarb (1988).
18 It would fit with standard accounts of logicism to be able to say that Russell therefore takes the propositions of mathematics to be analytic, but he refrains from so doing. In *Principles of Mathematics* (1903), he explicitly calls the truths of logic "synthetic judgments." Moreover, early in his analytic phase, his book *Leibniz* (1900), following Moore, argued against the possibility of analytic judgment in general. On this last point see Hylton (1990, pp. 16of.). Logicism becomes tied to analyticity, as opposed to logical truth, only in the late 1920s and early 1930s.

If formal logic provides the philosopher with tools for analysis, philosophical logic provides the philosopher with a new way of conceiving the business of philosophy. The philosopher is to provide an account of the logical form of propositions found in areas of traditional philosophy or the sciences. Thus, a philosopher might concern himself with the logical form of propositions about space and time or of propositions involving the notion of judgment, to take two examples from *Our Knowledge of the External World* (1914).[19] Philosophical logic provides an inventory of the possible logical forms of propositions. The philosopher then analyzes the propositions of some particular domain to find which of those forms such propositions have.[20] The view of philosophy as the analysis of logical forms of propositions within a special subject matter leads to a view of philosophy as composed of various and distinct logical problems. Russell writes of this as a movement to a scientific philosophy (1914/1981d, p. 85):

By concentrating attention upon the investigation of logical forms, it becomes possible at last for philosophy to deal with its problems piecemeal, and to obtain, as the sciences do, such partial and probably not wholly correct results as subsequent investigation can utilize even while it supplements and improves them . . . A scientific philosophy such as I wish to recommend will be piecemeal and tentative like the other sciences.

Only thus will philosophy progress in the way that other sciences do. The propositions of philosophy do not, however, on Russell's conception become just like the propositions of the special sciences; rather they remain *a priori* and depend only on logic, considered as the totality of knowledge about the possible forms of propositions (or facts). Thus, philosophical propositions are propositions detailing the logical structure of propositions within certain subject matters. Russell is therefore led to claim that "philosophy, if what has been said is correct, becomes indistinguishable from logic" (1914/1981d, p. 84).

19 The analysis of propositions involving the notion of judgment forms a large part of the general business of epistemology for Russell, as is clear in the suppressed "Theory of Knowledge" manuscript (Russell 1913/1984).
20 There has been some looseness in my manner of expression here and throughout. By the time of the external world program, Russell thought that logical form inhered ultimately in facts, not propositions. Russell's movement from the metaphysics of propositions in his earliest analytic period to the metaphysics of facts around 1910 is a complicated story that is immaterial to the points about Russell's epistemology of empirical knowledge that are our concern here. But see Hylton (1990, esp. chap. 8) and Goldfarb (1988).

The primary tool that drove the reduction of mathematics to logic and was to be used in a similar fashion in any reduction was the *theory of descriptions*. The theory of descriptions was Russell's mature response to what he termed "the problem of denoting" within his understanding of logic. The problem of denoting first arose for Russell in his 1903 book *The Principles of Mathematics*. In that work Russell put forward the view that a proposition is a complex of constituents and that, in the usual case, those constituents are what the proposition is about. Thus the proposition "Heloise loves Abelard"[21] is a structured entity consisting of Heloise, the relation of loving, and Abelard. However, certain propositions obviously contain constituents which they are not about, for example, "Every man is mortal." This proposition contains the constituent "every man" but is not about this constituent, which, after all, is a concept and hence not mortal.[22] Thus, Russell is led in 1903 to consider what we now recognize as quantified phrases to refer to denoting concepts that occur in propositions. Such propositions are, however, not about those concepts but about the objects denoted by the concepts.[23]

Implicit in Russell's 1903 theory of denoting is the idea that the surface grammatical structure of a sentence provides a good guide to the underlying logical constituent structure of the proposition.[24] Russell became suspicious of this idea by 1905, when he wrote his seminal essay "On Denoting" (1905/1973). Here Russell proposes that quantifier phrases are not associated with denoting complexes in the underlying propositions. Rather, in the propositions there is no constituent at all that corresponds to the denoting phrase. Thus, on the 1905 account there is no relation of denoting in anything like the sense that notion had in 1903; the domain of that relation has disappeared. The 1905

---

21 In my discussion of Russell, quotation marks do not mark names of linguistic entities (sentences, quantifier phrases), but rather names of logical entities (propositions, denoting complexes).
22 The suppressed argument here is, of course, that since "every man" is not mortal, the proposition "Every man is mortal" would be false if "every man" were what it was about. Since, however, the proposition is true (or, in any case, its falsity is not guaranteed on logical grounds), we must look for some relation between "every man" and humans that grounds the truth of the proposition in the right way. This is the relation of denoting.
23 *Denoting* is a logical relation between denoting concepts and the objects they denote, not between quantifier phrases and either denoting concepts or the denotation of denoting concepts. As Russell says (1903, §43), "The sense of meaning in which words have meaning is immaterial to logic." The problem of denoting is only obliquely related to language and has nothing whatever to do with reference.
24 As he notes in Russell (1903, §46).

theory replaces the theory of denoting with the analysis of descriptions in terms of quantifiers and identity which has become standard in logic since *Principia Mathematica*. Thus, the idea that there is an important analytic function in logic and philosophy, distinct from reading off the logical form of propositions from the surface grammar of sentences, comes to the fore for Russell in the theory of descriptions.[25]

We saw that the 1903 theory of denoting was in response to a question of philosophical logic concerning how certain propositions can be about objects (and/or concepts) that are not constituents of those propositions and can, conversely, contain concepts that are not what the propositions are about. In 1905 this concern is altered into an epistemological concern about how we can know anything about objects known only by description. To know something by description is to know a proposition in the verbal expression of which that thing is described by a phrase such as "the so-and-so." Thus, the following sentence (*) is a verbal expression of a proposition in which a fact about the center of mass of the solar system is a fact known by description:

(*) The center of mass of the solar system lies within the sun.

To know an object only by description is for all the facts known about an object to be known by description. Russell contrasts knowing something by *description* with knowing it by *acquaintance*. When one is acquainted with something (particular, universal, fact) one is presented with it. The question then is, How can one acquire knowledge by description of things?

The answer Russell (1905/1973, p. 119) proposes to this question is that "in every proposition that we can apprehend (i.e. not only in those whose truth or falsehood we can judge of, but in all that we can think about), all the constituents are really entities with which we have immediate acquaintance." This principle, which I shall, following Hylton (1990, p. 245), dub *the principle of acquaintance*, sets the goal of analysis. A proposition has been fully analyzed when all the constituents of it are entities with which one is acquainted. This analytic goal is supplemented with the technical machinery of formal logic to provide (Russell 1914/1981e, p. 115) "the supreme maxim of scientific philosophiz-

---

25 I shall refrain from saying anything about the notorious arguments of "On Denoting" against Russell's earlier views or against Frege's views on sense and meaning. Suffice it to say that the 1905 theory grounds the understanding Russell has of analysis during the external world period.

ing . . . : *Wherever possible, logical constructions are to be substituted for inferred entities."*

Given the line Russell takes on the apprehendability of propositions, the problem with inferred entities is clear enough. Being inferred and not presented, such entities cannot appear in any propositions that we can understand. Hence, the supreme maxim gains an ontological bite from its subservience to the principle of acquaintance. For, to construct an entity logically from those we are acquainted with is to show general rules by which to analyze any proposition that seems to have that entity as a constituent into a proposition in which only entities we are acquainted with occur. Thus, we legitimate our scientific ontology by defining it away in favor of the objects of acquaintance. As Quine (1981, pp. 83f.) writes,

[Russell's identification of external objects with sets of sense data] would afford translation of all discourse about the external world into terms of sense data, set theory, and logic . . . It would settle the existence of external things. It would show that assumption superfluous, or prove it true; we could read it either way.

It can be read either way because there is no distinction between these ways of reading it. What matters is that existence claims about external things become complicated existence claims, involving only terms with which we are acquainted. To define, Quine never tires of reminding us, is to eliminate.[26]

Of course, we are left now with the question of which entities one is acquainted with. Russell takes a broad line on this question. First, we are acquainted with sense data, that is, the particulars acquired in sensation. But we are also acquainted with logical constants and logical forms. Further, we are acquainted with certain universals (properties and relations), again through experience.[27]

Thus, the analytic enterprise in philosophy reaches for one goal: to reduce all propositions about any subject matter to propositions about things with which we are acquainted. Russell did this for mathematics by reducing it to logic. The same must be done for other fields of enquiry, only in these cases they will typically be reduced to logic and sense data, whether actually sensed or not (Russell's "sensibilia"). Russell presents his notion of the appropriate question of epistemology at the outset of his essay "The Relation of Sense-Data to Physics"

---

26 Compare, e.g., Quine's criticisms of Carnap's reduction conditionals (1969, p. 78).
27 Russell characterizes his notion of acquaintance in "On Denoting" (1905/1973, pp. 103f.) and, more fully, in a later essay (1911/1981b, pp. 152–5).

(1914/1981e, p. 108): "If [the theoretical objects of physics] are to be verified, it must be solely through their relation to sense-data: they must have some kind of correlation with sense-data and must be verifiable through their correlation *alone*. . . . But how is this correlation itself ascertained?" He answers his question by stating (ibid.): "We may succeed in actually defining the objects of physics as functions of sense-data." In this way he hopes to succeed in grounding the validity of physics solely in its relation to sense data (and logic) and show how high-level theoretical claims in physics actually can be understood.

It is clear that the principle of acquaintance has an empiricist flavor by the time of the external world program. But, as Hylton (1990, pp. 245ff.) points out, Russell always was committed to this principle in his analytic period. Its empiricist cast is superadded when the principle is treated as a constraint on analysis. That is, Russell's early view seemed to be in some ways more Kantian. We begin with an adherence to the principle of acquaintance and a commitment to the claim that we do have knowledge in some domain of enquiry. We then investigate how this knowledge is possible and claim that the fundamental objects necessary for this knowledge just are the objects of acquaintance in this domain. This seems to be how Russell's logicist reduction of mathematics proceeds. By the time of the external world program, however, Russell clearly sees the principle of acquaintance for empirical knowledge as playing a different role. A psychological or quasipsychological investigation of what might be legitimate candidates for acquaintance in empirical sensation constrains the analytic enterprise. This enterprise may, therefore, yield the result that the putative knowledge of a certain domain is not constructible from acquaintance. This active role for the principle of acquaintance in our epistemology of empirical knowledge yields the foundationalist and empiricist nature of Russell's epistemology.

Of course, Russell's notion that certain universals and logical primitives are among the entities we are acquainted with would be anathema to most empiricists. The idea of logical acquaintance is, of course, especially problematic. Russell's continued acceptance of it reflects the earlier role of the principle of acquaintance to some degree. But his reflections on the acquaintance we may or may not have with certain primitives – classes, propositions, or facts – exhibited especially in his suppressed 1913 "Theory of Knowledge" manuscript, indicate that here too the epistemological questions of acquaintance raise a genuine question about knowledge we may claim to have in logic.

Russell's external world program

Thus we see that Quine has understood the main import of the external world program.[28] It is crucial to Russell's epistemological program that all discourse concerning whatever domain be reducible to talk of that with which we are acquainted. The crucial domain of acquaintance for empirical knowledge is that of the hard data of sense. Knowledge by acquaintance is the privileged type of knowledge we have of sense data, and this is why the external world project has the form it does. Moreover, this epistemological program has clear ontological import, as when he claims to answer the metaphysical question "What is matter?" in his "Ultimate Constituents of Matter" (1915/1981f).[29]

Quine takes Carnap to be following the same lines of thought in the *Aufbau*, but also to be making significant improvements over Russell's own attempts at providing a systematic reduction of empirical discourse generally to discourse involving only sense data. It is evident from the passages from "Two Dogmas of Empiricism" and "Epistemology Naturalized" quoted earlier that the primary advantage Quine finds in the *Aufbau* as opposed to, say, Russell's "Relation of Sense-data to Physics," is the ingenuity of Carnap's logical manipulations. For example, Quine notes, Carnap is able to proceed from an autopsychological basis in his reductions, whereas Russell despaired and attempted only to reduce talk of physical objects to a language of sensibilia and not sense data. The crucial distinction here is that Carnap's basis is the sense data of an individual whereas Russell required not only the sensibilia of all epistemic agents at once but unsensed sensibilia as well.[30]

---

28 There are certain idiosyncracies to Russell's view of epistemology that lead to divergences between the external world program and typical sense-data empiricism. We have already noted Russell's broad line on the objects of acquaintance. Another such view is Russell's (e.g., 1915/1981f, p. 96) insistence that, since sense data form the basis of the construction of physical objects, they are themselves physical. Discussion of these issues lies beyond the scope of this outline of the main themes of Russell's epistemology.

29 Russell calls his answer to this question "realist" despite his assertion that sense data are the ultimate constituents of matter. This is not a "phenomenalist" answer, precisely because of the argument that the basis of physics must be physical, mentioned in note 28 to this chapter.

30 Quine's view on the advantages of Carnap's system is touted also by Carnap, who (§3) contrasts his own autopsychological system with Russell's heteropsychological one in more or less the same terms.

CARNAP'S *AUFBAU* AND RUSSELL'S EXTERNAL WORLD PROGRAM

We are asked, then, to view the *Aufbau* as simply a more thorough working through of Russell's external world program. This interpretation, however, is hard to sustain when one turns to the text. Consider the puzzles that await the reader in just the first sixteen sections. Things start out well in part I – Carnap gives Russell's "supreme maxim for scientific philosophizing" ("Wherever possible, logical constructions are to be substituted for inferred entities") as the motto for his book. Moreover, the early sections are full of references and allusions to both Russell's logicist reduction of mathematics to logic and his application of logic to empirical knowledge. It is perhaps a bit surprising that Carnap claims that (§3) the "most important suggestions for the solution as to how scientific concepts are to be reduced to the 'given' have been made by Mach and Avenarius" rather than referring to Russell, but at least he has enunciated the problem in an appropriately empiricist way and has cited the leading German positivists.[31]

The empiricist reader of the *Aufbau* begins to get uneasy when Carnap claims, in section 5, to be neutral toward the dispute between realists and Marburg neo-Kantian idealists on the issue of whether the mind constructs objects or merely apprehends them via concepts. On the other hand, empiricists may find themselves ambivalent or embarrassed by such disputes anyway, so maybe Carnap is simply trying to avoid an issue best left alone. Worries increase, however, when Carnap claims in section 10 that "science deals only with the structural properties of objects." When, in section 12, Carnap explains this claim, the empiricist reader is left deeply puzzled: "The contention of our thesis that scientific statements relate only to structure descriptions would, therefore, mean that *scientific statements speak of mere forms without saying what the terms and relations of these forms are*. This contention appears, at first, paradoxical." Whether paradoxical or not, this thesis is greatly at

---

31 It might be argued that Carnap's references to Ernst Mach and Richard Avenarius, as well as to Theodor Ziehen, Hans Driesch, and Walter Dubislav, in §3, are primarily aimed at keeping his German audience interested and that it would have been unwise for a German living in Austria in the mid-1920s to publish a book in epistemology that claimed that almost all of the best work was being done in England. I find this view overly cynical, however. Political factors were important, but Carnap underplayed neither his debts to nor his disagreements with Russell in the book, nor are his references to members of the German-speaking philosophical world just window dressing.

odds with what one would have expected on the empiricist reading of the work. Carnap seems to be saying that empirical scientific statements are somehow purely formal. No mention is made here of the crucial role for experience in questions of meaning and verification that is the stock in trade of the empiricist.

In section 16, Carnap tells us why scientific statements must be purely structural: "Science wants to speak of the objective; however, everything that does not belong to the structure but only to the material, everything that is concretely pointed out, is in the end subjective." Here we have a view of the objectivity of scientific statements that makes little sense from an empiricist point of view. Indeed, this account of objectivity makes the end point of empiricist reduction – the "given" in experience – the paradigm of the subjective and, thus, the antithesis of knowledge. At best, it seems that Carnap's motivations for reducing scientific concepts to experiential ones are rather more obscure than we had hoped. At worst, he seems to be presenting the epistemological problem in a direction exactly opposite to standard empiricism.

By the end of the book it is, moreover, quite clear that Carnap takes traditional empiricism[32] (§178) and Russell's own views (§176) to be as infected with metaphysics as any traditional epistemological project. Thus, his neutrality, as expressed in section 5, extends to such empiricist projects also. This is because he argues that his positive epistemological project agrees with the nonmetaphysical parts of *all* earlier epistemological projects while remaining neutral with respect to their metaphysical differences (§§177–8). As a complete, accurate, and informative account of Carnap's project in the *Aufbau*, therefore, the empiricist interpretation seems lacking. No bland suggestion that Carnap is following Russell as a matter of course seems adequate to Carnap's way of presenting the point and goal of his epistemological enquiries.

Carnap's distance from Russell can be seen by tracing through some of the consequences of Carnap's account of objectivity as structure. The general point about the structuralist account of objectivity standing at odds with empiricist reductionism can be sharpened when we consider

---

32   Empiricism can be read into Carnap's subjective or solipsistic idealism. Interestingly, Carnap does not think that empiricism, rationalism, and Kantianism are the traditional epistemological schools. Rather he thinks that realism, idealism, and phenomenalism are. Phenomenalism for Carnap, oddly from our point of view, is a two-world Kantian view that postulates things-in-themselves behind the appearances. Transcendental idealism is not this view for Carnap. Transcendental idealism is a version of idealism for Carnap that claims that all objects are "created in thought." See §177.

how it breaks from Russell's reliance on acquaintance. For Carnap, there is no immediate epistemic relation of acquaintance that grounds our knowledge and provides the end point for analysis. It is for this reason that, although the starting points of construction (or constitution) are much the same, Carnap and Russell view their projects quite differently. For Carnap, the language of sensation is the starting point of constitution because of the scientific fact – granted by all epistemological schools, according to Carnap, as we have noted – that our knowledge begins in sensation. But Carnap lacks any epistemological vocabulary of acquaintance to undergird the claim that this starting language is epistemically privileged or certain. Indeed, these epistemological terms – "acquaintance," "certainty" – are simply not to be found in the text. Such epistemological terms as there are, for example, "objectivity," would be misplaced if ascribed to the starting point of the system. The starting point is, as noted, the language of subjective experience, and the constitutional procedure will show us how we rise from this to the objective world of science.

The lack of an implicit single goal to analysis comparable to Russell's principle of acquaintance can also be seen from Carnap's consideration of multiple constitutional systems. Carnap (§62) presents various different physicalist bases possible for a constitutional system for unified science. He also considers (§63) a heteropsychological system. Such systems fulfill genuine methodological functions for Carnap, even though they are not epistemically ordered systems. A physicalist system, for example, would capture the point of view of the empirical sciences and show how all concepts of science would fit into one law-governed whole. Thus, Carnap writes (§59):

Since the task of empirical science (the natural sciences, psychology, the cultural sciences) consists, on the one hand, in the discovery of general laws, and, on the other hand, in the explanation of individual processes through their subsumption under general laws, from the standpoint of empirical science the constitutional system with physical basis represents the most appropriate ordering of concepts.

This multitude of possible constitutional schemes and the multiple philosophical and methodological tasks they fulfill indicate that Carnap has no epistemological function built into his notion of philosophical analysis.

A related difference between Russell and Carnap is found in their respective attitudes toward logic. As we have seen, Russell has an ante-

The Aufbau and the external world program

cedent epistemological point of view given in his adherence to the principle of acquaintance that allows him to have epistemological worries about the basic concepts of logic. This is not true of Carnap. No concerns of an epistemological nature about logic are in evidence in his book. Indeed, the role that structure plays in the account of objectivity indicates that logic must be in place before any epistemological question can be raised. In this way, Carnap's adherence to a Russellian theme of "logic as the essence of philosophy" actually goes deeper than Russell's own adherence to it.[33] Within the external world program, Russell uses the tools of logic in support of a prior empiricist epistemology of acquaintance. Carnap, by contrast, seeks to recast all of epistemology into a framework within which logical structure (and it alone) is presupposed. We have more than a change of tools in pursuit of an old project; we have a fundamental change in what counts as a philosophical project, given the new logic.

There may seem to be an irrefutable objection to the line I have been sketching. If Carnap is not following Russell's lead in the *Aufbau*, our objector may claim, how could we possibly make out Carnap's rejection of metaphysics? After all, the rejection of metaphysics simply follows from the doctrine of verification. Our inability to constitute the concept of, say, 'reality' in the metaphysical sense (cf. §176) from the experiential basis of the epistemological system is how we show that those concepts are illegitimate. If Carnap is to have an argument against metaphysics, he must be a verificationist and, hence, a Russellian empiricist, after all.

This argument is not correct, and it is instructive to see why. Carnap does not follow Russell's lead on questions of the relation of ontological issues to epistemology at all. This is indeed the central issue that divides the two *within the text of the* Aufbau *itself*. In the very section (§176) in which Carnap makes the point that metaphysical concepts are not constitutible within the epistemological constitutional system, he notes that this seems to agree with Russell's view. But he goes on to say: "this does not seem to be consistent with the fact that in Russell questions of the following sort are frequently posed, which (regardless of how they are answered) implicitly manifest a realistic conception: whether physical objects exist when they are not observed, whether other people exist, whether classes exist, etc." Precisely this sort of question, which is given an answer rather than rejected as meaningless in Russell, is what Carnap seeks simply to set aside. For Carnap, unlike Russell, the rejection

---

33 "Logic as the Essence of Philosophy" is the title of chapter 2 of Russell's *Our Knowledge of the External World*.

of metaphysics is not governed by the acceptance of an ontology of objects of acquaintance and a method that shows how to do without anything else. Carnap seeks to reject all questions of ontology; epistemology has nothing to say about such questions.

In fact, within Carnap's philosophical framework in the *Aufbau*, the role played by the argument of section 176 is minimal. Carnap takes no great pains in showing that metaphysical concepts are not constitutible in the epistemically ordered system. This is because if they were, they would be scientific concepts. But Carnap takes it as a presupposition of his dispute with the metaphysicians that both sides agree that metaphysical concepts are not scientific. The question at stake is what sort of concepts are employed in philosophy itself. Carnap's metaphysicians are in the business of employing metaphysical concepts such as 'reality' or 'essence' in giving a philosophical interpretation of science. Carnap is distancing himself from this point of view in his antimetaphysics, and for this task his epistemology plays only a limited role. We can see this, for example, from the fact that the physicalist constitutional system that Carnap takes as an alternative is also claimed to be metaphysically neutral (e.g., at §59). Nothing internal to the business of any constitutional system for empirical science is playing the major role in the rejection of metaphysics.

The important role is played, rather, by the logical language in which any and all constitutional systems are cast. The language of logic provides the metaphysically neutral vocabulary within which any and all philosophical discourse can be presented. The importance of the neutrality of logic is already given voice in Carnap's claimed neutrality in section 5. We have already noted that there Carnap claims that the very language of constitution as made out in the *Aufbau* is neutral between the neo-Kantian metaphysical thesis of objects created in thought and the realist thesis that objects are merely grasped in thought but exist outside of thought. For Carnap this dispute is misguided, because when we get clear on the language available to the philosopher engaged in constitution, neither of these theses is formulatable at all. All we are left with is the sequence of definitions of a constitutional system. This is the whole content of the epistemological perspective; no further external or interpretative questions are raised, and none need be answered (cf. §178).

Logic, thus, provides the philosopher with two things necessary for the rejection of metaphysics. It provides a general vocabulary applicable everywhere and that conditions the very possibility of judgment on any topic. This being the case, logic neither requires nor allows of deeper explanation in terms of metaphysics. The role of logic in conditioning the possibility of objective judgment cannot be explained through appeal to some particular doctrine, whether metaphysical or empirical (e.g., psychological). Logic is universal and, hence, fundamental and unavoidable for any theory. It is, therefore, universally available for exploitation by the philosopher. Logic also provides a new means of capturing the intent of traditional philosophical debates. Thus, as we have seen, old philosophical terms such as "constitution" itself can be given precise meaning within the language of logic. The universal applicability and expressive power of the new logic does all the serious work in the rejection of metaphysics. Carnap's most perspicuous statement of this view occurs not in the *Aufbau*, but rather in *Scheinprobleme in der Philosophie* (Pseudoproblems in philosophy) (1928), where he writes (§1):

It has frequently been stressed that the epistemological question of the grounding or reduction of one cognition to others must be differentiated from the psychological question of the origin of the content of a cognition. But this is merely a negative determination. For those who do not want to rest content with the expressions "given," "reducible," "foundational" or the like, or those who do not want to use these concepts in their philosophy, the task of epistemology has not been formulated at all. The goal of the following considerations is to formulate this task precisely. It will be shown that we can formulate the definition of epistemological analysis without having to use these expressions of traditional philosophy; we only have to go back to the concept of implication, the condition relation (as it is expressed in if-then sentences). This is, however, a fundamental concept of logic that cannot be rejected or even avoided by anyone: it is indispensable in any philosophy, in every branch of science.

This metaphilosophical role for logic – its place in clarifying the point and purpose of philosophy itself – is central to the project of the *Aufbau*. Carnap views the work as a call to arms for the scientific philosopher who feels that the endless disputes of metaphysics are not the product of the unfathomable depth of the issues, but rather of their inability to be expressed at all. The new logic is, thus, not a tool to use in pursuit of a reductive epistemological-cum-ontological project bequeathed to us by the British empiricists, but rather a way of reformulating the whole question of what is at stake in philosophy. Carnap's antimetaphysics is surely the consequence of a much more fundamental understanding of "logic as the essence of philosophy" than is Russell's empiricism of 1914.[34]

THE *AUFBAU* IN CONTEXT

These remarks lead naturally to the question of whether Carnap's epistemological thought in the *Aufbau* or, indeed, his logical empiricism generally ought to be interpreted as a vindication of an antecedently enunciated and independently understandable philosophical program, namely, traditional empiricism. Carnap's own view in the *Aufbau* is rather at odds with any view of the project as old philosophical wine in new formal bottles. The role of the new logic is much more important; it fundamentally changes the nature of philosophy itself. Old disputes and allegiances are set aside in favor of a common logical framework and a positive epistemological project.

The fundamental presupposition of this study of Carnap's early work is that the most fruitful way to approach the 1928 book is to take Carnap's own philosophical viewpoint seriously. This means taking seriously his desire to distance himself from strict empiricism. When he was writing this book, there was no project of empiricism that Carnap saw himself to be pursuing or vindicating. If he came to adopt the terminology of logical empiricism shortly thereafter, then this should be considered a development of his thought rather than a subsequent expression of what "was there all along." Moreover, the perspective will allow us to flag as a question to what extent *logical* empiricism is itself an elaboration of earlier versions of empiricism.

This work is primarily an examination of Carnap's epistemology in the *Aufbau*. My principal interpretative methodology is, therefore, to make Carnap's epistemological vocabulary and his account of the problem of epistemology primary. As we have seen, for Carnap the problem is how we achieve objective knowledge in the sciences despite the subjective origin of empirical knowledge in private sensation. The key to the answer is the idea that all streams of experience have a common form. This understanding of the problem of epistemology and its solution clearly has greater affinity to the Kantian critical philosophy than it does to foundationalisms of either the traditional empiricist or rationalist camp. Carnap does not seek to ground all knowledge as objective

---

34 For more on the question of Carnap's rejection of metaphysics, presented as a response to Coffa (1991), see Richardson (1992b).

through its connection to infallible rational intuition of first principles or certain deliverances of sensation.

Of course, the differences between Carnap's views and those of Kant himself are great. Carnap explicitly disavows the language of the "synthetic *a priori*." Nor does he desire to privilege Newtonian physics and Euclidean geometry – a project doomed from the word "go" in the context of knowledge in the exact sciences in the 1920s. With respect to the narrow point about the relationship between objectivity and form, Carnap differs from Kant in finding that logical form alone is sufficient to play the role of the form that guarantees objectivity. No room is found for the forms of "pure intuition" in the Kantian sense. These differences are not trivial. We shall see, however, that they are also not unique to Carnap. The most important of the neo-Kantian projects of the first quarter of the twentieth century also adhered to most or all of these differences from the original Kantian project. Consideration of the problem of epistemology as objectivity and the connection of objectivity to structure will, therefore, lead us through these neo-Kantian projects (Chapter Five), as well as Carnap's own pre-*Aufbau* work (Chapters Six and Seven).

From the point of view of the *Aufbau* itself, moreover, attention to the problem of objectivity as the core problem of the epistemology reveals an aspect of the work left wholly unexplored by the received view. Carnap provides not one but two related but distinct solutions to the problem of the objectivity of knowledge. On the one hand, he constructs a notion of objectivity within the system of scientific concepts itself via the construction of the intersubjective world of science (§§142–7). On the other hand, he also endorses the project of objectivity as pure logical structure (as was intimated in the passage quoted from §12) through his notion of a 'purely structural definite description' (§§14–16). Both of these projects can be viewed as methods of accounting for objectivity as a purely structural notion, but they differ in their notion of 'structure.' In the first case, the classical mathematical structure of physics is seen as the crucial objectifying structure for science. In the second, Carnap seeks to deploy the resources of logic to give a structural account of concepts that does not rely on this structure of the mathematized sciences but on the structure of type theory itself.

Let us call the general epistemological line that Carnap endorses "the structuralist account of objectivity." Similarly, let us call the two attempted solutions "the intersubjectivist project" and "the project of purely structural definite descriptions," respectively. The central issues for Carnap's own understanding of epistemology are, then, as follows:

What does Carnap commit himself to in accepting a structuralist account of objectivity? What are the details of the two different projects that are meant to express the import of this structuralism? Why are there two such projects? Ultimately, considerations of these issues will lead to a general examination of a central tension among Carnap's notion of epistemology guiding the technical projects, the centrality of structure in those projects, and his understanding of logic as type theory. In the end, we will be in the position to see why Carnap gave up epistemology by the mid-1930s and became the type of philosopher of science he became.

Before indulging in high-level interpretation, however, it will be best to review some of the features of Carnap's structuralist program and its two expressions. These aspects of the *Aufbau* are less well known than they might be, and we will have to engage in a fair bit of exegesis. In order to fix ideas, let us turn to this project first. The reader's patience is begged. In return, the author agrees to avoid mixing the fairly low-level exegesis with too many preliminary high-level interpretative remarks. A number of philosophical points that might be made will, therefore, be held off until Chapter Eight, when our background trip through the neo-Kantians and Carnap's pre-*Aufbau* work is finished and the whole of the interpretative perspective is finally available.

The exegetical remarks on the epistemology of the *Aufbau* will form the next two chapters. In Chapter Two, the focus will be on a more detailed discussion of the two halves of Carnap's epistemological problem – the subjective and the objective. Then we will move to a discussion of some of the principal features of the logical procedures he exploits in the project. The primary topics will be his account of purely structural definite descriptions and the procedure of quasi analysis. Chapter Three presents a broad outline of the constitutional system that Carnap presents in the *Aufbau*. Here, again, the main order of business will be the presentation of the two projects for objectivity.

CHAPTER TWO

The problem of objectivity: An overview of Carnap's constitutional project

IN this chapter we shall examine more closely the epistemological problem of the constitutional system of the *Der logische Aufbau der Welt*, as well as some of the technical means that Carnap proposes to use to solve this problem. Our first order of business will be to examine the import of the epistemological vocabulary used to motivate the projects of the work. This vocabulary emphasizes the subjective–objective distinction. It is incumbent upon us, then, to try to acquire a better sense of Carnap's use of these terms.[1] Most particularly, we must try to understand what is at stake in the claim that structure yields objectivity.

The main purpose of this chapter is to present Carnap's major motivating ideas as an introduction to his thought on objectivity. In Chapter Three, we shall examine his particular solutions to the problem of objectivity in the *Aufbau*. The point is to emphasize the crucial interpretative issues raised by the work on their own terms, while freeing ourselves from the need to cram their significance into ready-made philosophical pigeonholes. The puzzles that we will be left with at the end of these chapters and the question of how they arise within the philosophical context of Carnap's book will be our major concern in the remainder of the book.

---

1 "Objectivity" has recently reemerged as a central and vexed term in epistemology and metaphysics. For recent views on objectivity, see, e.g., Nagel (1979) and Putnam (1990). Within the history of science, the history of the concept of objectivity has recently become a topic of research. See, e.g., the papers from the symposium on objectivity published in *Social Studies of Science* 22 (1992), by Lorraine Daston, Ted Porter, and Peter Dear, respectively, and also Daston and Galison (1992).

KNOWLEDGE VERSUS EXPERIENCE: THE PROBLEM OF SUBJECTIVE ORIGINS

Let us recall the form of the epistemological problem that Carnap presents at the opening of his book: Knowledge, for any given agent, begins in the stream of experience of that individual. Individual experience is, however, the paradigm of the subjective; the qualitative particularities of any stream of experience are wholly private to the person whose experience it is. As such, the peculiarities of that experience cannot be communicated to any other agent. The problem is, then, to show how "it is still possible . . . to attain to an intersubjective, *objective world* that is conceptually comprehensible and, indeed, as one identical for all subjects" (§2). Carnap's solution to this problem is twofold. First, there are structural features in common among the individual streams of experience. Second, one can define the objects of knowledge wholly on the basis of such shared structural features of experience.

Carnap's most perspicuous statement of this structuralist view of objectivity, given in section 66, is worth quoting in full:

The problem now reads: How is science to come to intersubjectively valid statements if all its objects are constituted from an individual subject, if therefore all statements of science have in the end only relations between "my" experiences as their object? Since the stream of experience of any person is different, how is even one sentence of science to be objective in this sense, i.e., valid for every person, if it proceeds from his individual stream of experience? The solution to this problem lies in that of course the *material* of the individual streams of experience are completely different, or rather not comparable at all, since the comparison of two sensations or feelings of different subjects in the sense of their immediate given quality is nonsensical; but certain *structural properties* agree for all streams of experience. Science must restrict itself to such structural properties, since it is to be objective. And it can restrict itself to structural properties, as we have seen earlier, since all objects of knowledge are not content but form and can be represented as structural entities.

From the point of view of the formal logic of the *Aufbau*, this means that all streams of experience have some recognizably similar logico-mathematical structure. In practice, the streams of experience are conceived as ordered by a single relation, termed *recollection of similarity* (Rs), which holds between two elementary experiences of any given subject when one such experience is similar to a recollected representation of the other. (An elementary experience of an agent is a complete cross-section of experience for that agent at a given time.) The recollection of similarity relation is sufficiently structurally similar across agents to allow the objects of science to be defined from its structure. This procedure yields objects common to and identical for all agents. Before looking more at intersubjectivity and structure, let us note a few consequences of the subjective starting point of epistemological enquiry.

Presenting the problem of epistemology as the movement from subjective experience to objective knowledge brings with it important consequences. First, it provides the reason for the choice of the autopsychologically based constitutional system. Only because we are interested in capturing the epistemological order within the constitutional system do we choose such a system. But, as noted in Chapter One, this decision is not based on the idea that only the given in experience is real, nor even that the deliverances of sensation are the certain starting point for knowledge. Rather, it is based on the scientific fact and epistemological presumption of all philosophical schools (§178) – that knowledge begins in experience – that guides this choice. Moreover, since primitive experience is subjective and private, epistemological honorific notions like 'certain' simply do not apply to it.

Correlative with this, the subjective starting point of the epistemological constitutional system requires an endorsement of methodological solipsism. Methodological solipsism for Carnap amounts to "an application of the form and method of solipsism" (§64). Methodological solipsism is not a commitment to the truth of any judgment about the sole or preeminent reality of some particular epistemic subject, however. Methodological solipsism is simply a commitment to a type of constitutional order as the order that captures epistemological relations. It is that order toward which all epistemological schools tend. "Solipsist" or "autopsychological" are, moreover, not terms that have any determinate content prior to the constitutional project itself. They are not, therefore, metaphysical terms that must be imposed from outside of the constitutional system in order to make sense of the project as a whole. Carnap writes (§65):

"Methodological solipsism" [is] not meant as if it presupposed at the start a separation of the *"ipse,"* the "ego," from the other subjects, or as if one of the empirical subjects is set off and understood to be the epistemological subject. At the start, neither other subjects nor the ego can be discussed. Both are first constituted indeed simultaneously at a higher level. The choice of these expressions means merely that *after* the complete construction of the entire constitutional system, there are in hand differing domains that we call, in accordance with usual designations, the domains of the physical, of the psychological (i.e., of the auto- and heteropsychological), and of the cultural [Geistigen].

Thus (perhaps confusingly, given subsequent usage), for Carnap "methodological solipsism" amounts to the same thing as "neutral monism."[2] Since the meaning of these motivating distinctions among objects occurs only within the system, the basis for any system is, at the start, neutral. Thus, he continues in section 65 to claim:

The characterizations of the basic elements of our constitutional system as "autopsychological," i.e., as "psychological" and as "mine," first has a meaning when the domains of the nonpsychological (at first, the physical) and of "you" have been constituted. Then, however, it is thoroughly meaningful for distinguishing this system form from the other system forms with either a general psychological or a physical basis.

How, then, can we understand what it is we are trying to do in providing a constitutional system prior to actually doing it? In particular, how are we to understand the starting point of the epistemological constitutional system as "subjective"? That is, how are we to understand Carnap's argument that the epistemic order requires an autopsychological basis (§§54, 64)? Surely we are occupying a philosophical point of view outside any constitutional system in giving such arguments. Perhaps, therefore, we need a prior, metaphysical standpoint before we can understand the motivation for Carnap's epistemology.

This is precisely what Carnap seeks to deny. He argues that we are not employing metaphysical terms in such considerations. Rather, we are engaged in discussions in the as yet unreconstructed sciences. That is, in our example, the notions of 'experience' and 'autopsychological' are psychological, not metaphysical, notions. Thus, for instance, in his preliminary discussions of the lower constitutional levels (§§75–94), Carnap is happy to relate what is being done in the constitutions through discussing them in relation to cognitive facts within the as yet unreconstructed language of psychology.

Indeed, Carnap's account of the elementary experiences and the basic relation of recollection of similarity are wholly informed by Gestalt psychological findings about human experience. This is an empirical constraint that is built directly into the basis of his epistemological

---

2 On issues around solipsism and neutral monism in positivism and logical empiricism, see Hamilton (1990, 1992).

system. Psychology is where we must look if we want to know what human experience is like. Thus, for example, in defending the idea of the epistemic primacy of complete cross-sections of experience and, therefore, the choice of the elementary experiences as the basis elements, Carnap writes (§67): "Contemporary psychological research has confirmed more and more that in the various sense modalities, the total impression is epistemically primary, and that the so-called individual impressions, from which one is subsequently accustomed to saying the perception is 'composed,' are first achieved through abstraction therefrom." Carnap's desire to capture epistemic primacy and his endorsment of looking to the sciences for the indicators of primacy are, therefore, his sole reasons for demanding that the basis elements have this holistic structure.

Therefore, the findings of the empirical sciences, and especially psychology, are used within the epistemically ordered constitutional system from its very basis. Of course, these findings of psychology are themselves tentative and subject to revision. In this way, the constitutional system is itself subject to change (cf. §106), motivated wholly by changes in our best scientific knowledge in psychology and the other sciences.

Hence, the subjectivity of the starting point is motivated by empirical psychology, and our knowledge of empirical psychological theories will be clarified by the constitutional system motivated by its findings. The constitutional project can be seen, therefore, as a project of clarification of the basis of scientific knowledge from within. The concern with the connection of objective concepts in the sciences reflects and makes precise the partially unarticulated and intuitive procedure used by the scientists. It is for this reason that Carnap calls it a "rational reconstruction of the process of cognition" (§100).

STRUCTURE AND OBJECTIVITY

We now have a tolerably clear understanding of how Carnap means to delimit his epistemological starting point – how he conceives of the subjective. But what of the goal of objectivity? His claim that all scientific objects are (§66) "not content but form and can be represented as structural entities" requires clarification. What is motivating Carnap's views here? What, in the end, does it mean to be a structural entity?

Carnap, in effect, has two paradigm cases in mind. In an early discussion of objectivity in empirical science (§16) it is clear that physics exhibits a position as the preeminently objective empirical science: "In physics we easily notice this desubjectification, which has transformed almost all physical concepts into pure structure concepts." Furthermore, although Carnap is at pains to stress the objective status of other sciences, it is clear that the objective status of those sciences is derivative upon the objectivity of physics. Of the constitution of the physical world, Carnap writes (§136):

> The goal of this constitution consists in the introduction of a domain that is determined through mathematically expressible [fassbar] laws. The laws are to be mathematically expressible in order that with their help certain conditions can be *calculated* from others, which determine them. The necessity of the constitution of the physical world rests furthermore on the circumstance that only it, but not the perceptual world . . . permits a univocal, contradiction free intersubjectification (§§146–9).

However, there is another paradigm that informs the structure of the constitutional system and the account of objectivity it subserves. This is the constitutional system of the concepts of mathematics given by Whitehead and Russell in *Principia Mathematica* (§12). But Carnap's remarks about the relation between the logicist reduction of mathematics to logic and the constitution of the concepts of empirical science in the autopsychological constitutional system underscore the oddity of his structuralist project. In section 12 he writes:

> Whitehead and Russell, through deriving the mathematical disciplines from logic, have shown in all strictness that mathematics . . . only makes such structural claims. The situation, however, seems to be completely different in the empirical sciences: *an empirical science must know whether it speaks of persons or villages. This is the decisive point: empirical science must indeed be able to distinguish between such different objects* [Gebilde]; it does this at first mainly through definite descriptions with the help of other objects [Gebilde]; finally, however, the definite description takes place through structural descriptions only.

Here we see again Carnap's epistemological differences with Russell. The point is not that the logicist reduction was an epistemological success because it reduced all mathematical concepts to ones with which we have acquaintance (and, in this way, provided a preeminent example of constitutional epistemology to be taken over into empirical science). Rather, logicism acquires its epistemological point by reducing mathematical concepts to purely formal ones, where logic is simply the locus of form. It is this connection between objective scientific concepts

Structure and objectivity

and pure form that we seek to extend to empirical science and capture in the constitutional system.

Thus, Carnap seems to assimilate the empirical sciences to the formal sciences here. That is, it seems that the goal of constitution reaches in both cases back to the purely structural, as given in logic. It would seem, then, that the structuralist project divorces science entirely from the empirical realm – that, in Carnap's hands, empirical science achieves objectivity by, in the end, severing its ties to empirical reality in just the way mathematics and logic do.

Care must be exercised here, however. For 'reality' is itself a concept that has a determinate, objective sense for Carnap only by finding its place within the constitutional system (§§170–8). Thus, presenting the interpretative problem as one of the connection between the constitutional system and empirical reality threatens to beg rather large questions against Carnap's understanding of what he is doing. It is more useful to think about what role logical structure is meant to play in Carnap's project for the objectivity of empirical judgment. The question then becomes whether he can still maintain a clear distinction between logico-mathematical concepts and empirical ones, given the objectifying role he envisages for logic. For surely Carnap does want to maintain a distinction between logic and empirical science, even if this difference cannot be adequately captured in terms of a philosophically primitive understanding of concepts "connecting to empirical reality."

More appropriate for our task, then, is to consider Carnap's project with respect to objectivity in the *Aufbau* in relation to similar projects in the philosophical air at the time. Here, we can gain a degree of understanding of the epistemological point of Carnap's project by looking at a disagreement that arose among the neo-Kantians, to which Carnap refers in section 12. Members of the Southwest school of neo-Kantianism, especially Heinrich Rickert, argued against the unity of science by maintaining that the type of concept formation used in the natural sciences was incapable of capturing the particularities of individual objects. A representative selection from Rickert's seminal book *The Limits of Concept Formation in the Natural Sciences* (1929/1986, pp. 38f.) asserts:

We must realize the significance of the fact that all natural scientific or generalizing concept formation ignores the concrete reality of and individuality of unique empirical reality . . . A natural scientific representation that proceeds by generalizing no longer refers to this or that distinctive real thing. On the contrary, it abstracts from all properties that constitute objects as these distinctive realities, the very properties that are essential to their status as real entities.

Thus, he claimed that any genuine science of the individual must use a different type of concept formation, one based in empathy, or *Verstehen*, which captured the individual in its particularities and was employed by the human and cultural sciences.

This objection to natural scientific concept formation need not rely on a realist account of how concepts are constituted from experience. That is, it need not be taken to presuppose that fully determinate objects are given as such in experience and that natural science forms concepts via abstraction. Rather, the question is wholly one of whether schematizing, scientific concept formation is capable of constituting individual objects of knowledge. If we lack the ability to capture the particularities of individuals via a notion of concept formation based in logico-mathematical form, we would need to endorse a different notion of concept formation for individual concepts. This is just what Rickert seeks. The challenge to a project such as Carnap's would then be to show how formal logical means of definition suffice to capture determinate, unique empirical objects.[3] What Carnap must provide is a method of concept formation that succeeds in capturing the individuality of the concepts used in the sciences generally.

On this issue, Carnap remarks (§12):

Recently the demand for a "logic of individuality," that is, for a method of conceptual manipulation that is fair to the particularity of individual given things [Gegebenheiten] and does not seek to comprehend these through step by step confinement in species concepts (classes), has been repeatedly raised (in connection with the thought of Dilthey, Windelband, Rickert) . . . I only want to point out that the concept of structure in the theory of relations forms a suitable basis for such a method.

He favorably cites Ernst Cassirer's (1910/1953, chap. 4, §9) response to Rickert here as well. Carnap follows Cassirer in claiming that Rickert has simply misunderstood the nature of the scientific concept as a class rather than relational notion. He returns to this issue in the discussion of the form of the basis in section 75, where he writes: "Cassirer has

---

3 'Object' is being taken here in the widest sense, in accordance with Carnap's admonition of §1, as I noted in Chapter One. The point is not to distinguish concepts from objects but to indicate how precise, determinate significance accrues to any scientific concept or object. This explains the fluidity of my mode of expression here; given the argumentative context, this is scarcely avoidable.

shown that a science that has the goal of determining the individual through lawful connections without losing its individuality must use, not class ('species') concepts, but relational concepts, since these can lead to the formation of series and, thus, the erection of systems of order."[4]

Cassirer's response to Rickert derives from his general view that the form of the scientific concept is the functional concept of mathematics, not the generic, abstractive concept of Aristotelian logic.[5] Rickert, however, takes the particularity of the individual empirical object to be captured by the qualitative particularities of our experience or empirical intuition. Against this, Cassirer claims that the objective notion of individuality is found not in fleeting and private experience, but in the unique place of the object in a system of scientific laws. He writes (1910/1953, pp. 224f.):

> It is not evident that any concrete content must lose its particularity and intuitive character as soon as it is placed with other similar contents in various serial connections, and is in so far "conceptually" shaped. Rather the opposite is the case; the further this shaping proceeds, and the more systems of relations the particular enters into, the more clearly its peculiar character is revealed . . . The individual in its peculiarity is threatened only by the universality of the blurred generic image, while the universality of a definite law of relation confirms this peculiarity and makes it known on all sides.

This kind of functional connection first determines the identity of the object. As a functionally unique member of a system of relations, the object is rationally constituted. Cassirer writes (1910/1953, p. 149):

> The chaos of impressions becomes a system of numbers . . . It is true that, in the symbolic designation, the particular property of the sensuous impression is lost; but all that distinguishes it as a *member of a system* is retained. The symbol possesses its adequate correlate in the *connection* according to law that subsists between the individual members, and not in any constitutive part of the perception; yet it is this connection that gradually reveals itself to be the real kernel of the thought of empirical "reality."

As we saw in the passage from section 75 of the *Aufbau* quoted earlier in this section, Carnap thinks that Cassirer has understood the methodological situation quite well. Where Carnap differs from Cassirer is in

---

4 This remark is again explicitly within a discussion of the controversy between Cassirer and Rickert.
5 We shall examine Cassirer's views at greater length in Chapter Five.

his commitment to the logic of *Principia Mathematica* as the operative logic of relations that provides the technical resources to carry out his own project. Carnap, thus, has a precise and powerful formal logical tool that he employs to formulate Cassirer's insight and sketch of how the process can go forward. The definitional tool he describes that will determine the individual via its place in the relations in which it stands is the *purely structural definite description* (hereafter, *PSDD*) (§12).

Before we look at Carnap's example of a purely structural definite description, we can get a good sense of the conditions it is meant to fulfill by looking at a related project to which Carnap objects – the project of "implicit definition" of scientific concepts, as exploited in Moritz Schlick's (1925) *Allgemeine Erkenntnislehre* (General theory of knowledge).[6] Schlick essentially takes up the challenge Rickert lays down by seeking to extend David Hilbert's technique of implicit definitions to the concepts of empirical science. Carnap finds this approach to be wanting in several respects, and his objections can sharpen our understanding of the point of the project of giving purely structural definite descriptions.

In the *Allgemeine Erkenntnislehre*,[7] Schlick notes the importance of interconnected networks of laws of nature for the understanding of the world and the prediction of future events, that is, the epistemic importance of the world of physics. He also puts forward the thesis that sensory images – for which he frequently (and confusingly) uses the favored Kantian term "intuition" – are too "fleeting and variable" (Schlick 1925, §6) to serve as a basis for scientific knowledge.[8] Thus, in this work Schlick sets himself the task of clarifying and interpreting scientific knowledge in a way that does not view sensory experience as the locus of such knowledge. He, too, emphasizes the structure of sci-

---

6 For more on Schlick's project in *Allgemeine Erkenntnislehre*, see Oberdan (1990, 1993, 1996), Lewis (1991), and Turner (1996).

7 All quotations from *Allgemeine Erkenntnislehre* are taken from the Blumberg translation.

8 We have already seen Rickert using the term "empirical intuition" in this context, and it is clear that Schlick has only empirical intuition in mind. Strictly speaking, it might be more felicitous, from the point of view of keeping Kantian distinctions straight, for all these philosophers to have used the term "appearance" – the undetermined object of intuition – or "impressions" (*Empfindungen*) here. For Kant, empirical intuitions presuppose the forms of pure intuition and are not fleeting and variable in the appropriate way. Here, as elsewhere, care must be taken not to confuse the issues by presupposing that experience is a mere play of sensations. Precisely this issue marks a distinction between empiricism and Kantianism.

ence as a whole to explain how science both yields and employs completely precise concepts.

Schlick's connection with the challenge of the Rickert wing of neo-Kantianism is clear from the following account he gives of what he is doing (1925, §3): "There is in fact only one method that can yield scientific knowledge in the strictest, most genuinely valid sense and thus satisfy the *two* conditions under discussion: to determine the individual completely and to achieve this determination by a reduction to that which is most general." The method he endorses is the mathematical method of implicit definition, developed and exploited by David Hilbert (1899) in his work on the foundations of geometry. This method is, according to Schlick, our way of capturing the individuality of the elements of empirical reality through general concepts.

Implicit definition, or *definition by axioms,* proceeds via the laying down of certain axioms in which appear concepts that are not independently defined and stating that those concepts are simply whatever makes those axioms true.[9] Thus, in his formalization of geometry, Hilbert said that the concepts such as 'Point,' 'Line,' and 'Plane' that occurred in his axioms were whatever make those axioms true. In this way, the concepts used in the axioms are implicitly defined by general truths that hold of these concepts. For example, the concepts 'point' and 'line' are partially defined by the general truth that "For any two distinct points there is a line such that those points lie on that line."

Schlick sees this mathematical method as providing a response to the demand that Rickert makes. Implicit definition determines concepts on the basis of general truths about those concepts, and it does so completely. The second conjunct is true because the words for the concepts are stipulated as designating whatever makes the axioms true. There is no further constraint placed on the concepts. Hence, there is no appeal to intuition here, whether of an empirical or *a priori* nature; our concept 'line' is not given through lines constituted by us or given to us in intuition.

For Schlick, rigorous natural science must also define its concepts via implicit definition if it is to "determine concepts completely and thus to attain strict precision in thinking" (1925, §7). But on the face of it, the

---

9   It is, of course, more usual now to express this point in what Carnap termed "the formal mode of speech": The terms occurring in the axioms refer to whatever makes the axioms true. This became the standard only after the metamathematical and metalogical turns of the late 1920s and early 1930s, however, and is not how either Schlick in his book or Hilbert in his early work on geometry presented the idea.

concepts of natural science cannot simply be defined by the fact that they fulfill this or that consistent axiom system. One and the same axiom system can, for example, give the structural characteristics of a sequence of railroad stations and a sequence of telephone connections. But these things are different from the point of view of natural science. That is, implicit definition determines concepts in relation to one another but does not determine the connection between such concepts and empirical reality at all. Schlick himself puts the matter this way (1925, §7):

Implicit definitions have no association or connection with reality at all; specifically and in principle they reject such association . . . A system of truths created with the aid of implicit definitions does not at any point rest on the ground of reality. On the contrary, it floats freely, so to speak, and like the solar system bears within itself the guarantee of its own stability.

This is a large unanswered problem in Schlick's thought on scientific knowledge in *Allgemeine Erkenntnislehre*. Ultimately, he seeks to mitigate it by claiming that what is at stake here is the precision of scientific thinking and that this is where the structural aspects of implicit definition are exploited; the precision of scientific theorizing is the same as the precision of mathematical thinking: Both are purely formal. Thus, if, in the end, Schlick must allow for empirical intuition to creep back into science – in order to provide some indication as to which of many possible axiom systems is true of empirical objects – this yields no worse a consequence than the well-known empiricist position that the truth of judgments in the empirical science "is not absolutely guaranteed" (1925, §11). The precision of science is saved, but we can never know with absolute certainty whether the axiom systems of theoretical science capture the structure of the world.

This answer, however, simply changes the question from what Schlick claimed it was in the passage just quoted. This answer requires that objects be given in empirical intuition as such and thus sets aside the project of defining objects via their conceptual interconnections. In Schlick's original formulation of the problem, and for Carnap, the relation of structure and science goes deeper; it is to explain not the precision of science but its objectivity – its ability to make claims about the world at all. On Carnap's view, if we eventually had to rely on the individual's subjective experience in defining scientific concepts, those concepts would themselves be irreducibly subjective. Science would altogether cease to be about an objective world that is identical for all of us. That is to say, Schlick's eventual endorsement of implicit definition, which defines concepts through the assertion of various judgments, leaves open the possibility that those judgments are not precisely true of anything in reality. For Carnap, until and unless we have precisely and structurally defined concepts, the making of judgments in any significant sense is impossible. The issue of the truth or falsity of any particular judgments, including those of our favored axiom systems, is secured only by our ability to make objective judgments at all.

Carnap's logicism provides him with both the means to criticize a project of implicit definition such as Schlick's and an alternative paradigm of concept formation. Carnap argues for a logicist rejection of Hilbert's formalism and, hence, also of the method of implicit definition, even within the mathematical sciences. The logicist program in mathematics differs from the formalist program in that, although both provide axiom systems from which (it was thought) all mathematical theorems could be derived, the logicist alone provided definitions of the mathematical concepts that were symbolized in the axiom system. Thus, the Russellian account of arithmetic differs from that given by the Peano axioms in that *Principia Mathematica* also provides definitions of the basic concepts of the Peano axioms, for example, 'number' and 'successor.'[10] It is this additional feature which allowed Carnap to conclude that the logicist program alone provided an explanation of the *objectivity* of arithmetical knowledge.

Carnap presented his reasons for this assessment of logicism and formalism in his 1927 essay entitled "Eigentliche und uneigentliche Begriffe" (Proper and improper concepts; hereafter *EUB*). The principal focus of this essay was a discussion of proper (*eigentlich*) concepts and their relation to improper (*uneigentlich*) concepts. "Proper concepts" are those which are explicitly defined within a constitutional system, whereas "improper concepts" are those only implicitly defined via the axioms of this or that axiom system. Within the domain of proper concepts, Carnap further distinguished empirical concepts from formal concepts. "Formal concepts" are the concepts of logic and mathematics (as given in *Principia Mathematica*) whereas "empirical concepts" are (EUB, p. 356) "the concepts of real objects."

Carnap was at pains in his essay to establish that the concepts of natural science are all proper concepts and yet to explain the nature and

---

10 There are many ways to formulate the Peano axioms. They can be formulated such that 'number' and 'successor' are the only primitive concepts, however. See Russell (1919, chap. 1).

usefulness of axiom systems as implicit definitions of improper concepts. He made three distinctions between proper and improper concepts. First, proper concepts do, whereas improper concepts do not, fulfill the law of *tertium non datur*. Within the framework of type theory, the claim that proper concepts fulfill the law of *tertium non datur* amounts to the following: Consider a concept represented by the symbol ϕ. Then for any object, α, such that ϕα is meaningful, ϕα is either true or false. That is, any object of appropriate type either falls under the concept or it does not. As the concept represented by ϕ is also of some particular type, it can serve as an argument for predicates of higher type. So, since *tertium non datur* also holds for these concepts, we arrive at the following fact about proper concepts: For any concept, Φ, such that Φϕ is meaningful, Φϕ is either true or false.

This last claim is, of course, untrue in general of concepts implicitly defined via axiom systems. In order to implicitly define a concept, an axiom system need only be consistent. This very weak condition on the axiom system makes the last claim fail for a large class of improper concepts. Carnap's example (EUB, p. 363) is as follows:

Axiom System I:

1. The field of R has three members.
2. R and the ancestral of R are irreflexive.
3. R is intransitive.

Axiom System I "defines" the concept 'R.' The models of Axiom System I and, hence, of R allow, however, of two nonisomorphic structures. The arrow diagram for R can be of either of the following types:

$$\circ \rightarrow \circ \rightarrow \circ \qquad \circ \leftarrow \circ \rightarrow \circ$$

But the structural properties of R are different (obviously) in these two diagrams. In particular, since Axiom System I allows these two models, the sentence "R is one-to-one" is meaningful but neither true nor false. R, as defined by Axiom System I, neither has nor lacks the property of being one-to-one.

What is crucial to the argument here is that one-to-oneness is a structural property of relations. As such, it must be meaningful to ask of a given relation if it is one-to-one or not, and, thus, every proper relation either has this property or not. But relations specified by some consistent axiom systems are not specified sufficiently to determine whether they have this structural property. Thus, these axiom systems surely do not count as definitions of the relations mentioned in them.

The second distinction between proper and improper concepts that Carnap finds is the following. He claims that (EUB, p. 367) "It belongs to the essence of a proper concept that for every object it is in principle decidable whether that object falls under that concept or not; in fact with sufficient knowledge of the object this decision is also practically feasible." This, however, is not the case with concepts improperly defined by axiom systems. Consider Carnap's example of the natural numbers, as defined by the Peano axioms. This axiom system allows of many interpretations, including any physically existing infinite sequence of spheres (if there is any such series). The question, Is this sphere a number? is, however, meaningless in abstraction from the entire interpretation. If this sphere is part of the infinite sequence of spheres which forms an interpretation of the axiom system, then, within this interpretation, the sphere is a number; if we interpret the axiom system using an interpretation based on spatial or temporal points, then the sphere is not a number. No amount of knowledge that we can gain of the sphere will, however, provide a univocal answer to the question as to whether the sphere is a (Peano) number. The question therefore lacks an answer, and *tertium non datur* fails here as well.

This last difference between proper and improper concepts is related to (Carnap [EUB, p. 370] calls it a "symptom" of) the final and ultimate distinction Carnap claims for these two kinds of concepts. Carnap states (EUB, pp. 371–2):

> The sign of an improper concept is the sign of a variable which is based on a certain axiom system in such a way that the sentential [satzartigen] signs in which it appears are to be made into proper sentences through a specific kind of supplementation to the axioms of the axiom system.

Carnap puts forward the view that improper concepts are mere placeholders – variables – through the use of which one can become familiar with the formal consequences of certain axioms. Thus, the theorems of Peano arithmetic, for example, are best thought of as abbreviated forms of long, purely logical theorems in conditional form beginning with a universal quantifier binding each nonlogical symbol and having as antecedent the conjunction of the axioms and having as consequent the putative theorem.

This way of viewing axiom systems and the implicitly defined concepts they contain gives substance to the brief remarks Carnap makes about implicit definition in section 15 of the *Aufbau*. Carnap there states that implicit definition can lead only to analytic statements about the (improper) concepts so defined. This is certainly not sufficient for a system of scientific concepts. Carnap points to the need to define the concepts of science such that contentful, empirical statements containing the signs for those concepts can be made. In "Eigentliche und uneigentliche Begriffe," Carnap puts the point this way (p. 372):

Empirical concepts are constituted step-by-step in the systematic constitution of [our] knowledge of reality. As a member of this constitution every empirical concept has immediate relation to reality. In contrast to this, improper concepts chiefly float, so to speak, in the air. They are introduced through axiom systems, which are themselves not in immediate relation to reality.[11]

So what Carnap needs in his constitutional system for empirical concepts is a method of definition which is formally sufficient for a step-by-step constitution of the entire system of scientific concepts, but one which is superior to implicit definition in that it maintains connection between the defined concepts and empirical reality – or, more precisely, that allows for synthetic, empirical knowledge. This is, of course, not necessary for the logicist constitutional system for mathematics given in *Principia Mathematica*. Whitehead and Russell's system shows the concepts of mathematics to be proper concepts, but they are also shown to be formal rather than empirical concepts. Thus Carnap needs to go beyond the system of *Principia Mathematica* in the definition of empirical concepts as well.

It is the need to preserve empirical knowledge and synthetic *a posteriori* judgments that constitutes the requisite connection with empirical reality. Thus, Carnap's use of metaphysical language in the passage just quoted is wholly metaphorical. It should be clear that what is doing all the philosophical work for Carnap throughout his discussion in this essay is simply the status of *tertium non datur* as a logical truth. Its apparent failure for implicitly defined concepts indicates that concepts are not adequately specified by such axiom systems. What is, therefore, necessary for the well-foundedness of both ϕ and α is that we can make sense of $\phi\alpha$, and thus not-$\phi\alpha$ *because* "$\phi\alpha$ or not-$\phi\alpha$" is a logical truth and,

---

11 This passage appears to contrast improper concepts with empirical concepts. Carnap's point is, however, that implicit definition of empirical concepts leaves them without relation to the empirical realm. Formal concepts, even when properly defined as in *Principia Mathematica*, still lack this relation to empirical reality, but that is not a problem, as we shall see later in the chapter.

ipso facto, meaningful. The contact with "reality" requisite for empirical concepts is just this requirement of sense, which is driven by adherence to the logical truth of *tertium non datur*. In the case of empirical concepts, this means finding a sense for empirical judgments involving those concepts. Carnap hopes to fulfill all these desiderata in his procedure of purely structural definite descriptions. It is to this procedure that we now turn.[12]

PURELY STRUCTURAL DEFINITE DESCRIPTION

A "purely structural definite description" (PSDD) picks out an object uniquely on the basis of structural features of the relations in which it stands to other objects in a domain. It relies only on the structural features of the relations, that is, on those features of it that are preserved in the arrow diagram or list of n-tuples (where the objects related by the relation are given arbitrary designations). For relations among empirical objects, these structural features are typically only empirically known. Such a definite description, according to Carnap (§13), has the advantage that we do not have to rely ultimately on experiential ostension of any object in the domain as the ground of the sequence of definite descriptions for the objects in that domain. Thus, the purely structural definite descriptions fulfill the desiderata we have for the definitions of empirical objects for objective science: They rely only on the structure of experience; it is an empirical matter that experience has a structure that permits them; and no prior determination of any of the objects in immediate acquaintance is presupposed by or expressed in the definitions.

We can illustrate the essential features of purely structural definite descriptions through a simplified version of the railway example Carnap provides in section 14. Imagine a city with a very simple subway system that has the following structure: There are two lines, one running east and west and the other running north and south. The two lines intersect at exactly one station, where passengers can make free transfers from one line to the other. Let us suppose that this station is called "City Center." Suppose further that the eastern terminal of the

---

12 Thus there is an inaccuracy in Friedman's (1987, p. 542, n21) claim that Carnap "endorses" Hilbertian implicit definition in §15. Although Carnap does positively claim "scientific importance" (as shown by Schlick) for such definitions, the bulk of this part of §15 is meant to underscore the advantages of Carnap's definitional method over implicit definition. Compare also Carnap's remarks at §121 and EUB, p. 373.

Carnap's constitutional project

system is six stations from City Center, the western terminal is five stations from City Center, the northern terminal is four stations from City Center, and the southern terminal is two stations from City Center. Call these stations, respectively, "East," "West," "North," and "South." The relation of nextness between stations is the important one for the construction. Let us call it "R." This relation has enough structure that we can uniquely define all the stations from it via Carnapian PSDDs. We can, through these definitions, then introduce names for the stations as defined terminology into our language.

The feature of the structure of R that allows the formation of PSDDs in this case is the existence of stations with differing numbers of neighbors. The vast majority of the stations have exactly two neighbors. The four terminal stations, however, have only one neighbor each, and one station (City Center) has four. This last station gives us our easiest entering place for the PSDDs. Using the abbreviation in (1), we can use the truth of (2) to introduce the term "City Center" into our language via (3):

(1) $\Phi x =_{df} (\exists y)(\exists z)(\exists w)(\exists v)[(Rxy \& Rxz \& Rxw \& Rxv \& y \neq z \& y \neq w \& y \neq v \& z \neq w \& z \neq v \& w \neq v) \& (\forall u)(Rxu \to (u = y \lor u = z \lor u = w \lor u = v))]$

(2) $(\exists x)(\Phi x \& (\forall y')(\Phi y' \to y' = x))$

(3) City Center $=_{df} (\imath x)\Phi x$

With (3) in hand we can use structurally specifiable differences to distinguish the terminal stations. The crucial fact is that the chains of the R relation are of different length for each terminal station. For example, South is only two stations from City Center. This fact can be captured within the bounds of purely structural definite descriptions in the obvious but long-winded ways: There is one and only one station with exactly one R-neighbor and which stands in relation R to some station that stands in relation R to City Center. The remaining stations can then be defined by the lengths of R-chains leading to them from the defined stations. Once we have all the terminals defined we can define all the other stations via the length of the R-chains from them to City Center and the terminals. All difficulties are thereby resolved.[13]

Definition (3) meets the requirements of a purely structural definite description as Carnap presents the notion in section 13. It uniquely picks out a single object from the field of the relation R that fulfills a condition, Φ, which in turn is specifiable in terms of R and logical terms

---

13 The details are left as an exercise in tedium for the insomniac reader.

alone. Since R is not itself an object in the domain in question, but rather a relation over that domain, there is no problem induced by the fact that it appears in the definition. Similarly, no object in the domain is ostensively pointed out or introduced as part of the primitive terminology of our language. Finally, it is, of course, only the (in our case, imagined) empirical fact that this system has a neighbor relation of this structure that allows these definitions to work.[14]

Of course, if the relation(s) chosen do not have the structural characteristics necessary for structurally specifying the individual objects in their domains, this is not simply the end of the matter. In such cases, Carnap counsels us to expand the number of relations we look at in trying to come up with the structural definite description: Start with further geographical relations, and expand the number and kind of relations until each station is uniquely determined. Any subjectively different stations, to continue the example, which are indistinguishable even after we have considered all relations from all branches of science among them must be deemed objectively indistinguishable "not only for geography, but for science in general" (§14). Thus there is no *a priori* guarantee that this method will meet with success, but it alone can guarantee objectivity. In section 13, Carnap goes so far as to allow that even "the total domain of all objects of knowledge" may not in fact be ordered in a system of purely structural definite descriptions (constitutional system) but says "it is a necessary presupposition of the possibility of an intersubjective, purely rational science" that such a system is possible.

The type theoretic structure of logic and the existence of relations among relations provide the solution to a related difficulty. Carnap is faced with the problem of specifying all the concepts of science purely structurally. But it is clear that relations considered in isolation can share structure. Thus, a simple structuralist account would not be able to distinguish, for example, any two equivalence relations defined over domains of the same cardinality when these relations are considered in isolation. Carnap's guiding idea is that by embedding these relations and the objects over which they hold in a rich enough structure of further relations, each of the relations will be purely structurally defin-

---

[14] A system with only two stations, each of which is the other's only neighbor, is obviously too structurally impoverished to yield any system of PSDDs for the stations. We would have to bring different relations and, presumably, a larger object domain of which the stations were only a small subclass to bear before we could get the definitions going.

able. To use Michael Friedman's terminology (1987, p. 528), such "locally" structurally identical relations can be distinguished by their places in the overall "global" network of relations. Thus, Carnap exploits the idea that relations over objects at some type level are themselves individuals in the domain of other relations of higher type to achieve the rich structure of relations needed to achieve a constitutional system for total science.

It is this strategy of uniquely determining all the objects (concepts and relations) of science that grounds the project for achieving objectivity via PSDDs. Each relation is ultimately uniquely determined by its position in the whole nexus of relations. This is meant to answer an objection one might bring to our example of a PSDD in definition (3). We said that this definition meets the requirements for a PSDD because no element of the domain was ineliminably mentioned in it. But, of course, the relation, R, itself is ineliminably mentioned in the definition. Thus, definition (3) counts as a PSDD within a constitutional system for total science only on the presupposition that R itself has already been or subsequently will be given a PSDD of its own. Nothing Carnap has said in his example of section 14 and nothing that I have said in following this example have lent any plausibility to the claim that we can do this.

Again, we must be careful in what we are asking Carnap for here. Surely Carnap is not in a position to provide a blanket *a priori* guarantee that this can be done in any particular case. The method of giving PSDDs for relations via their unique place in the whole network of relations must, however, be possible if objective science is possible. Thus, it is a methodological presupposition of the constitutional project that the method will work for the epistemologically ordered constitutional system for the totality of science (or indeed any such total constitutional system). How it can proceed is no more difficult to understand than it is to understand how the PSDDs for the object domain of R were formulated. Thus, although the example does not yet show how elimination of essential reference to particular relations is possible – doing that would require that the entire constitutional system already be in place – it does show how the constitutional system can proceed given that it has gotten started. This is to be achieved by not merely quantifying over relations but by picking them out by definite description according to their purely structural but empirically given relations within the whole network of relations. That is, the uniqueness of the described relation is logically presupposed in the definition but is only empirically ascertainable. The empirical nature of the guarantee of the uniqueness of reference of the structural definite description is meant to give content to the idea that the constitutional system is a constitutional system for empirical concepts, as opposed to the formal concepts of mathematics. This finds its expression in Carnap's distinction between logical and empirical theorems within the definitions of the system.

There is, of course, more to be said here. There are serious worries still about the viability of the structuralist project. These worries are manifest in the *Aufbau* itself in sections 153–5, in which Carnap attempts to define away the basic relation itself. Here the tension between objectivity as form and the empirical basis of knowledge comes out with clarity. The discussion of these sections must wait for its proper place in the outline of the constitutional system, however.

QUASI ANALYSIS

There is one other general technical problem that Carnap's conception of the constitutional project entails, regardless of the constitutional order chosen. Carnap conceives of the basis of any constitutional system as consisting of one or more relations holding over a domain of primitive elements. The basis elements have no primitive qualities; that is, the relations are not supplemented by primitive property descriptions. Thus, methodologically, the basis elements are free of qualities. Indeed, the qualities that hold of the basis elements are among the things that must be constitutionally defined. So, he needs to devise a general method of constituting properties from relation descriptions. His solution is the procedure he terms "quasi analysis."[15]

The point of quasi analysis is to allow the construction of properties of individual basis elements from the relations that hold among those elements. Formally, therefore, the procedure of quasi analysis is an extension of the method of abstraction used by Whitehead and Russell in their work on the foundations of mathematics. Perhaps the most famous use of their method of *abstraction* (or *analysis*) is as part of the logicist definition of the natural numbers. Consider sentence (*):

(*) The earth has (exactly) one moon.

Logicists worried what meaning could legitimately be assigned to such a sentence. Very roughly, the idea was to think of (*) as expressing the

---

15 The process of quasi analysis has engendered a good deal of the secondary literature on the *Aufbau*. I have used Goodman (1953) throughout the following discussion. For other literature, see, e.g., Kleinknecht (1980), Lewis (1969), Mormann (1994), and Proust (1989 [1986], §4, chap. 2).

claim that the predicate "is a moon of the earth" is satisfied by exactly one object, that is, that the class of objects satisfying the predicate is a one-membered class. This, in turn, helps the logicist account of number claims only insofar as the notion of 'one-membered class' can be explicated without a primitive notion of 'one.'

This is where the method of abstraction comes in. The idea is that a primitive relation of equinumerosity can be brought in to aid the definition of the number of a class. Consider a relation of equinumerosity for classes which holds just in case there is a function that maps each element of one class onto exactly one member of the other. The notion of a one-to-one function can itself be understood in terms of the existence of a relation and the existence and uniqueness of relata of that relation. Thus, it can be expressed in wholly logical terms. This will do the trick for the logicists. Equinumerosity is a logical notion that either obtains or fails to obtain between any two classes.

The method of abstraction now allows particular equivalence classes of the relation of equinumerosity to be formed. For example, we can define the class "zero" as the class of all classes equinumerous with the empty set. (The empty set is itself definable as, say, the class of all things not identical with themselves, that is, the extension of the predicate "not identical with itself.") "One" can then be defined as the class of all classes equinumerous with zero (since zero turns out to be simply the class containing only the empty set). The meaning of the asterisked sentence is then given by the following sentence:

(**) The extension of "is a moon of the earth" is an element of one.

The crucial notion for Carnap, if not for the particular purposes of the logicists in this case, is that here we have a property of an object (in this case, a class) defined from a relation over such objects (in this case, the relation of equinumerosity between classes).

The extension of this to the empirical realm is clear enough. To take the particular example of Carnap's "elementary experiences" (*elex*), we want, for example, to be able to claim

(#) Elementary experience, $elex_{23}$, has a red dot in a particular point of the visual field.

The idea is to try to construct from the basic relation among the elementary experiences the class of the elexes that have a red spot at that point of the visual field. The meaning of this sentence is then that $elex_{23}$ is an element of the class of such elexes. Carnap has no other way to make sense of any property ascription to the elexes, since they are understood to be primitive and, thus, without properties somehow independent of the constitutional project itself. Carnap calls such constructed properties "quasi properties" and the process by which they are constituted "quasi analysis."

Formally, then, quasi analysis is simply an extension of the notion of analysis. The distinction Carnap draws between analysis and quasi analysis is epistemological. He introduces the notion of analysis with these words (§70): "In proper analysis, we are concerned not with propertyless points or indivisible unities, but rather with objects that have various constituents (or characteristics). Analysis consists in inferring these constituents, which are at first unknown, from other data, for example, from a relation description." Quasi analysis, on the other hand, is not a process by which one infers properties of complex objects from relations among them. It is, rather, a process of constituting quasi constituents or quasi qualities from relation descriptions holding over propertyless points or indivisible unities. Thus, quasi analysis is, Carnap tells us (§74), "synthesis in the linguistic garb of an analysis." The properties that the basis elements are eventually said to have are not analyzed from complex basis elements but are logical constructions from these elements, classes of the elements derived from the basic relations given at the start of the system. Thus, analysis and quasi analysis are formally identical procedures for Carnap. They differ only in their constitutional and epistemological roles. Analysis presumes an antecedent fact of the matter about the properties of complex objects and tries to recover such properties from relations among those objects. Using formally identical techniques, quasi analysis seeks to constitute classes that play the role of the properties for objects that are constitutionally primitive. That is, in quasi-analytic contexts there is no independent or antecedent sense in which the objects standing in the relations have properties; they have only those properties that are definable in a quasi-analytic way.

The formal identity between analysis and quasi analysis aids with the exposition of Carnap's formal concerns. In situations such as the one just discussed, analysis consists in the definition of equivalence classes from a given "equivalence relation." Any relation that is reflexive, symmetric, and transitive is an equivalence relation; equinumerosity, for example, is an equivalence relation. Carnap's quasi analysis cannot rely on the basic relation(s) being equivalence relation(s), however. He needs a more general procedure, since his relations might be rather differently structured. There are two ways in which Carnap thinks that the method of analysis must be extended if it is to be applicable to the basic relation of the system actually presented in the *Aufbau*. These extensions are necessary in order to exploit the structure that a genuine recollection of similarity relation is likely to have.

Let us recall the sort of thing that Carnap must try to construct. He needs to construct, for example, the colors in the visual field of a given elementary experience. If it were the case that the visual field contained only a single color for any given elex, then he could perhaps (somewhere not too far up the constitutional order) simply use the method of analysis to create the equivalence classes of a color identity relation for the visual field. He cannot, however, do that if (as seems reasonable) the visual field can contain more than one color. If this is the case, then the only way to define a class of elexes that have, say, a particular shade of yellow somewhere in the visual field is not via any equivalence relation but by what Carnap will call a *part identity relation*. This relation captures the idea that a given object is partially (qualitatively) identical to another. For example, the class of elexes with a specific shade of yellow in the visual field might contain one elex that also has a shade of blue in the visual field and a second one that contains a shade of red in the visual field. These two elexes are part identical to one another – they both contain that yellow shade – but the first will also be part identical to other elexes to which the second is not. In other words, it is clearly the case that quasi analysis must be applicable to nonequivalence relations. A part identity relation is a similarity relation only; it fails to be transitive.

We can understand Carnap's attempted solution to the problem of extending the construction of classes from equivalence relations to similarity relations through a consideration of examples drawn from Nelson Goodman's *Structure of Appearance* (1953). Here, I shall follow Goodman in giving examples that Carnap would think of as following the method of analysis rather than quasi analysis. I shall not lose sight of the distinction between analysis and quasi analysis, however, and I shall return to it when responding to Goodman's philosophical concerns with quasi analysis.

Let us consider a world of six individuals and three properties. Each of these properties is a color; they are, respectively, a particular shade of red, blue, and green and will be designated r, b, and g. We shall designate the individuals by the first six arabic numerals for the natural numbers (1 through 6). To say that object 4 is green and only green, I shall write "4. g."

Before we get to more complicated situations, I shall start with an easy example in which each object has one and only one color. Such a world might look like this:

$$
\begin{array}{lll}
1.\ r & 2.\ b & 3.\ g \\
4.\ b & 5.\ b & 6.\ r
\end{array}
$$

Proper analysis is a process whereby we would recover these properties of these objects from a relation holding among them. For example, we might have the relation of color kinship – where one object is color akin to another just in case they have a color in common.

Given the extensionalist framework within which we are working, to recover the properties amounts to no more than giving a procedure that recovers the appropriate classes of the individuals. In our simple case the classes we want to recover are the three classes {1,6}; {2,4,5}; and {3}. Similarly, in this case, the relation of color kinship has a very simple structure. It is reflexive, symmetric, and transitive over the field; hence, it is an equivalence relation. Its ordered pair list is:

⟨1,1⟩; ⟨1,6⟩
⟨2,2⟩; ⟨2,4⟩; ⟨2,5⟩
⟨3,3⟩
⟨4,2⟩; ⟨4,4⟩; ⟨4,5⟩
⟨5,2⟩; ⟨5,4⟩; ⟨5,5⟩
⟨6,1⟩; ⟨6,6⟩

The way to recover the appropriate classes is simple: A color class is a class of objects all of which stand in the relation of color kinship to one another and such that there is nothing outside the class that stands in the color kinship relation to all members of the class. The first conjunct disallows classes such as {1,2}: The members of this class do not stand in the color kinship relation. The second conjunct disallows classes such as {2,4}: There is an individual outside this class that stands in the color kinship relation to all the members of the class, namely, 5. The classes we want are the largest classes all of whose members are color akin.

This is a very easy case to understand, precisely because we have an equivalence relation in this case. The color kinship relation divides the field into equivalence classes. These equivalence classes are precisely the classes we are looking for. Thus, in such a case, not only is there no element outside the color class that stands in the relation to *all* the elements inside, but there is no element that stands in the relation to *any* of the elements. This is, however, a special case. Since each individual has one property, the classes constructed from the kinship relation to serve as quality classes do not overlap.

Let us complicate our picture by making our imagined world slightly more realistic. In this example, our individuals can have one or more colors. In such a case, color kinship will now be a part identity relation and, thus, a similarity relation. An example from Goodman has the world consisting of the following individuals:

1. br	2. b	3. bg
4. g	5. r	6. bgr

Given this tally of the individuals, we can list the classes our analytic procedure must deliver: {1,2,3,6}, {1,5,6}, and {3,4,6}. We can also construct the pair list of the color kinship relation:

⟨1,1⟩; ⟨1,2⟩; ⟨1,3⟩; ⟨1,5⟩; ⟨1,6⟩
⟨2,1⟩; ⟨2,2⟩; ⟨2,3⟩; ⟨2,6⟩
⟨3,1⟩; ⟨3,2⟩; ⟨3,3⟩; ⟨3,4⟩; ⟨3,6⟩
⟨4,3⟩; ⟨4,4⟩; ⟨4,6⟩
⟨5,1⟩; ⟨5,5⟩; ⟨5,6⟩
⟨6,1⟩; ⟨6,2⟩; ⟨6,3⟩; ⟨6,4⟩; ⟨6,5⟩; ⟨6,6⟩

Can we reconstruct the classes from the pair list? It seems that we can without trouble through the selfsame idea. The color classes, which Carnap calls *similarity circles* (§70) (owing to complications noted later in this chapter), are again those classes of the elements such that any two elements are related by the relation and no element outside the class is related to everything inside. Indeed, in the given case, this recipe yields exactly the three classes we want.[16] In these cases where transitivity fails, Carnap's idea is that the similarity circles constructed in this way will distinguish between overlaps that do not indicate a shared property and those that do indicate a shared property.

Before considering Goodman's concerns about this aspect of Carnap's project of quasi analysis, let us conclude our exegesis of the formal aspect of the project. So far, the relations we have considered are

---

16 If this is not obvious, Goodman (1953, pp. 158–60) goes through the case in detail.

Quasi analysis

part identities – relations that indicate that two objects agree in one or more quality. The relation that Carnap has available for quasi analysis in the constitutional system actually outlined, however, is not a part identity; it is a *part similarity*. Two elementary experiences stand in this relation, so to speak, not merely if they agree in a constituent, but also if they share similar constituents.[17] Thus, similarity circles defined by this relation in themselves yield only classes of part similar individuals, and further work must be done to carve the similarity circles into quality classes.[18] Again let us employ Goodman's (1953, pp. 165–8) detailed exposition as our guide.

If we continue to think in terms of analysis, rather than quasi analysis, to motivate the process, we can put the basic ideas as follows: Let us think of a relation of color similarity that holds between two individuals just in case the first has a color that is similar to a color exhibited by the second. (Because this is a symmetric relation, it matters not at all which is considered first or second.) Consider a similarity circle based on this relation: It contains not merely individuals that share a color but individuals that have similar but not identical colors. How do we get the right classes: The ones containing only objects sharing the *same* color? The idea is to look at how the similarity circles overlap. Carnap (§§72, 80–1) considers an analogy with what he terms the "color solid": The color solid is a three-dimensional array of colors, ordered by hue, saturation, and brightness. Imagine this three-dimensional solid sphere (or ball) constituted by small overlapping spheres. For example, imagine the color sphere covered by similarity spheres, each of which captures similar shades of color.[19] How would we define the individual points (colors)? Geometrically, the points are the largest portions of the whole sphere undivided by the small overlapping spheres, and that is how to define them.

This is, then, the guiding analogy: The quality classes are the largest

---

17 This way of putting the matter gets things backward. The systematic difference between part identity relations and part similarity relations, for Carnap, is given in the structure of the class of similarity circles constructible from these types of relation (as we will see later in the chapter). The terminology is confusing since both part identity relations and part similarity relations are similarity relations, not equivalence relations.

18 The fact that part similarities do not yield quality classes via the process of constructing similarity circles is the reason why similarity circles are so named, and not called "quality classes."

19 In this case the similarity holds over the colors themselves rather than over the colored individuals of the original case.

classes of individuals wholly inside a similarity circle and undivided by the overlapping similarity circles. Think, for example, of the similarity circle "centered" on a particular shade of yellow. The quality class for that shade of yellow would be the largest subclass of that similarity circle undivided by other similarity circles – the circles "centered" on nearby shades of yellow. In practice this amounts to the following first attempt (cf. Goodman 1953, p. 175): A class of individuals, q, is a quality class just in case (i) each element of q is contained in every similarity circle to which any element of q belongs (this bars individuals that find themselves in other similarity circles) and (ii) for every individual not in q there is some similarity circle which contains all of q but not that individual (this gives us maximal classes).

This actually does not work, because of a crucial disanalogy in the two cases (the color solid covered by densely packed color similarity spheres, and the colored individuals arranged in similarity circles based on a color similarity relation). In the case of the color solid itself, a small sphere centered on a particular shade of yellow – say, the yellow in the Swedish flag – does not overlap any sphere centered on any shade of blue. The overlaps occur only with spheres of nearby colors. With the colored individuals, however, there can be overlaps between similarity circles "centered" on widely disparate colors. For example, if among our individuals is a Swedish flag, this will fall into yellow and blue similarity circles. Thus, our condition (i) is too strong; we do not want to throw the Swedish flag out of the class of things exhibiting the shade of yellow in the flag simply because it is in another similarity circle for blue things that most of those yellow things are not in. What we want to do is separate the nearby colors that are lumped together by the similarity relation. We do not care about overlaps from similarity circles from far afield. Carnap distinguishes these cases as "essential overlap" and "accidental overlap" (§§80–1), respectively.

But how are we to distinguish accidental from essential overlap? Carnap (§§81, 112), in essence, proposes to treat accidental overlap as "uncommon." Thus, the first condition of the definition is revised to read (cf. Goodman 1953, p. 176): (i) Each element of q is contained in every similarity circle within which at least half of the elements of q belong. Thus, our Swedish flag is no longer a problem, since the blue similarity circle within which it finds itself contains at most a few more elements of the class of things exhibiting the yellow of the flag.

There are a couple of points about quasi analysis on the basis of part similarity relations that should be noted. First, given that relations do not come tagged as being part identities or part similarities, how do we decide whether the simpler or the more complicated quasi-analytic procedure should be followed? Carnap (§72) argues that the difference between part similarity and part identity relations is itself a matter of the structure of the initially constructed similarity circles. If, after the construction of the similarity circles in accordance with the simple procedure, there are large multiple overlappings, then we must proceed to the second step. Otherwise, we can treat the similarity circles as quality classes immediately. Thus, the difference between part similarity and part identity relations is not a difference between whether the relations capture qualitative identities or similarities among the individuals; that would contradict the epistemological starting point and constitutional reason for the quasi-analytic process itself. Rather, it is a matter of the structure of the relations alone — a matter exhibited by the structure of the overlapping of the similarity circles constructed from them.

Finally, as Goodman (1953) stresses, the complicated process of quasi analysis on the basis of part similarity does more than simply solve a problem posed by a complicated system of mutually overlapping similarity circles. It also crucially provides an ordering of the qualities, based on the size of the essential overlaps. This ordering of qualities is exploited in the further constructions. For example, classes of qualities have to be linked together and distinguished from other classes of qualities, as when we distinguish tactile from visual qualities. Thus, the more complicated procedure is in accord with Carnap's methodological need for relational structures; the complicated quasi-analytic procedure yields not a mere list but a structure of qualities. Thus, we are not stymied in the search for further constructions.

GOODMAN'S OBJECTIONS TO QUASI ANALYSIS

Perhaps the second most famous objections (after Quine's) to Carnap's project in the *Aufbau* are Nelson Goodman's technical objections to quasi analysis. Thus, I would be remiss not to discuss those objections here. In the end, I shall argue that Goodman's objections are indeed objections to analysis on the basis of similarity relations, but not to quasi analysis on the basis of similarity relations. Goodman does not adequately distinguish between the technical congruence and the epistemological or constitutional noncongruence of these notions in Carnap's project.[20]

---

20 My response to Goodman is similar to and has been informed by those found in Proust (1989 [1986]) and Mormann (1994).

Recall Carnap's condition for the analytic and quasi-analytic construction of similarity circles on the basis of similarity relations: The similarity circles are those classes each of which is such that any two elements within it are related by the similarity relation and no element outside it is related by that similarity relation to everything inside. Goodman notes that as an analytic process this recipe can easily fail. An example based on one given in the preceding section of this chapter is seen in the following world:

    1. br   2. b   3. bg
    4. g   5. br   6. bgr

Here, the only difference from the original case is that individual 5 is both blue and red and not merely red. This does not disturb our target class for the quality red, which remains {1,5,6}. But, if we form the pair list for color kinship and then find the similarity circles, this class is not among them. That is because there are individuals not in this class which are color akin to every member of the class, for example, 2. The problem is that all red individuals are also blue individuals. Carnap (§70) calls red a "companion" of blue in such a case. Hence, Goodman (1953, p. 161) calls this the "companionship difficulty."

Goodman also notes a second way in which analysis via similarity circles can fail. Consider the following world, differing from the original only in the colors exhibited by 2 and 5:

    1. br   2. br   3. bg
    4. g   5. gr   6. bgr

In this case the two classes we should arrive at for blue and red are, respectively, {1,2,3,6} and {1,2,5,6}. Neither of these classes are similarity circles, however. Both of these are proper subclasses of the class {1,2,3,5,6}, which is a similarity circle. What has gone wrong here is that all the members of this similarity circle are pairwise related, but there is no quality in common to all of them. Goodman (1953, p. 164) calls this problem the "difficulty of imperfect community."

In a large number of cases, analysis based on similarity circles simply fails to return the right classes. Thus, it is fatally flawed as a method of analysis. As intimated earlier, Carnap himself noted the companionship difficulty (§70). He called cases of companion qualities "unfavorable circumstances" and claimed the method of similarity circle analysis works when there are no "systematic connections of qualities." Presumably, Carnap would be tempted to call the imperfect community problem another unfavorable circumstance.

Goodman is skeptical about this invocation of "unfavorable circumstances." He notes that "unfavorable" need not mean "unlikely." After all, given the nature of color vision, might not there be systematic connections between two very slightly different shades of blue (Goodman 1953, p. 161)? (Consider a shade of blue that most of us see only in the fading evening sky and, hence, in momentary experience containing other shades very close to this one. This seems a likely candidate for companionship. Or, again, a rare shade of green that I have seen only in my lover's eyes would presumably be a companion of black for me, since her pupils are black.) More importantly, there is a grave risk that invoking "unfavorable circumstances" is simply circular (Goodman 1953, pp. 162, 164), amounting to nothing more than saying that the method works except in those cases where it fails.

These problems with analysis are problems that Goodman sees with quasi analysis also. For example, Goodman writes (1953, p. 161): "Although this section [§70] describes only a process to which quasianalysis is analogous, the analogy is so close that we have here the essence of Carnap's method of dealing with the problem of abstraction." But, if we recall the differences between analysis and quasi analysis, the situation seems more complicated. The crucial point is that in quasi analysis there is no independent way to characterize the classes the procedure is meant to yield. This is precisely the difference between quasi analysis and analysis. In analysis we assume we have individuals possessed of properties and ask for a way of recovering those properties from a relation description. In quasi analysis, all we have is the relation description and we seek to construct classes that will count as quasi qualities of these pointlike individuals.

Consider, for example, our last world, the one exhibiting the imperfect community problem. To turn this into a quasi analysis problem, we would have to remove the initial listing of qualities of the individuals and present only the relevant relation description. Thus we would start only with the following pair list:

$$\langle 1,1 \rangle; \langle 1,2 \rangle; \langle 1,3 \rangle; \langle 1,5 \rangle; \langle 1,6 \rangle$$
$$\langle 2,1 \rangle; \langle 2,2 \rangle; \langle 2,3 \rangle; \langle 2,5 \rangle; \langle 2,6 \rangle$$
$$\langle 3,1 \rangle; \langle 3,2 \rangle; \langle 3,3 \rangle; \langle 3,4 \rangle; \langle 3,5 \rangle; \langle 3,6 \rangle$$
$$\langle 4,3 \rangle; \langle 4,4 \rangle$$
$$\langle 5,1 \rangle; \langle 5,2 \rangle; \langle 5,3 \rangle; \langle 5,4 \rangle; \langle 5,5 \rangle; \langle 5,6 \rangle$$
$$\langle 6,1 \rangle; \langle 6,2 \rangle; \langle 6,3 \rangle; \langle 6,4 \rangle; \langle 6,5 \rangle; \langle 6,6 \rangle$$

There is no sense in which this pair list "ought to" yield the class {1,2,3,6} as a similarity circle. Indeed, this pair list is identical to the one we could read off from the following world:

1. g   2. g   3. gr
4. r   5. gr   6. gr

In this case, the right classes for analysis to yield would be {1,2,3,5,6} and {3,4,5,6}, which is what the method of similarity circles does yield.

The proper question for quasi analysis is not, Does it yield the right classes? There is no telling what the right classes are, independently of the results of the quasi-analytic procedure itself. What, then, is the relation between analysis and quasi analysis, and what role does discussion of unfavorable circumstances play for Carnap?

The discussion of analysis is motivational and heuristic. Carnap presents a method for constructing classes from relation descriptions that captures an intuitive idea of what a quality is and that works, in a number of cases, to recover the right classes of elements, that is, the classes of objects that do in fact share a property. It is true that sometimes it does not work – sometimes the color kinship relation does not exhibit the right structure to allow the quality classes to be recovered. But in such cases, maybe another relation would help, or perhaps qualities are not distributed in a way that can be recovered by any technique. Nevertheless, a method of some power for recovering properties has been discovered.

But the constitutional problem solved by quasi analysis is quite different. It is not a matter of *recovering* properties from relations; rather it is a matter of defining classes that play the role of properties, given only the structure of a relation. Carnap claims that the method of quasi analysis is useful for this. Indeed, it is more than just useful; Carnap claims not that this method works "in unfavorable circumstances" but that it will always work. In discussing quasi analysis, Carnap (§81) says, for example,

A more exact investigation, for which there is here no room, teaches, however, that these interferences in concept formation through quasi analysis [e.g., the unfavorable circumstances yielding a companionship problem] only appear if circumstances are present, under which the actual process of cognition, that is, the quasi analysis intuitively carried out in actual life, does not lead to normal results.

What is Carnap saying here? Again, we can see the point by looking at our latest examples: the world exhibiting imperfect community, and the alternative two-quality world that yields the same pair list. Carnap is not saying that quasi analysis on the pair list yields the wrong results in cases of imperfect community. Rather, he is saying that if the pair list for color kinship is the one we drew up, then quasi analysis yields the two classes it does *and* any agent who had that pair list would conceptualize the world in accordance with the two- and not the three-quality way. For such a person, there would be two qualities arranged in the way shown. This is, I take it, an expression of Carnap's methodological commitment to Gestalt psychology; the Gestalt of the color kinship relation comes first, and qualities are derived from it alone – both in the actual process of knowledge and in quasi analysis. In this sense, in cases of quasi analysis, sensitivity to unfavorable circumstances is a virtue that allows it accurately to reflect the dependence of conceptualization on the empirically given structure of experience.

The notion of "normal results" warrants comment also. For, if there is a normal result, there is some external perspective from which to make this judgment. But this perspective is again empirical psychology. Psychology tells us which color qualities are normal for humans to perceive. The working posit is that the color kinship relation for most of us will then exhibit the structure that allows just these qualities to be constructed. We do not have a pair list of this relation handy, of course, so this does not amount to an empirically testable claim. But then the claim that the reconstruction will yield precisely the results of intuitive concept formation done in our cognitive life is not a straightforwardly empirical claim, and so we ought not to be surprised if it is untestable.

We can treat Goodman's further objections to the more complicated case of analysis and quasi analysis on the basis of part similarity relations in a similar fashion. Goodman (1953, p. 176) considers the offered way of dealing with the problem of the Swedish flags as another case of barring unfavorable circumstances. Suppose, for example, the world contained nothing either yellow or blue but Swedish flags. Then there would be identity between the yellow and blue similarity circles and thus no way of constructing a distinction between (this) blue and (this) yellow. Indeed, the way Carnap distinguishes accidental and essential overlap basically broadens the companionship problem. Goodman (1953, p. 177) identifies the condition that must hold for the process to yield the right results: "We must now assume that fewer than half the [individuals] having any given quality q also have one or another of any group of mutually similar qualities other than q." This is a very strong assumption. Consider that presumed shade of blue I have seen only in the fading light of the evening sky. I can construct the quality class of that shade of blue only if fewer than half of those experiences have been accompanied by a visceral feeling of well-being (since we must divide visual and emotional qualities only higher up the system). Conceptual wealth is, it seems, purchased at a price.

Needless to say, I think Carnap's response here would be the same as in the earlier cases of "unfavorable circumstances." His methodology commits him to the priority of relational structure. Thus, I see no reason why he should deny the psychological conjecture that someone whose experiential life showed a particularly odd structure would arrive at very skewed concepts, that is, would ascribe properties at variance to the properties most people would ascribe to objects. Quasi analysis gets high marks for respecting this putative cognitive fact.

Goodman's particular concerns dissolve when we respect the constitutional difference between analysis and quasi analysis. In cases of quasi analysis, there is no external perspective against which to check the constructions for correctness; quasi analysis is not constrained by antecedent or independent matters of fact about the qualities of the objects related by the similarity relations. Indeed, to think it was so constrained would be to obviate the need for quasi analysis at the outset and to dismiss Carnap's methodological priority of relations over primitive properties for the basis elements. Goodman's objections do, of course, underscore the need for an account of the standards of constitutional adequacy, the status of notions such as 'unfavorable circumstances,' and the possibility of an external perspective constraining the constitutional system. These topics will concern us throughout the remainder of this work.

CHAPTER THREE

An outline of the constitutional projects for objectivity

W E are now in a position to undertake a closer examination of the details of the actual projects for achieving objectivity presented in *Der logische Aufbau der Welt*. An outline of Carnap's levels of constitution is, therefore, in order. In this way, we will be able to see what Carnap is doing in his two projects. Again, many questions about constitution and the order of the definitions will not be addressed in order to focus our attention solely on the question of the way the constitutional system explicates the objectivity of scientific claims.

THE LOWEST LEVELS OF THE CONSTITUTIONAL SYSTEM

The constitutional system meant to mirror the epistemic primacy relation begins, as we have noted, from a single relation, the "recollection of similarity" relation (*Rs*), over total cross-sections of experience at a time. Carnap's first order of business in the constitutional system is to constitute the rich texture of individual psychological life, the autopsychological domain, from this slender basis (cf., esp. §§108–20). Our primary concern is with the role of the autopsychological domain in the construction of objectivity, so I shall only sketch the definitions here. Of primary importance for our purposes is the final accounting of the autopsychological domain and the transition to the world of physics.[1]

Before discussing the definitions, there is a noteworthy aspect of

---

1 Greater detail on the definitions at the lowest levels of the system can be found in Goodman (1953, chap. 5). Throughout my discussion of the constructions, I have used the abbreviations for Carnap's key terms that George used in his translation, most of which were taken over from Goodman's work. I have done this to facilitate cross-referencing my discussion with the original text and also with Goodman's more detailed discussion.

The constitutional projects for objectivity

Carnap's procedure that warrants a brief mention. In accordance with the methodological strictures of "purely structural definite description" (*PSDD*), the definitions depend only on the structure of the recollection of similarity relation, but this structure is itself only empirically known. Thus, Carnap (§106) distinguishes between empirical and analytic theorems of the constitutional system. Of this distinction he writes (§106): "Transformed into propositions about the basic relation(s), an analytic theorem results in a tautology; an empirical theorem indicates empirical, formal properties of the basic relation(s). In realistic language: the analytic theorems are tautological statements about concepts . . . ; the empirical theorems express an experientially known state of affairs." Thus, Carnap is distancing himself here from the Kantian synthetic *a priori*. Empirical theorems are, therefore, capable of being captured as structural claims but are known only empirically. The status of knowledge that is at once empirical and purely formal will remain a primary question for us throughout our examination of Carnap's book.

The beginning steps of the constitutional system are straightforward. The basic relation of the system, the recollection of similarity relation, is introduced in section 108. The empirical theorem (theorem 1) that guides the rest of the constitutional definitions states that Rs is asymmetric. Intuitively, this is because Rs is a *recollection* of similarity. Thus, it encodes a temporal ordering. The agent whose elementary experiences are ordered by Rs is thought of as having an experience and recollecting the prior experiences similar to it. We can then (§109) construct the set of the elementary experiences (*elex*) as the field of the Rs relation.

Rs, for the same reason it is asymmetric, is also irreflexive. Rs is, therefore, not a similarity relation and, so, is not a candidate for quasi analysis. A similarity relation, "Part Similarity" (*Ps*), however, can easily be defined from Rs by collecting together any pair consisting of two elementary experiences that are related by Rs or are identical.[2] In other words, two elexes are part similar just in case one elex has been recollected as similar to the other or they are the same elex (§110):

$$Ps(x,y) =_{df} Rs(x,y) \vee Rs(y,x) \vee x = y \quad (x,y \in elex)$$

---

[2] "Part Similarity" is a particular relation and should not be confused with the general notion of a 'part similarity relation' discussed in Chapter Two with reference to quasi analysis. Part similarity relations and part identity relations are species of similarity relations. Only after the business of quasi analysis will it be knowable (as an empirical theorem, though not mentioned as such) that Ps is a part similarity relation.

The lowest levels of the constitutional system

Ps is clearly reflexive and symmetric and would be so regardless of the structure of Rs. Thus, Carnap's first analytic theorems (theorems 2 and 3) are the theorems that say Ps is reflexive and symmetric.

Ps is, therefore, by definition a similarity relation and a candidate for quasi analysis. Carnap's next order of business is then to define the class of similarity circles (*similcirc*) constructed by quasi analysis on Ps (§111). Given that these similarity circles collect together enormous numbers of elexes into classes of mutually similar experiences, Carnap presumes that there will be very large mutual overlaps among the similarity circles. He, therefore, engages in the second part of the complex quasi-analytic procedure: He defines "quality classes" (*qual*; cf. §112) from the similarity circles by admitting solely those classes that are divided only by "accidental" overlaps.[3]

Next, Carnap defines a relation, "part identity": Two members of elex are called "Part Identical" (*Pi*) just in case there is a quality class to which they both belong (§113). This is the basic point of the construction of quality classes; quasi analysis is meant to yield classes of elementary experiences that agree in some quality or other. Moreover, as we noted in Chapter Two, the more complicated quasi-analytic procedure yields an ordering of quality classes. Carnap exploits this order in his further definitions. The first definition states that two quality classes are considered "similar" (*Sim*) just in case each element of one is part similar to each element of the other (§114). Similar quality classes are intuitively those that are qualitatively close to one another. For example, suppose we have one quality class for a particular shade of blue, another for a similar shade, and a third for an auditory tone. Some elements of the first quality class may be similar to elements of the third, given that we are still dealing with total cross-sections of experience. The leading idea, though, is that each member of the first class is similar to each member of the second but not so to the third. This procedure will allow the various sense modalities to be pried apart from one another. The relation, Sim, is a reflexive and symmetric relation between quality classes (theorem 4).

The constitutional definitions begin to get a bit more complicated at this point. Carnap next (§115) considers the chain (Frege's ancestral) of the Sim relation; call this "Sim_{po}." The intuitive idea is that two quality classes stand in this chain, Sim_{po}, just in case there is a sequence of zero or more quality classes, such that each is similar to the next and which

---

3 Compare the discussion of accidental and essential overlap in Chapter Two.

leads from the first quality class to the second. Sim_{po} is reflexive, symmetric, and transitive.[4] Thus, we can define the class of abstraction classes for it, that is, the class of quality classes that can be linked by chains of similar quality classes. Carnap terms these abstraction classes the "sense classes" and the class of them, "Sense." The guiding idea is that, for example, there is always a way of tracing through mutually similar qualities all the way from one color shade to another far from it (barring unfavorable circumstances), but there is never a way to trace in this way from a color shade to, for example, an auditory tone. Sim, moreover, defines an ordering among the quality classes within any member of Sense. Thus, Carnap proposes to distinguish among the various members of Sense via the structure of the order that Sim induces within them. In particular, he seeks to use the topological definition of "dimension" to distinguish the visual sense class and all the other sense classes. The visual sense class, "Sight" (§115), is defined as the one and only element of Sense that has exactly five dimensions as ordered by Sim. It would seem that the existence of exactly one such class is an empirical theorem guiding the definition, but Carnap fails to mention this explicitly.[5]

Carnap's business in section 116 is to introduce sensations and divisions within the class of elementary experiences induced by them. The idea is that sensations are the quality exemplifications of an elex, that is, a given experience is said to be a sensation of a given quality just in case that quality is exemplified by that experience. Somewhat more formally, the class of "sensations" (*sen*) is the class of all ordered pairs consisting of an element of elex and a quality class to which that elex belongs. The relation of "simultaneity" (*Simul*) between two sensations is defined to hold just in case they have the same elex as the first member of the ordered pair. Carnap will use sensations and simultaneity to define two divisions in experience. The first exploits the structure of simultaneity: Simul is an equivalence relation. Hence, we can again construct its abstraction classes. Carnap calls this class Div_1. A given member of Div_1 is just the class of all the sensations of a given elex, that is, the class of all the qualities that are exemplified by that elex.

---

4 Indeed, the chain operation will always yield an equivalence relation from a similarity relation. Sim_{po}'s status as an equivalence relation should, therefore, count as an analytic theorem. Carnap uses this status but does not officially designate it as a theorem.
5 The five dimensions are, intuitively, the three dimensions of the color solid and the two dimensions of the visual field. Constitutionally, of course, this intuitive statement is reversed. For example, the color solid is defined as a particular three-dimensional subclass of Sight and so on.

The lowest levels of the constitutional system

Carnap then defines the second division of qualities of the elex – a relation, Div_2, that holds between the class of quality classes of an elex and that elex. Thus, whereas a given sensation is an ordered pair of an elex and a particular quality class containing it, a member of Div_2 is an ordered pair of the whole class of quality classes of an elex and that elex. He then defines a class, div_2, as the domain of Div_2. Thus, a given member of div_2 is simply a class of quality classes – the ones containing a particular elex, though that elex does not appear in the definition. The distinction between Div_1 and Div_2 is the distinction between the quality exemplifications of a given experience, which Carnap calls "sensations," and the class of the qualities of that experience in general.

The order of business of sections 117–18 is the definition of two distinct orders within the five-dimensional order of the visual sense, Sight.[6] Carnap is seeking to distinguish between the places in the visual field and the colors. There are complications that need not concern us. The guiding idea is to define the visual field first. Here we exploit the idea (§88) that different place identical qualities cannot occur in the same elex. (That is, the visual qualities of a given elex are such as to allow the same color in different places, but not different colors in the same place.) Thus, place qualities have exclusion properties not shared by color qualities. This is not to say that two color qualities might not be mutually exclusive, however, so care must be taken. Carnap (§§88, 117) argues that rather than look at exclusive classes directly, we can define a visual field place as a nonempty class of quality classes, all of which are contained in one similarity circle of the exclusion relation among quality classes but not in any other such similarity circle.[7] This defines the class of visual places, "place." Two quality classes are "place identical" (*Plid*) just in case they belong to the same place class. Place classes are "place proximate" (*Proxpl*) just in case a quality class in one of them is similar (*Sim*) to a quality class of the other. Proxpl again orders the class of place classes. Thus, Carnap (§117) claims as an empirical theorem that the dimension number of the place classes ordered by the Proxpl relation is two.

---

6 The motivations for various of the technical ideas exploited by Carnap are discussed at some length in §88. I pass over them with no comment, as the details of the constitutional definitions at this level play no great role in the constitutional ideas behind objectivity.

7 In the first edition, Carnap had used the term "abstraction class" rather than "similarity circle" in this definition but, as pointed out by Goodman (1953), the exclusion relation is not transitive, so no abstraction classes can be defined.

The constitutional projects for objectivity

The order of colors is then constructed, with the help of the order of places. Carnap (§118) defines a relation over (visual) quality classes, "color identity in proximate places" (*Colidprox*), on the basis of proximate places and similarity of quality classes. "Color identity" (*Colid*) is simply the chain of the Colidprox relation. The class of color classes is just the class of abstraction classes of Colid. Then a relation of "proximate color" (*Proxcol*) is just the similarity relation restricted to the class of color classes (rather than the whole class of quality classes). The order of Proxcol is the color solid, and Carnap claims as another empirical theorem that this order has three dimensions.

The final note (§120) of the early sections of the constitutional system is about a preliminary time order among the elexes. Carnap claims that the chain of the Rs relation, which will be irreflexive, asymmetric, and nontransitive, may be considered a preliminary time ordering. It does not have all the properties of a full temporal ordering – some pairs of elexes are not related by Rs_{po} at all, so there are gaps – but it does have some of them. Moreover, as already noted, Rs is intuitively a relation involving recollection, so it implicates a temporal order in any case. By the end of these sections of the constitutional system, then, Carnap has constructed the whole class of perceptual qualities and sensations. In particular, he has distinguished the class of visual qualities, the class of visual field places, and the color qualities, and has placed the elex into a preliminary time sequence as well as into a general system of qualities exhibited by them. Moreover, he has established some empirical theorems about the structure of the visual field and the color solid, positing that they are, respectively, two- and three-dimensional. These structural features of the autopsychological realm will be exploited in the further constitutional definitions by which we attain to the physical world.

THE CONSTITUTION OF THE WORLD OF PHYSICS

The movement from the autopsychological world to the world of physics is the locus of Quine's principal worries about the methodology of the *Aufbau*, as we noted in Chapter One. In this section we will be in a better position to understand Quine's worries. More than that, however, we will discover the role Carnap sees the constitution of the world of physics as playing in the constitution of objectivity. This latter aspect of the discussion is more important for our purposes, given the interpretative perspective I have been urging. Again, I shall begin by outlining Carnap's constitutional order.

After an introductory section (§123), Carnap proceeds directly to the constitution of physical space-time (§124). In this he diverges from the constitutional order of Bertrand Russell. As Carnap notes, Russell, in his epistemological writings, especially *Our Knowledge of the External World* (1914), constituted visual things first and then constituted space and time as relational structures among these things. Carnap proposes, instead, to constitute the whole of physical space-time at once, prior to the constitution of visual things. The advantage over Russell's procedure is, according to Carnap, greater adherence to the supreme maxim of scientific philosophizing: By constituting the entire physical space-time at once and then embedding the visual things in it, the unperceived spatiotemporal points are constituted rather than inferred from the behavior of visual things.

Ultimately, the difference from Russell is important. Carnap constitutes four-dimensional physical space-time as a pure world of numbers and, therefore, as a logical object. It acquires its status as *physical space-time* not from having its properties constituted or inferred from the behavior of perceptual objects but through the coordination of physical state magnitudes to the points of this heretofore purely logical object.[8]

Having given reasons for proceeding directly to the constitution of physical space in section 124, Carnap spends the next three sections spelling out the conditions to be fulfilled by the constitution of physical space. The raw materials for this construction are the two-dimensional spatial and one-dimensional temporal structure of visual qualities. As it turns out, the constitution crucially involves temporality and yields physical space-time. The conditions on the constitution of physical space-time and the assignment of the constituted qualities to the points of this space-time are given in section 126 and translated into realistic language in section 127. The idea is essentially that physical space-time is to be the abstract Euclidean space of the minimal dimensionality requisite for the fulfillment of the twelve constitutional conditions of sections 126–7. These conditions for the assignment of the perceptual qualities to points of space-time are motivated by certain known scientific facts (e.g., the speed of light) and certain methodological posits

---

[8] Carnap (§124) also eschews the idea of constructing three-dimensional visual space before the construction of physical space. He sees this as an avoidable step, from a logical point of view. He relies, thus, on the idea of constitution theory as a rational reconstruction of the process of cognition, to avoid having to make this superfluous step. The constitutional process need not contain this step merely because of the psychological reality of three-dimensional visual space.

The constitutional projects for objectivity

(e.g., the postulation of the laziest perceptual world consistent with the actually perceived qualities).

The idea is this: We use the qualities of the elex ordered by the preliminary time order to assign qualities to space-time points. We do this by projecting these qualities outward from a continuous world line of a "point of view." We do the assignment such that we assign the qualities of the elex to world points that are (virtually) simultaneous with that elex: for example, we assign close-by color qualities of the elex to points separated only by small angles. Moreover, we are always guided by the attempt to assign qualities to maximize certain types of continuity.

There are, thus, two correlative investigations in these sections. Carnap is at once considering the methodological rules by which to assign qualities to space-time points and considering the minimal number of space-time dimensions that allows a univocal such assignment. That physical space-time has four dimensions is, thus, not required absolutely but stems from the constraints of dimensionality given by the two-dimensionality of the visual field, the continuity requirements of the rules, and the "empirical determination" that an assignment can be univocally carried through for a four-dimensional manifold.

We shall not pause to consider the desiderata of sections 126–7 in any detail (they are easily understood), but I must mention a few important matters about the constitution of physical space-time and the assignment of perceptual qualities to physical space-time points. First, it is in this assignment that Quine sees Carnap as betraying the reductionist nature of the constitutional system, and hence as vitiating the entire purpose of the program of the *Aufbau*. As Quine writes (1953/1961, p. 40),

Statements of the form "Quality q is at $x;y;z;t$" were, according to [Carnap's] canons, to be apportioned truth values in such a way as to maximize and minimize certain over-all features, and with the growth of experience the truth values were to be progressively revised in the same spirit . . . [B]ut [this] provides no indication, not even the sketchiest, of how a sentence of [this] form . . . could ever be translated into Carnap's initial language of sense data and logic.

Quine is certainly correct. The assignment of qualities to space-time points via these rules of assignment seems not to cohere with the ideal of translational reduction at all. A major change of method has occurred here, unannounced by Carnap.

Quine's claim about the undefined nature of the "is at" relation is

The constitution of the world of physics

exacerbated by another feature of Carnap's constitution of the distribution of qualities to physical space-time points. As noted by Quine (1953/1961) and as explicitly stated in Carnap's criterion 12 in section 126, the assignment of qualities to points is supplemented and sometimes even altered as we continue to constitute objects (especially physical and intersubjective objects) higher up the constitutional hierarchy. That is, the assignment of perceptual qualities is subsequently corrected by the assignment of physical quantities, for reasons we shall see shortly.

For the moment I shall simply flag this instance of methodological change in the *Aufbau* and tip my hat to Quine for having uncovered it so forcefully. I am not yet in a position to say much about why Carnap did not think it a particular problem for the project. This is an issue we shall return to at some length hereafter. As a preliminary remark, however, it should be noted that Quine's criticism is fully based on a reductionist understanding of Carnap's epistemology in the *Aufbau*. If explicit definition from sensation is *not* the ultimate goal of Carnap's project – if, rather, the goal is a structuralist account of objectivity – then the immediate connection between the project and the method of explicit definition in the sense of the definitions of the autopsychological realm is severed. There may be other ways to reach the goal than via explicit definition. Moreover, given the status of physical space-time as a pure world of numbers and hence as a logical object, Carnap may well think that he has an alternative route to objectivity available. I shall have more to say of this in the sequel, however.

Having assigned the visual qualities to physical space-time in accordance with the desiderata of sections 126–7, Carnap proceeds to define visual things in section 128, as bundles of world lines of visual qualities that stay in spatial proximity relations over protracted segments of time. Certain peculiar features of "my body," especially its continuous proximity to the "point of view" and its open surface, allow it to be singled out from among the class of visual things (§129). Visual things are supplemented through the addition of tactile qualities, assigned to points of space-time: A tactile quality is assigned to a world point where the corresponding part of "my body" is (§130). Among other benefits, this allows "my body" to become a topologically closed tactile-visual thing. Now we can constitutionally describe the sense organs of "my body" as parts of it and in this way constitutionally distinguish the remaining senses (§131). Now we can constitute the additional sensory qualities associated with the other senses and assign them also to points of physical space-time (§133).

In section 132, Carnap aims to complete the domain of the autopsychological by constitutional introduction of unconscious objects. This is done so that "we can constitute the domain of the autopsychological as a domain in which a more complete lawfulness of processes holds than in the subdomain of the conscious objects." Carnap pleads ignorance of the constitutional forms of the unconscious objects. This is due to the fact that the autopsychological objects are studied only in psychology. Hence, their properties were (and are) far from completely known – given the rather primitive state of psychological theory in Carnap's time (and our own).

Having all these tools in hand – particularly the assignment of perceptual qualities to the points of physical space-time – Carnap can constitute perceptual things in section 134 analogously to his constitution of visual things in section 128. The perceptual world is then the space-time world, with perceptual things imbedded in it. This perceptual world is completed in section 135 in a way analogous to the assignment of unseen color spots on the basis of seen ones in sections 125–7. Assignments are made in such a way as to maximize the rule-governed nature of the perceptual world, either temporally, where assignments are made so as to induce the regularity of processes partially observed, or spatially, where assignments are made in such a way that the unperceived spatial qualities are, *ceteris paribus,* taken to be analogous to the perceived qualities of the thing in question. These two assignments correspond to the psychological categories of "causality" and "substance" (§§132, 135). They induce regularity within the perceptual world insofar as it can be made regular (since only physics can be made completely subject to law).

The next constitution in Carnap's chain of constitutions is the constitution of the physical world, in section 136. The world of physics is to be constituted as "a pure world of numbers," that is, quantitative values of the physical state magnitudes are assigned directly to the points of space-time considered as numerical coordinates. (The physical state magnitudes are the quantitative concepts found in the laws of physics, e.g., 'force,' 'mass,' and 'acceleration.') This leads to the constitution of a domain which is fully expressed in numerical terms and determined by mathematical laws – the laws of mathematical physics. This allows the calculation of physical magnitudes based on the values of the magnitudes that determine them. Thus, Carnap's view of the physical world is one which resolves it into a fully mathematical manifold.

There is an important antireductionism also present in section 136.

The constitution of the world of physics

The state magnitudes that are used to formulate the laws of physics and that are assigned values for each point of space-time are not "unambiguously determine[d]" by the constitutions given in the previous steps of the constitutional system. That is to say, neither the laws of physics nor even the concepts in terms of which they are expressed (the state magnitudes) are fully determined by the constitutions prior to the constitution of the physical world. Carnap indicates that various systems for physics are all equally confirmed by the evidence. He holds out hope that an unambiguous choice among these various possible systems of physics will be made eventually but notes that this choice will be "guided by methodological principles, for example, the principle of the greatest simplicity."

This statement indicates that Carnap endorses the idea that there is a conventional element within physics. The assignment of state magnitudes to the points of physical space-time is not uniquely determined by the perceptual qualities assigned to those points in the constitution of the perceptual world. Thus the perceptual world determines neither the state magnitudes that are chosen as the elements of the physical world (these are determined by the laws of physics – laws which are themselves not determined by the perceptual world) nor even the numerical values these state magnitudes receive for each space-time point. Carnap stresses that the relation between the assignments of qualitative properties to space-time points and the assignments of their quantitative physical properties is a one-to-many relation. That is, the quantitative properties of space-time points determine univocally their qualitative properties through the mathematical laws of physics and the constitutional definitions that link the two kinds of property. The qualitative properties, however, do not univocally determine the physical properties – not even after the state magnitudes are themselves determined by the laws of physics.

Thus, Carnap seems to acknowledge the difficulty that gave rise to Quine's later objections to this part of the *Aufbau*. A system of explicit constitutional definitions would not yield this antireductionist stance. In section 136 the concepts of physics are explicitly claimed not to be definable on the experiential basis. The qualitative world of perception does not determine the mathematical world of physics. If definitional reduction to sensation were the goal of this constitution of the world of physics, Carnap's own discussion would undermine his project. Clearly, his endorsement of this antireductionism is important evidence that explicit definition is not the goal of this part of the project. The goal seems to be, rather, the elucidation of the unique role that the superadded mathematical structure of the world of physics provides for the question of the objectivity of science.

Thus, for Carnap's epistemology, the most important aspect of the constitution of the physical world is its necessary role in the subsequent constitution of the intersubjective world. In section 136, it is not altogether clear why Carnap believes that the physical world can be intersubjectivized whereas the perceptual world cannot. He seems to indicate that the fully mathematical structure of the world of physics, its complete rule-governedness, is what yields this result. In section 133, however, he stresses the idea that the assignment of perceptual qualities to space-time points varies from subject to subject and, hence, "cannot be carried out in a unique and consistent way." The interaction of these two ideas and the manner in which they guide the subsequent constitution of the intersubjective world will be addressed in the next section.

Carnap concludes chapter B of part 4 by constituting two additional physical objects that are crucial to his constitution of the heteropsychological and intersubjective worlds. First, in section 137 he constitutes man as a biological species. Second, he constitutes the "expression relation" which holds between certain autopsychological events and certain physical behaviors of "my body" that "express" these states. (The intuitive idea is that physical motions of my body express my state of mind, for example, if I fling my manuscript out the window, this expresses my frustration with the editing process.) The species man provides the individuals for whom Carnap intends to constitute the heteropsychological realm. The expression relation is the primary tool for this constitution.

THE CONSTITUTION OF THE INTERSUBJECTIVE WORLD

Chapter C of part 4 of the *Aufbau* traces the constitution of the heteropsychological domain and, on the basis of that, the constitution of the intersubjective world. After these constitutions, Carnap constitutes the cultural objects (§§150–2) and then considers the possibility of eliminating the recollection of similarity relation in accordance with the project of purely structural definition description (§§153–5). The latter topic is discussed in the next section of the present chapter; the former does not introduce any new epistemological issues and, therefore, is not considered here.

The constitution of the intersubjective world

After a preliminary section (§139), Carnap proceeds to constitute the realm of the "heteropsychological" (§140), that is, the psychological processes of the other human beings, on the basis of their physical behavior and an extension of the expression relation (already constituted). The expression relation must be extended because it was defined as a relation between "my" physical behavior and the psychological events which that behavior expressed, whereas for the heteropsychological realm the relevant behavior is, of course, the behavior of others. In essence the idea is to introduce psychological states in the mental life of others which are of the same kind as the states expressed by "my" behavior when I behave in the same kind of way in which the other person is behaving. (Thus, if a reader throws this book out the window, that is seen as "expressing" her frustration and will allow us to constitute her mental states.)

The rather meager psychological stream attributed to the "other" individuals by this constitution is supplemented again by state and process laws indicating, respectively, the simultaneous occurrence of two psychological states and the succession of two states. Following this, a further supplementation of the psychological realm of the "other" is made with the introduction of unconscious events. In this way, the mental life of the other members of the species man is constituted in a fashion which makes their mental life virtually as rich and regular as "my" own.[9]

In the next section (§141) Carnap introduces the "sign production" relation. This is again a relation between certain physical behaviors of human beings – their vocalizations and writing – and the entities signified by these behaviors. This relation "make[s] possible a broadening of the constitutional system, an increase in the number of constitutible objects of almost all kinds."

Despite the obvious benefits that accrue to the constitutional system through the introduction of the sign production relation, the constitution of this relation is difficult, for it is an enormous task to translate the conjectural rules by which we attempt to determine the significance of the signs of others into the language of constitution theory. In section 142, Carnap considers a related relation, the "reporting relation," which

---

9 It should be noted that the constitutional procedure here, just as did the procedures in the constitution of the world of physics, presuppose the availability of scientific laws. In particular, Carnap's procedures assume we have available a rich mentalistic psychology, though one that finds its evidential basis in the behavior of people.

obtains between sign productions consisting of sentences and the states of affairs reported by those sentences. One might say – although Carnap does not – that the sign production relation is the reference relation restricted to individual lexical or semantic items, whereas the reporting relation is the same relation for entire semantic complexes.[10] Although Carnap's examples indicate that he is a compositionalist, holding that the state of affairs reported in a report is a complex of the objects signified by the individual signs that compose the report, he emphasizes that the reported state of affairs is first understood and that this allows us to infer the significance of the individual words (contextual understanding).[11] Due to their similarity and connection, I will follow Carnap and use "designation relations" as a general term covering both of these relations.

The importance of these two relations for the development of the constitutional system is twofold, Carnap tells us in section 144. First, a reliable report informs me of a state of affairs of which I may not have had knowledge before. Moreover, the report informs me that this state of affairs is known to the author of the report. Thus the physical and heteropsychological (and the higher-level cultural) realms can be greatly enriched by utilizing these relations.

Before going into more detail about the constitution of the sign production relation and the reporting relation, we would do well to note that Carnap clearly distinguishes between these relations and expression relations.[12] The expression relation is a relation between a physical behavior and a psychological state which is manifested in this behavior: for example, the relation that might exist between a feeling of frustration and the flinging of a manuscript out a window. The designation relation is a relation between a physical object and an object it represents: for example, the relation between the following five ink characters – Venus – and the planet Venus. What complicates matters at times is the fact that some of the designating physical objects are also physical behaviors of humans, but even in this case the two relations

---

10 Carnap does not say this, because at the time he had logicist concerns that we cannot make sense of reference; compare §161.
11 In how far this is meant to capture for the realm of meanings the Gestalt account of psychological priority is not spelled out. I would suppose that Carnap is here, again, being driven by Gestalt psychology as well as the methodology of the logicism of his teacher, Gottlob Frege.
12 In this, he must be following Frege. For Frege's distinction between judgment and the venting of psychological states see, e.g., "Der Gedanke" (1918/1977). Compare also Ricketts (1982, pt. 1).

must be held to be distinct. Carnap puts the point admirably in section 19 when he writes:

In many cases, the same physical object stands, at the same time, in an expression and in a designation relation to the psychological. In such cases, the relations can and must be distinguished very well from one another. Spoken words, for example, are in every case, expressions of something psychological, regardless of what their content concerns; this is because they betray something of the momentary psychological state of the speaker through the sound of the voice, the tempo, rhythm, etc. and also through the choice of words and manner. Beyond this, however, the words also have a meaning.

The constitution of the designation relations is the business of sections 141–2 of the *Aufbau*. As material for this constitution we have the physical world already constituted from "my" perceptual world, and certain methodological criteria *per* section 136. Among these physical objects are the signs themselves, whether as marks on paper or as sound waves emanating from some – the humans – among those physical objects. Our task is to correlate these privileged few objects with all the physical objects. If we can achieve this constitution, we will have achieved something of fundamental significance, because we will have enriched the constitutional system in the two ways mentioned earlier. First, the expression and sign production relations are our only entering wedges into the psychological events of other people; the realm of the heteropsychological can be constituted only on the basis of these relations. Second, because it is possible for someone else to experience and talk about physical objects not experienced by me, the designation relations will allow me, in a way that reflects the methodological rules of section 136, to constitute additional physical objects, thus enlarging the physical realm.

Carnap attempts to give rules for the assigning of weights (to objects, relative to a sign production and to states of affairs, relative to a report) in order to constitute the linguistic relations. The rules Carnap gives seem quite naive and insufficient for the task. Consider these remarks about rules for assigning weights to objects for a given sign production in section 141:

The rules would, among other things, roughly say that the weight assigned to a physical thing in relation to a sign production rises if the thing is close to the body of the sign producer at the time of the sign production; furthermore, if it stands in certain relations (namely, the stimulus relations) to the sense organs of the sign producer or, secondarily, if it was near to the sign producer or in a

The constitutional projects for objectivity

stimulus relation to his sense organs, not at the time of the sign production, but shortly beforehand.

Carnap also indicates that the rules would assign higher weights to objects somehow physically salient in the environment of the sign-giver. Such rules might be sufficient in a world where people utter only observation reports, but in a world where people discuss their friends in distant lands, the question of human rights, and the logic of *Principia Mathematica*, they seem quite impoverished.

Given Carnap's expressed goal of providing a mere outline of the higher constitutional levels, it would be unfair to make too much of the inadequacy of his remarks on these constitutions.[13] They may, however, seem to be in principle inadequate. Carnap claims that the domain of the heteropsychological (and, therefore, the domain constituted on the basis of the heteropsychological – the cultural) can be constituted only after the designation relations in question are constituted. Thus it would seem impossible for heteropsychological and cultural objects to be designated or reported on, since they are unavailable at the time when the linguistic relations are constituted. This, it would seem, is in direct violation of Carnap's principle (§19): "All objects, inasmuch as they are objects of conceptual knowledge, . . . can in principle be designated."

The objection is, however, mistaken. Carnap does allow for higher-level constitutions to reach back, as it were, and affect constitutions upon which they are based. Only in this way will the designation and reporting relations do one of their two principal jobs: enlarge the physical world. We noted earlier that other people can report on states of affairs of which I have no experience, space-time regions which my body had no access to – say, their recent stay in Japan. But how is this to work on Carnap's scheme? Before I can take my friend to be reporting on events in Japan, I have to constitute the reporting relation itself. And

---

13 Carnap, after all, begins the chapter in which these constitutions are discussed by saying (§139): "For the further levels of the constitutional system, we must satisfy ourselves with giving only as many hints as are necessary to recognize the *possibility* of a constitution of the object in question on the basis of previous constitutions." Furthermore, he declares the constitution of the sign production relation is (§141) "more difficult than any of the constitutions we have hitherto undertaken" and that the constitution of the reporting relation is (§142) "still more complicated" – strong words from someone who has already constituted the physical world from sensation. Clearly, Carnap would like more help from psychologists and linguists here than he finds available.

when I do that, the physical world *is* restricted to the physical objects I have observed and their interrelations (suitably supplemented so that the physical world has a thoroughgoing causal structure). How, then, can my friend report on events wholly unfamiliar to my experience, objects as yet unconstituted?

The answer is, I believe, to be found along the following lines. Employing a certain definitional procedure, we are led from the basic relation to the constitution of the physical world. Among the objects in the physical world are the human beings. The fact that a certain class of individuals can be brought together as a biological species indicates that there are certain regularities to be found exclusively among those physical objects labeled "human." This leads to a different way of organizing my experience, which leads to the constitution of additional physical objects. For, among the states of affairs which I experience are the linguistic behaviors of these human beings, in which they discuss objects previously unknown to me. That is, having reached a high enough level of constitution resulting from pursuing one line of organization of the data of experience, I, for the first time, realize other ways of organizing the selfsame data to arrive at additional objects of experience – objects I have "experienced" only through the linguistic behavior of other people. Put another, more realistic and less Carnapian way: Once we have the biological species man in hand, certain regularities of human behavior are explainable only by expanding the population of physical objects.

A similar account may be given in the case of the constitution of the sign production and reporting relations themselves. Our problem was to determine how, given the availability only of "my" world of physics, it is possible for other people to designate or report on their own psychological states – states which can be constituted only on the basis of these designation relations. The answer here goes as follows. Just as the physical world was enriched by employing a new method of organizing the data of experience, once a sufficiently high level of organization of that data has been reached, this selfsame high level of organization leads to the constitution of additional heteropsychological objects. Less abstractly, the heteropsychological realm is partially constituted via the expression relation; however, it is greatly increased by the designation relations. Certain experiential regularities in the behavior of human beings are brought into lawlike connection only if we constitute additional heteropsychological entities as the designata of certain sign productions.

Thus we see that no new procedures are introduced when we get to the designation relations; rather, the designation relations stand in the same kind of relation to objects constituted on their basis as the physical world itself does. At no one stage of the constitutional system is the physical world constituted *in toto;* rather, a four-dimensional manifold is constituted, and individual objects are imbedded in this manifold via a variety of routes, based on experience and certain methodological maxims. Similarly, at no stage are the designation relations constituted *in toto;* rather, certain rules for determining weights are given, such that any subsequently constituted object can in principle be found to be designated by some sign production.

If no new problems arise for the designation relations, at least we can see more clearly how pressing the methodological problems are in Carnap's higher-level procedures. The designation relations are not constituted as pair lists at any level; they are in principle supplemented all the way up. Thus, it is clear that no constitutional definition of them, in Carnap's official sense, is possible at all. Similarly, although each physical object (and, we shall see later, each intersubjective object) is constituted at some level of the constitutional system, at no level is the physical world as a whole constituted. We are again left with the puzzling feeling that Carnap has simply set aside the strictures that give the point of his epistemological exercise. Again, however, I think the place to begin in considering this puzzle is to consider where Carnap is going in these definitions: to the objective world of science.

Thus, without making any claim that the mysteries of Carnap's use of the designation relations in the constitution of the heteropsychological realm have been solved, let us proceed by granting him this use and see how the intersubjective world is constituted from it. On the basis of the expression, sign production, and reporting relations, Carnap has constituted other humans not merely as physical objects, but as epistemic subjects in their own right – complete with their experience of the world around them. Now we can proceed, using the mental states attributed to the other humans, to reconstruct how they have constituted the world. This process is reconstructed by applying the same constitutional definitional forms that formed the basis of the construction of the autopsychological world to our recently gained knowledge of the mental lives of other human beings.

So, for example, I have constituted a physical object (M) from my elementary experiences. Further, this physical object has been constituted as a human being within the biological realm. As such I have constituted, via the last-outlined procedure, certain psychological events in the life of this person. I can now apply the same constitutional forms to this basic relation for M as I applied to my own. Using the notation introduced by Carnap in section 145, we can say that the heteropsychological realm we have constituted for a person, M, amounts to a specification of the recollection of similarity relation for M, or "Rs_M." Using the constitutional procedures that we used on Rs to get eventually to the physical world, we can start with Rs_M to constitute "the world of M." This constitution of the world of M on the basis of Rs_M is called "the constitutional system of M" or "S_M." At the autopsychological level these analogously constituted entities will be in complete structural agreement. For example, identical constitutional operations on Rs and Rs_M will both yield the result that the visual field is two-dimensional – though of course in the first constitution I have constituted "my" visual field, whereas in the second I have constituted M's visual field.

The fact that the same constitutional forms are being used in both the constitutional system based on "my" experiences (S) and the one based on the experiences of S (S_M) means that for the lowest, autopsychological levels of the respective constitutional systems there is a quite thoroughgoing "constitutional analogy" (§146). Thus, for example, Ps_M (part similarity in S_M) has the same derivation relation (compare §121) as Ps; that is, the constitutional definition of Ps_M differs in logical form from the constitutional definition of Ps only in that Ps is defined on the basis of Rs whereas Ps_M is defined in terms of Rs_M. This similarity of constitutional form is mirrored in these lower constitutional levels by a similarity in the empirical facts that hold of the constituted objects and that drive the additional constitutions. For example, just as the visual field turns out to be the one sense modality with five dimensions in S, so too does the (visual field)$_M$ turn out to be the one sense modality with five dimensions in S_M.

Both the "constitutional analogy" and the empirical coincidence begin to break down higher up the constitutional hierarchy. Thus, for example, certain objects for which the constitutional analogy holds in S and S_M begin to diverge in their empirical properties. The visual-tactile thing that is constituted in S_M analogously to the way "my body" is constituted in S will, for most choices of M, differ greatly empirically from "my body"; after all "my body" (mb) has all the empirical traits of my body whereas "my body"$_M$ (mb_M) – that is, M's body from M's point of view – has the empirical traits of M's body. So, too, does the constitutional analogy between constitutional forms begin to disappear in the higher levels of the constitutional system. For example, once we have constituted physical space-time in S, most of the remaining constitutional definitions take the form of assigning objects to the points of this space-time via, for example, noting the metrical relations of these things to my body. In general, however, these same metrical relations will not merely not pick out the same things in relation to M but will not pick out anything at all.

The breakdown of constitutional analogy is, however, met with a corresponding rise of a different relation between the objects of S and S_M (§146): "a one-to-one correspondence holds between the world of physics in S and that in S_M, such that the same spatiotemporal and qualitative . . . relations that hold for the physical world points in S_M also hold for the coordinated world points in S." This correspondence is what Carnap (§146) calls "intersubjective correspondence." He introduces notation for this as follows: given an object, O, that has been constituted in S, the object in S_M that intersubjectively corresponds with O is denoted by "O^M."

The idea can best be put in the following way. Consider two constitutional systems, mine and M's, and the constitution of my body as a physical object in both. Let us call my body as constituted in my system "mb." Now, there are two objects in the constitutional system of M which are similar to mb. First, there is an object which has a constitutional definite description in M's system analogous to mb's in mine. Call this object "mb_M." This object is not my body, however; rather it is M's body as constituted from M's point of view. The two entities mb and mb_M do not agree on very many physical characteristics in general. (M weighs more than I do, for example.) However, there is an object in M's world of physics which has virtually all the physical characteristics that mb has in mine, among them localizability at the same point in physical space-time. Call this object "mb^M." This object is my body once again, but from M's viewpoint; it intersubjectively corresponds to mb but is constituted via a very different constitutional definition.

We can enlarge the scope of these remarks to include all the people constituted by me – not only M but N, P, and so forth. In each of the constitutional systems for these people there will be objects which intersubjectively correspond to any given object in my constitutional system, that is, which share all or virtually all of the physical properties of some object in my constitutional system. Of course, these intersubjectively corresponding objects are not constituted via the same constitutional definitional forms in their constitutional systems as the object to which they correspond in mine.

Carnap proposes (§148) that for each object O of my constitutional system, we take the abstraction class of the objects in all the constitutional systems which intersubjectively correspond to O to form the "intersubjective object" (*Int'[O]*). Similarly, we call a property of or statement about an object "intersubjectively communicable" if all the objects intersubjectively corresponding to that object also have the property or make the statement true. Carnap claims that the intersubjective objects form the object domain of science and that the formulation of intersubjectively communicable statements is one of the principal aims of science (§149).

In what sense is the world of physics ineliminably implicated in the process of intersubjectivizing for Carnap? Well, first, the world of physics must be in place before the issue can be raised in any serious way within the constitutional framework. That is, it is only as physical objects that other epistemic subjects are first recognized. Thus, the question of intersubjectivity cannot be addressed until the world of physics is in place. In this sense, the construction of the world of physics first allows the way out of a solipsism within which no epistemologically interesting question can even be raised.

More apropos Carnap's remarks in sections 133 and 136 (as noted earlier), however, is the following. The regularity induced in the world of physics of an agent by the constitutional procedure allows her to do two crucial things. First, she can precisely specify objects at a time via their quantitative properties, including especially their distances and directions relative to herself. This is true of any other agent, M, also. Included in this specification is their spatial relations to one another. Given the identity of the laws of physics for each, all that is needed to find the intersubjective objects is a mapping of these spatial relations onto one another – and the metrical structure of space-time provides an easy way to do this.

Why would this not work at the level of the perceptual world, though? There, too, the spatiotemporal structure is fully specified. The only difference is that the assignments to the space-time points are qualities, not physical quantities. Here, the easiest way to think about this is, I believe, methodologically. What do the laws of physics and the quantitative structure of physics provide, on Carnap's view? The added structure provides the means to calculate the physical state magnitudes at some space-time points from those of other space-time points. This limits the degrees of freedom in the assignment of such magnitudes. Given a rich enough subset, the physical magnitudes are fully determined everywhere. Any observed variations from the calculated values can be investigated – either through an investigation of the intervening medium or through a psychophysical investigation of the observer.

On the other hand, the assignment of qualities to space-time points in an attempt to directly intersubjectivize the perceptual worlds breaks down. There are too many degrees of freedom. Since there are no laws specifying how these qualities go together in spatial regions or evolve over time, there are too many possible such worlds. Any assignment is as good as any other. Moreover, if there is a disagreement over qualities at a given point, there is no epistemic recourse. There is no further investigation to turn to for resolving the dispute.

Thus, on Carnap's view, the mathematically precise structure of the world of physics does two things at once. It ties down the degrees of freedom in the assignment of magnitudes to space-time points. It also, thereby, changes disagreement over assignment from mere difference (given lack of recourse to any further investigation) to genuine dispute and contradiction. This is the hallmark of intersubjectivity: It changes mere agreement and disagreement genuinely into assent and dissent about a determinate subject matter.

Intersubjectivizing, then, begins with this mapping of physical worlds of individuals onto one another. Carnap argues, however, that we can intersubjectivize the other object domains also. Thus, for example, once we have the intersubjective object corresponding to person N, designated $Int'(N)$, we can intersubjectivize N's mental life. Each of us constitutes N constituting the world from his elementary experiences ordered by the relation of recollection of similarity. We can easily form the abstraction class $Int'(Rs_N)$, which is the intersubjective object that we talk about when discussing N's recollection of similarity. Thus, although intersubjectivizing can proceed only through the mathematical forms of the physical world, once we intersubjectivize the physical world we have the ability to intersubjectivize for all realms. The intersubjective world is a world that contains the riches of all the sciences, including psychology, sociology, and economics.

This is, then, Carnap's first solution to the problem of objectivity. Utilizing the mathematical structure and law-governed nature of the world of physics, mappings from one person's world of physics onto another's can be done in a univocal way. The class formed from such objects is the intersubjective object that is available to all agents and that grounds the possibility of intersubjective judgment. It would seem that the constitution of the intersubjective world, extended in the end to the realms of the psychological and cultural sciences also, gives Carnap what he wants: a structural solution to the question of objectivity that grounds the possibility of scientific objectivity in all the sciences.

THE ELIMINATION OF Rs

Despite having finished his outline of the constitutional system on this high note, Carnap raises one final worry. The constitution of the intersubjective world does not fulfill the project of giving purely structural definite descriptions (PSDDs). Even if we grant the (false) assumption that Carnap's constitutional definitions are explicit definitions, in the sense required by the official project, there remains one primitive, undefined term at the basis of the system. This is, of course, the term for the basic relation itself. Thus, in sections 153–5, Carnap returns to the project of giving a purely structural definite description for each term of the system and asks whether it is not possible to finish the dematerialization of science by structurally defining the recollection of similarity relation (Rs) itself.

The strategy is this: Take a constitutional definition fairly high up the system, one that relies on "empirical theorems" about Rs. Since this definition relies on fairly sophisticated empirically given structural facts about Rs, we define Rs as the one and only relation that allows this definition. Carnap chooses the definition of the visual sense as the one and only sense modality of exactly five dimensions. We use the definitions of all the terms in this claim to translate this into a complicated claim expressed in the language of logic and Rs. We define away the basic relation, then, as the one and only relation that permits the constitution of the visual sense in just this way. If we can do that, we can show how to translate all scientific discourse into purely structural terms.

This strategy has a fatal weakness, however – indeed it is the weakness we uncovered in going through the simplified railway example in some detail in Chapter Two. Carnap must rely on empirical ascertainment of the structure of the relation; in essence, he must rely on ostension at the level of the whole structure of the primitive basic relation. Why is this? It is so because of a problem that Carnap himself remarks on in section 154. Consider a permutation mapping, f, of the elexes onto themselves (and assume it is not the identity map). Then consider a relation, Rs', defined as follows:

$$Rs'(e_i, e_j) \text{ if and only if } e_i = f(e_k), e_j = f(e_m), \text{ and } Rs(e_k, e_m).$$

Given the resources of type theory, Carnap has no trouble showing the existence of Rs'. Moreover, Rs' is clearly isomorphic to Rs. Thus, any structural fact about Rs that permits the definition of the visual sense in

The constitutional projects for objectivity

the way Carnap does can be mirrored exactly by a definition of the visual sense' with Rs' playing the role of Rs. Thus, the uniqueness claim for Rs in the attempted PSDD for it fails.

The problem is precisely that structure is preserved by the definitions. Thus, if some highly complicated constitution from Rs has a certain structure, performing the same constitutional operations from Rs' will yield something else of the same structure. Carnap's attempted solution to this difficulty is to restrict the class of relations that can serve as possible bases. He claims that the permuted relations expressed in the recipe just given are "unnatural or nonexperiencable." The constitutions from them are even less likely to correspond to anything in mental life than are the relations themselves. He introduces a primitive notion, 'foundedness,' to cover only "natural or experienceable" relations. As so patched, the definition of Rs now reads: "Rs is the one and only founded relation that permits the definition of the visual sense in just this way."[14]

The patching does the trick only if foundedness itself can be considered a logical notion. Thus, Carnap seems to undercut the very structuralist idea underlying PSDD with his final move. For this structuralism can work only if a notion like 'experienceable' or 'ostendable' for relations is finally absorbed into logic itself. This is precisely what Carnap tries to argue in section 154. He considers the notion of 'foundedness' to be akin to the notion of the 'universal quantifier,' a logical notion ultimately referring to domains of application. The crux of the argument is contained in the following sentences: "Logic is not a particular domain, but rather contains those propositions which (as tautologies) hold of objects of any arbitrary domain. From this it follows that it must consider those concepts that allow of application to any domain. And to these concepts 'foundedness' does indeed belong."

This argument seems extraordinarily bad. The analogy with the universal quantifier is obscure and misleading. Foundedness is, after all, nothing more than an undefined property of relations and plays nothing like the role of the quantifier. There is something important going on here, however. The argument can be reconstructed as saying that without the notion of foundedness it is impossible to define any domain over which the logical truths are true. Carnap's constitution theory is his attempt to give the one and only general account of objects that is possible from his perspective. If, ultimately, no objects can be constituted without the notion of foundedness, no domain of objects is

---

14 These concerns are brought out forcefully in Friedman (1987) and Hart (1992).

The problem of objectivity

available at all. A logic that is unable to provide the notion of a real object is incapable of explaining the objectivity of judgment. But it is clear that this is what logic must be able to do for Carnap.

Let us leave that argument as our best attempt to breathe life into Carnap's remarks in section 154. At the very least, even if there is an argument that is not wholly *ad hoc* for considering foundedness to be a logical notion, Carnap can fulfill his project of providing PSDDs for the concepts of science only by ultimately changing the very logic he is working with. Type theory must be augmented with foundedness. Moreover, foundedness seems to smuggle directly into logic precisely the difficulty to be overcome. This is convenient, given Carnap's inability (which we noted in Chapter One) to raise any serious questions about the epistemological status of logical truth, but in the end, it looks to be too convenient.

THE PROBLEM OF OBJECTIVITY

So far, I have been engaged in a fairly flat-footed exegesis. Clearly, in presenting the two projects for objectivity and other aspects of Carnap's epistemological project, I have paid special attention to those places where Carnap most closely addresses his particular understanding of the general problem of epistemology. But, to this point the discussion has certainly not settled any issue, nor indeed has it gone very far in helping us to understand how Carnap arrived at this epistemological position in the first place. It is the latter issue that provides the crucial clue to Carnap's thinking about objectivity, structure, and knowledge.

In particular, I have suggested a new perspective from which to consider the issues presented by Carnap's process of intersubjectivizing. Carnap does change his constitutional methods at this point. But, unencumbered by a prejudice about the empiricist nature of his project, we must reconsider what is happening here. In various sections of the *Aufbau* and in the procedure of intersubjectivizing, Carnap clearly indicates that it is the extra, superadded formal structure of mathematically expressed physical concepts and laws that is crucial for the intersubjectivity of knowledge. Moreover, he explicitly disavows the reductionism that seems so naturally to be the point of his constitutional procedure, regardless of whether this is taken to be empiricist reductionism or some other kind. If one were to search for a maxim to sum up the process of intersubjectivizing in the *Aufbau*, one might say: "Experience becomes objective knowledge only via the imposition of further mathe-

The constitutional projects for objectivity

matical structure not given in experience." Thus, science goes beyond experience only formally, not materially.

This general account is quite different from the project of giving purely structural definite descriptions, which presupposes that the given structure of experience is *sufficient* for objective knowledge. Here the operative notion of structure is logical, not mathematical. But with this understanding of structure and its role in knowledge, Carnap comes perilously close to the type of conflation of empirical and logical knowledge for which he criticizes the project of implicit definition. The existence of other relations over the elexes with the structure of Rs is provable given Carnap's logical framework; the uniqueness of this structure to Rs is, thus, disprovable. Thus, Carnap's particular way of eliminating Rs is suspect, as is the claim that we should want to eliminate it anyway. At the very least, the empirical content of knowledge and the structuralist account of objectivity, interpreted in accordance with the procedure of giving PSDDs, seem to be in substantial tension.

This curious situation cries out for illumination. We still need a better sense of why Carnap would conceive of epistemology in these terms. For this reason, it is time for us to back up. We have already noted the generally Kantian tone of the epistemological vocabulary that Carnap employs. We have also seen that he was at pains to use the structuralist project to defend and extend Ernst Cassirer's account of concept formation against that of Heinrich Rickert. We have noted the antireductionist and conventionalist elements in Carnap's procedure of intersubjectivizing.

This neo-Kantian and conventionalist background, I submit, is the crucial one to explore to understand Carnap's account of the epistemological problem and its solution in the *Aufbau*. It is to this background that we now turn. By first noting some crucial ambiguities in Kant's own account of the synthetic *a priori*, we will be in a position to see the crucial methodological maneuvers of the neo-Kantians from whose works Carnap took his project. This background will enable us to think more seriously about Carnap's early work. From his 1921 dissertation through his 1926 monograph *Physikalische Begriffsbildung*, Carnap explicitly distanced himself from strict empiricism, adopted a conventionalist methodology in physics, and used broadly neo-Kantian epistemological categories. His designation for the work in this period is revealing: "critical conventionalism." This work places the *Aufbau* in a new light. Rather than read it in terms of Carnap's subsequent development, it is surely more historically appropriate to locate it within the evolution of his thought. In his 1921 dissertation, Carnap began his philosophical work as an unreformed neo-Kantian. In *Der logische Aufbau der Welt*, he presents a generally neo-Kantian epistemological problematic while claiming neutrality among the earlier epistemological schools of thought. Only by 1934 or so was Carnap happy to call himself an empiricist, though of a new, logical sort. But by this time he had also rejected the project of his 1928 book and, indeed, the whole project of epistemology.

For Carnap, the project of epistemology is the project of structuralist objectivity. Uncovering two distinct, but related and intertwined, accounts of objectivity in the *Aufbau* indicates that the project was already under great strain in 1928. An exploration of what the project was for the neo-Kantians and how it changed with Carnap's technical, formal-logical point of view will show us more clearly what those strains were and why Carnap could not be satisfied with either of his technical projects in the 1928 book. We will then be able to understand why a failed *Aufbau* led to epistemology naturalized for Quine, but to logical empiricist philosophy of science for Carnap.

CHAPTER FOUR

The background to early Carnap: Themes from Kant

WE have had occasion to note Carnap's advocacy of Kantian themes in his early philosophical thought. But, of course, Carnap is not adopting Kantianism in all its details – too many aspects of Kant's own philosophical thought were rendered implausible, if not simply exposed as mistaken, by scientific and mathematical advances in the nineteenth and early twentieth centuries. Carnap's early views are much more substantially informed by the views of the scientific neo-Kantians of the early twentieth century. These neo-Kantians both took considerable insight from Kant's own work and significantly changed some central Kantian tenets. Thus, for an understanding of Carnap, it is the work of the neo-Kantians that is of primary importance. Nevertheless, the best place to start in examining the work of the neo-Kantians is with the metaphysical and epistemological positions of Kant himself and the problems that arose for these positions in the evolution of scientific, mathematical, and logical theorizing in the years between Kant and Carnap. With this in hand we will be better able to see the continuities and discontinuities between neo-Kantian and Kantian thought. Thus, in this chapter we shall reconstruct some themes in Kant's account of the synthetic *a priori* and its role in objective, theoretical knowledge. In the next, we shall see how the twentieth-century neo-Kantians take up these themes in the post-Einsteinian era.

THE KANTIAN PROBLEMATIC

In this section I will briefly review some of the major themes in Kant's account of scientific and metaphysical knowledge, as presented in the *Critique of Pure Reason* (Kant 1781 / 1787 / 1965)[1] and related documents.

---

1 Hereafter I cite the *Critique of Pure Reason* (Kant 1965) in the standard form, by edition and page number (ed. 1, 1781 = A; ed. 2, 1787 = B), in parentheses in the text.

The Kantian problematic

I will then explain how post-Kantian scientific advances rendered some details of Kant's account implausible. This section is meant only as a broad overview of certain aspects of the problem situation that confronted the neo-Kantians. In the next section the discussion will turn to a more detailed look at three notions of the synthetic *a priori* in Kant, their connections, and their relation to other aspects of the Kantian epistemological picture.

Kantian speculative philosophy provides an examination of the conditions of objective knowledge, with an eye toward the question of whether such objectivity is possible in metaphysics. In this way Kant is led to his fundamental philosophical question: "How is synthetic *a priori* knowledge possible?" Synthetic *a priori* knowledge is, roughly, substantive knowledge of the world known independently of experience. Kant argues that this is the type of knowledge that rationalist metaphysics must be. On the one hand, it is meant to be a body of substantive truths, not mere analyses of concepts. On the other hand, these truths are (allegedly) discoverable by pure thought independently of any experience.[2] Kant, therefore, seeks to answer his fundamental question in order to resolve his deep uncertainty about the possibility of objective knowledge in metaphysics. Fortunately, there are two bodies of synthetic *a priori* knowledge available to Kant that provide him with independent material for the consideration of his question: pure mathematics and pure physics. Thus, the synthetic *a priori* does not stand or fall with the possibility of metaphysics; rather the conditions under which synthetic *a priori* knowledge is possible can be examined by considering mathematics and physics, and then we can ask whether these conditions extend also to the metaphysical case.[3]

By calling pure mathematics, including geometry, and pure physics, which for him contained in the main (reformulations of) the Newtonian laws of motion, synthetic *a priori* knowledge, Kant is not simply begging the question against an empiricism that seeks to account for either or both of these disciplines as purely analytic (say, as Humean relations

---

2   Indeed on the extreme Leibniz–Wolffian rationalist view, sensation is simply a source of confused representation of the intelligible world of pure thought. Thus, experience is a source only of error and confusion, so everything knowable in the strictest sense is knowable *a priori*. Thus, metaphysics is the paradigm of the knowable.

3   In this discussion, I am using an order of explication more in keeping with the analytic method of the *Prolegomena of any Future Metaphysics* (1783) than the synthetic method of the First Critique. This is a matter of convenience, given that my main interest here is the positive story relating the synthetic *a priori* to scientific knowledge, not the detailed questions of the proper explanatory order in transcendental philosophy.

of ideas) or as synthetic *a posteriori* deliverances of sensation. Rather, on the one hand, Kant argues that an examination of the inference structure of mathematics and geometry reveals that they employ reasoning patterns not expressible within logic as then understood, that is, Aristotelian syllogistic reasoning. Hence, no notion of analyticity or conceptual explication is available within the Aristotelian, syllogistic logic of the time that can ground any viable account of mathematics or geometry (let alone any part of physics) as analytically true.[4] On the other hand, in the Transcendental Analytic, Kant proffers the view that the very notion of an epistemically probative matter of fact of experience presupposes both pure mathematics and the pure principles of the understanding (which stand in a close connection to the principles of pure physics) and, hence, that these domains cannot themselves be derived from experience.[5] Thus, Kant's presupposition of the availability of synthetic *a priori* disciplines in the sciences does not preclude a substantive response to the different understanding of these disciplines that the empiricist has.

As is well known, Kant's examination of the conditions of the possibility of synthetic *a priori* knowledge yields the result that every synthetic judgment requires a *synthesis* of two distinct types of representations, intuitions and concepts. *Intuitions* are immediate representations received passively by the mind, whereas *concepts* are mediate representations of objects that express the spontaneity of thought. Empirical intuition is given in sensation and, thus, involves the faculty termed *sensibility*; empirical concepts are derived or abstracted from sensation by a faculty termed the *understanding*. The result of this doctrine requiring the combination of intuitions and concepts in objective judgment is that rationalist metaphysics, which seeks to discover objective truths

4 This argument will be explored at greater length in the next section of the present chapter. For a vastly more detailed and subtle account see Friedman (1993, esp. chaps. 1 and 2).
5 That is, the Humean skeptical argument against causation, for example, relies on the availability of an unproblematic notion of experiential matter of fact as the epistemic starting point. From this starting point, Hume argues against the availability of an objective notion of causality. Kant's position is that the Humean starting point requires the objectifying principles of the Kantian faculty of the understanding and the whole of the underlying categorical framework that it entails, including the very notion of causality that Hume rejects. Thus, Hume's position is incoherent, because he misunderstands the relation of the pure concepts of the understanding to experience. This point recurs in my brief discussion of the "Refutation of Idealism" in the next section of the present chapter. Here I follow the much more richly detailed account of the situation given in Kitcher (1986).

about purely intelligible objects in abstraction from all use of the sensibility, is impossible; no objective judgments are possible beyond the bounds of the forms of sense, for no intuition adequate to any such supersensible idea is possible.

We have seen that, to some degree, doubt is the mother of Kantian philosophy, but not general skeptical doubt about the possibility of objective knowledge in the sciences. The main doubt is the doubt about whether objectivity can be extended to a nonsensible, metaphysical realm. This is a local doubt, resulting from the poverty of metaphysical theorizing in comparison with its mathematical and scientific counterparts. Thus, Kantian philosophy is not primarily a system of first philosophy designed to answer skeptical doubts about scientific knowledge. Nevertheless, Kant does undertake an explanatory burden with respect to such knowledge in his philosophy. For, his philosophy does not merely point out the status of the synthetic *a priori* as the principles of the objectification of sensation into experience. Rather his philosophy seeks, in addition, to explain how these principles can play that role. This requires what Kant called his "transcendental turn" and his "Copernican revolution in philosophy."[6]

The rationalist metaphysician invites us to consider ourselves as striving to attain to knowledge of a realm of objects beyond experience through pure thought. Thus, the rationalist requires that we somehow attain *a priori* knowledge of "things as they are in themselves." Kant claims, in the preface to the second edition of the First Critique, that this view makes the possibility of *a priori* knowledge wholly inexplicable, and he urges a change. He enjoins us to consider the view that "we can know *a priori* of things only what we put into them" (B viii). That is, objects must conform to our faculties of knowledge, and, thus, our *a priori* knowledge extends only to the principles that express the contribution of our faculties of knowledge to objective representation. In accordance with this, the business of philosophy changes from an attempt to give *a priori* principles of a realm beyond experience to an examination of the forms of the faculties of knowledge that synthesize

---

6 Thus, Kantian philosophy is not meant to replace the justificatory practices of mathematicians and (Newtonian) physicists with something more epistemically correct – say, more evident axioms. Rather, Kant points out the unique status accruing to certain principles in exact science and explains how these principles can come to play this role. This can lead to reformations of scientific practice, especially where such practice is informed by metaphysical concerns (e.g., Kant's rejection of the two contending views in the Newton–Leibniz debate over the nature of physical space), but such reformations are not the primary motivation for the transcendental turn.

the material of sensation to yield objective knowledge. This is Kant's "transcendental turn."

Having discovered that synthetic judgments must contain a synthesis of intuitions and concepts, the transcendental turn requires the investigation of two distinct cognitive faculties: the sensibility and the understanding. Both of these faculties have purely formal components that lead to synthetic *a priori* knowledge. The "forms" of the sensibility are space and time, and this explains the *a priori* status of mathematical and geometrical knowledge. The "pure forms of the understanding" are revealed in the logical functions of judgment as understood in Aristotelian logic. These, when considered as pure functions of thought of an object of intuition in general, in transcendental logic, yield the *categories*. These, in turn, yield the "pure principles of the understanding" when schematized under the pure form of time, as the most general form of intuition.[7]

The content of Kant's synthetic *a priori* principles is quite rich. In particular, Kant argues that Euclidean geometry is synthetic *a priori* knowledge and, hence, a doctrine of substantive yet necessary truths about the world. Similarly, Newton's laws of motion also have the status of synthetic *a priori* truths for Kant.[8] Thus, the Kantian synthetic *a priori* is in essence strong enough to impose a unique system of mathematics and physics upon the manifold of empirical intuition. This system of mathematics and physics takes us beyond the play of sensation to the regular, law-governed world of Newtonian physical objects.[9]

Thus the machinery of faculties of knowledge and their forms explains the *a priori* knowledge we possess in mathematics and physics and limits any *a priori* knowledge to the twin cognitive sources of objective judgment. It thereby explains the mistake of the rationalist metaphysicians' understanding of the subject matter of metaphysics. More-

---

7 Time is a more general form of intuition than space, because, although outer intuitions have location in space and time, inner intuitions have location in time only.
8 The status of the laws of pure physics is quite complicated. They are transcendentally grounded via the pure principles of the understanding and gain genuine empirical content via moments of the empirical concept of matter. This is the argument of Kant's *Metaphysical Foundations of Natural Science* (1786/1985).
9 Thus, Kant is led from what he calls a "general metaphysics of possible objects of experience" to a metaphysics of corporeal nature (1786/1985). The use of the term "metaphysics" should not confuse us here; the rationalist metaphysics that Kant is arguing against has no room for either a general metaphysics in Kant's sense nor certainly a metaphysics of corporeal nature. For more on the project of the *Metaphysical Foundations of Natural Science* see Friedman (1993, chap. 3), Buchdahl (1992), and the essays in Butts (1986).

over, by defining *reason* as the faculty of inference, Kant can explain the persistence of metaphysical modes of thought. Kant argues, in the Transcendental Dialectic, that the systematizing function of reason leads naturally to attempts to theorize beyond the bounds of sense, in order to induce a final and complete system of knowledge. Thus, for Kant, metaphysics is not a theoretical understanding of a purely intelligible world, but the misuse of reason beyond the bounds of the conditions under which objective knowledge is possible.[10]

There are many attractive aspects to Kant's account of knowledge. Chief among these is the way it both respects and illuminates the scientific knowledge of his time.[11] Unfortunately, this tight connection with the scientific knowledge of his time leads to the most serious objection to the Kantian picture. Kantian philosophy seems to have no resources to explain the revolutionary changes that occurred in physics, mathematics, and logic in the nineteenth and early twentieth centuries. Euclidean geometry, Newtonian physics, and Aristotelian logic, which form the *a priori* core of objective knowledge on the Kantian view, were each either overthrown or fundamentally reconsidered in the course of the decades after Kant. There could scarcely be a more embarrassing fate for allegedly synthetic *a priori* principles, such as Newton's laws of motion, than to be rejected as inadequate within the development of the exact sciences themselves. It seems, then, that precisely Kant's deep philosophical account of the science of his time disqualifies Kantian philosophy from extending beyond the world of classical physics to the world of Einsteinian physics, non-Euclidean geometry, and modern logic.

Consider, for example, the development of non-Euclidean geometries in the nineteenth century. Kant seems to have literally no way of even conceiving of this possibility.[12] On Kant's account, Euclidean geometry both describes the structure of our form of outer intuition and

---

10 The ideas of reason give the entering point of Kant's practical philosophy in the Third Antimony, which deals with the "idea of freedom." So, they have a positive role to play in the full critical project; fortunately, this story lies beyond the scope of our current concerns, but see Allison (1990), Beck (1960), and Wood (1970).
11 Readers interested in the details of the connection of Kant's philosophy to the science of his day may examine Friedman (1993), Buchdahl (1992), and Butts (1986).
12 In the sense of real, not logical, possibility. The synthetic status of the truths of geometry do allow the logical possibility of the concept of a two-sided closed figure; the *a priori* status of those truths disallows the real possibility of an object falling under such a concept. Mathematical truth is not logical consistency within a system for Kant.

must be presupposed for any objective, experiential judgment to be possible. The latter characteristic disallows any empirical testing of Euclidean geometry, considered as one among a number of alternative and competing geometrical systems of physical space. The former characteristic disallows, so to speak, *a priori* doubts about the validity of Euclidean geometry. The invocation of the form of the faculty of intuition as an explanation of the synthetic *a priori* status of Euclidean geometry would misfire badly if we could somehow raise doubts about whether Euclidean geometry really captures that form. This would be to raise skeptical questions that would undermine the whole transcendental turn.[13]

Thus, the development of non-Euclidean geometries and the rigorization of analysis, leading ultimately to the development of modern logic and modern axiomatic approaches to geometry, yield a radically transformed understanding of the mathematical enterprise in which Kant's account simply does not apply. Similarly, the development of the theory of relativity radically reforms the structure of physics. This renders, in effect, Kant's attribution of *a priori* status to Newton's laws of motion a refutation, rather than the clinching argument, of his philosophical account of scientific objectivity. Kant's account of Newtonian physics gives Newton's laws of motion the status of principles that must be presupposed in order for any objective experiential judgment to be possible at all. Just as in the case of geometry, then, Newtonian physics cannot be empirically refuted or subject to, so to speak, other *a priori* rivals. Kant lacks, therefore, any way of conceiving the real possibility of its overthrow.

Nevertheless, throughout the nineteenth and early twentieth centuries many philosophers who were primarily interested in epistemological and methodological questions about natural science took their inspiration at least in part from Kant. Although this is perhaps in part explainable as deference to Kant's status as the preeminent philosophical force in Germany throughout the nineteenth century, there are sys-

---

13   That is, if the invocation of the forms of the intuition, for example, were interpreted as indicating a wholly separate philosophical access to these forms, independent of the principles of geometry and mathematics used by the exact sciences, then this invocation would fail to do precisely what it was meant to do: explain the role that those mathematical principles play. I am taking a stand in the text on a much-contended interpretative issue: the role of intuition in Kant's understanding of geometry and mathematics. I shall elaborate on this in the next section of the present chapter.

The Kantian problematic

tematic reasons for this also.[14] First, a number of philosophers were deeply suspicious of the imposing metaphysical systems of the world being promulgated by Hegel and others in the nineteenth century. Despite the Hegelians' claims to be engaged in something like the Kantian transcendental project, the Hegelian dialectic seemed to subvert Kant's order of philosophical critique. Whereas, for Kant, the possibility of metaphysics was to be investigated through philosophical understanding of the conditions of objectivity in the formal and natural sciences, the Hegelians sought to install metaphysics as the realm of absolute truth through uncovering contradictions within the sciences. Philosophers and scientists dubious about the value of Hegelian metaphysics attempted to reinstate the spirit if not the letter of the Kantian project: Hegelian metaphysics stood as much in need of critique as the metaphysics of Leibniz, and the way to do this was to reflect philosophically on the epistemological lessons of the most successful sciences of the day.[15]

Second, although the Kantian account of science had itself come to grief, no other traditional project could be pointed to as having been vindicated in the revolutionary advances science was making. Neither the old rationalist or new Hegelian metaphysical systems seemed to provide even the beginnings of an understanding of what was happening in science. Similarly, traditional empiricism seemed no better here. Consider, again, the development of non-Euclidean geometries. Kant had already pointed out the poverty of the claim that Euclidean geometry was an analytic discipline relating ideas of points, lines, and so on to one another. The development of non-Euclidean geometries appeared to show, on the one hand, that there was a serious question about which geometrical system the physical world instantiated but, on the other hand, that mathematicians could investigate all of these geometrical systems in a purely *a priori* way. The former may have seemed to make the geometrical structure of physical space the subject for empirical investigation, but the latter was still incomprehensible for traditional empiricism.

---

14 Kant may well have enjoyed this status in the nineteenth century because the richness of his philosophical project made it of continuing attractiveness to philosophers of wide-ranging interests. The claim, therefore, that "Kant was widely followed in Germany because he was the preeminent German philosopher" sounds suspiciously like putting the cart before the horse.

15 A typical call for a "back to Kant and reintegration of philosophy with the sciences" view is found in Zeller (1862). This was a particularly important such call, given Zeller's Hegelian pedigree, as is noted by Ward (1890/1927).

Early Carnap: Themes from Kant

Indeed, the existence of non-Euclidean geometries raises serious questions about the abstractionist account of concept formation employed by the empiricists. The traditional empiricist holds that all our ideas are abstracted from our impressions. Consider the parallel postulate and its negations. The empiricist seems to have three unpalatable options here. First, she can claim that our ideas of point, line, and parallel are analytically connected, so that the parallel postulate is either analytically true or false. Even putting aside Kant's insight into the poverty of Aristotelian logic, the empiricist now runs into insuperable difficulties in explaining the mathematicians' *a priori* investigations of all the systems – even those containing the analytically false postulate – and, especially, the mathematicians' relative consistency proofs for the systems. Second, she could claim that the parallel postulate states only a putative matter of fact of experience. The same problem with understanding *a priori* mathematical geometry arises here; at best, mathematicians would have to be viewed suspiciously as engaging in only the first half of the hypothetico-deductive method, never remembering to test their hypotheses empirically. Third, the empiricist could claim that our geometrical ideas are so vague as to make the parallel postulate neither an analytic relation of ideas nor an empirical matter of fact. This does not allow us simply to assume the truth or falsity of the principle, however. For now the parallel postulate violates the empiricists' strictures about what is knowable. This option puts geometry in the same basket with metaphysics: Both are to be rejected as unknowable for the empiricist.[16]

Not only were none of the rivals to the Kantian project in a better position to account for the developments that rendered Kantian philosophy implausible; there were some aspects to the Kantian account that still seemed important and illuminating. Kant's synthetic *a priori* had drawn attention to the special role played by the principles of geometry and the laws of motion in Newtonian physics. These principles were presupposed in the Newtonian system, and only on the basis of these presuppositions did the whole system get off the ground. Kant's synthetic *a priori* seemed to capture something methodologically compelling, therefore. Principles playing this constitutive methodological role could, perhaps, be found in all scientific theories.[17] Thus, for

---

16 Of course, there are famous stories of geometrical empiricism in the nineteenth century, but the question is how the empiricist can understand mathematical practice in general, which seems not driven by concerns with empirical testing.
17 This claim is deliberately ambiguous. It can be read with the existential quantifier for the principles falling within or without the scope of the universal quantifier for

100

The synthetic a priori

example, a number of scientists and philosophers found "conservation principles" to play the methodological role of the synthetic *a priori* within nineteenth-century dynamics and electromagnetic theory. The principle of the conservation of energy seemed to be neither a logical truth about an antecedently understood concept of energy nor simply a matter of fact about energy that was discovered by science. Rather, it was presupposed in the physics of the day and seemed to constitute in part the physical significance of the concept of energy as understood by the physicists employing that theory. Thus, the Kantian story seemed to have uncovered an important part of the story of the methodology of scientific knowledge production.

Any attempt to use Kantian philosophy as a key to understanding scientific knowledge, therefore, had to come to a new understanding of the synthetic *a priori*. Indeed, there are separable aspects to the notion of the synthetic *a priori* in Kantian philosophy. Perhaps some deep lessons could still be found in the Kantian approach by disentangling these strands of Kantian thought.

THE VARIOUS NOTIONS OF THE SYNTHETIC *A PRIORI*

There are three distinct strands of thought at stake in the notion of synthetic *a priori* knowledge within Kant's speculative philosophy.[18] All three of these ideas have already made an appearance at various places in the preceding section of this chapter. Once we have disentangled them we can get a better sense of what thinkers interested in the philosophy of science early in the twentieth century might have found attractive in the Kantian position.

Kant introduces the notion of the synthetic *a priori* in the introduction to the First Critique. If we combine his introductory definitions of *a prioricity* and synthetic judgment, we arrive at the nominal definition of the synthetic *a priori*. For Kant, *a priori* knowledge is knowledge (B 2) "independent of experience and even of all impressions of the senses." The distinguishing features of *a priori* judgments are that they are necessary and universal (B 3). Additionally, synthetic judgments are amplia-

---

scientific theories. As we shall see in Chapter Five, the neo-Kantians tried both approaches; indeed, they frequently tried both at once.

18 There are more notions than this in play in his critical philosophy in general. Both the practical philosophy and the account of judgments of taste bring further complications to the notion of the synthetic *a priori*. Again, happily, we shall consider only the speculative philosophy here.

tive (B 11), that is, the predicate concept does not lie within the subject concept. Therefore, we have a "synthesis" of a subject concept with a predicate concept, since the latter is not derived from a simple analysis of what is already thought in the subject concept itself. We arrive, then, at the nominal definition of the synthetic *a priori* as substantive knowledge of the world, knowable independently of experience and hence necessarily true.

The claim that there is synthetic *a priori* knowledge in this nominal sense is surely at odds with traditional empiricism. That there is such knowledge is not, however, at all obvious. The claim that there is such knowledge rests, for Kant, on the philosophical insight he brings to bear on the notion of analyticity available within the framework of Aristotelian logic. Kant's nominal account of the synthetic *a priori* is, thus, augmented by his division of objective representations into concepts and intuitions, his understanding of the synthetic *a priori* as principles about the pure forms of these representational types, and his explanation of how we can know such principles through assignment of these forms to the mind.

Suppose, for the purposes of this argument, that the necessity or *a priori* status of mathematics and geometry, for example, is granted. Kant's insight is that the poverty of logical structure in Aristotelian logic renders it impossible for these disciplines to be analytic disciplines. Space, for example, as conceived of within geometry, is a single, infinitely large object that is infinitely, indeed continuously, divisible. Thus, space is both a single representation and contains infinitely many other representations (the spatial points, for example) within it. The notion of a general concept, taken over from Aristotle, cannot ground either of these aspects of space. Neither the singularity of space nor the way it contains an infinite number of spatial points (lines, etc.) can be guaranteed by the logical resources available at the time. The idea is that both the uniqueness claim ("There is one and only one space") and the claim about infinite representations within space (say, the denseness of space: "For any two points there is a third between them") require a logic of relations and of quantifier dependence. These resources of modern logic were simply not available in Kant's day. Thus, no concept of space subject only to the confines of concepts understood in classical logic is adequate for the conception of space necessary for geometry. Therefore, one can understand geometry as a branch of knowledge only by seeing it as involving another form of representation, intuition, that grounds the truth of its claims.

For example, within modern quantification theory we can represent

The *synthetic* a priori

the structure of the points of Euclidean space through axioms that provide a theory of order. Thus, denseness (*D*) can be handled with an axiom involving a notion of 'betweenness' among points and quantifier dependence in which the existential quantifier is within the scope of the universal quantifiers. If we symbolize using "*P*" for 'point' and "*B*" for 'between,' we get:

(D) $(\forall x)(\forall y)(((Px \& Py) \& x \neq y) \supset (\exists z)(Pz \& Bxzy))$

The essential use of relational predicates, the identity relation, and quantifier dependence puts (D) beyond the limits of representation in a language of Aristotelian logic. In this sense, given that logic is the theory of conceptual knowledge, the representation of space cannot be conceptual. Kant, therefore, reinterprets the source of our knowledge of the structure of the points in Euclidean space as involving constructive procedures in pure intuition. Essentially, Kant conceives of the axioms of Euclidean geometry as procedures for the intuitive construction of, for example, lines and circles. These procedures can be combined and iterated indefinitely. The structure of Euclidean space is, in this way, constructed from these basic procedures, as is done in the straight-edge-and-compass proofs of traditional Euclidean geometry. We today conceive of geometry in terms of, say, a first-order axiom system that involves certain nonlogical primitive concepts (such as line, point, and between) and allows the purely logical deduction of the theorems from the axioms. For Kant, however, there is no notion of logic underlying axiom systems in this way. Rather, the axioms themselves codify certain primitive nonlogical constructive inferential operations.[19]

The *a priori* status of the knowledge of geometry and mathematics grounds the claim that the intuitions (space and time) they are about are themselves *a priori*. Thus, space and time are intuitive representations, the properties of which are revealed in geometry and mathematics and which can in this way be known independently of all experience.

The distinction between concepts and intuitions provides the key to understanding how concepts not analytically connected can be synthesized in a synthetic judgment. They are combined through their connection with intuition. In a synthetic *a posteriori* judgment, concepts are combined through their relation to empirical intuitions subsumed under them. In pure synthetic *a priori* judgments, *a priori* concepts are

---

19 Here I follow the much more detailed interpretation of the role of constructions in pure intuition given in Friedman (1993, chaps. 1 and 2).

Early Carnap: Themes from Kant

synthesized through their relation to pure *a priori* intuition. Thus, the synthetic *a priori* principles of mathematics and geometry involve the schematizing of mathematical or geometrical concepts to construct those concepts in pure intuition. Also, the synthetic *a priori* principles of the understanding go beyond the purely formal principles of pure general logic to schematize the pure concepts of the understanding under the pure intuition of time. In this way, those principles provide the formal principles of knowledge of objects in general.

This is, then, the second understanding of the synthetic *a priori* in Kant. The distinction between synthetic and analytic judgments and the idea that discursive conceptual knowledge finds its foundation solely in logic leads to the recognition of a second type of representation that underlies objective judgment. Thus, we arrive at the distinction between concepts and intuitions. Each is involved in any synthetic judgment, whether empirical or *a priori*. The synthetic *a priori* results when pure *a priori* intuition plays the role of the representation mediating nonanalytically connected concepts. Only two types of concepts can be so conjoined: the concepts of mathematics, including geometry, and the pure concepts of the understanding. Pure intuition and pure concepts of the understanding are understood as pure forms of the corresponding faculties of representation, understanding, and sensibility. Thus, synthetic *a priori* principles are purely formal principles of the types of representation required for there to be representations of objects at all.

From a modern point of view, there seems to be a tension between this second understanding of the synthetic *a priori* and the first. The first notion stressed the contentful, ampliative nature of the synthetic *a priori*; the second stresses its purely formal nature. Now, it is clear that the synthetic *a priori* is not purely formal in the sense of pure logic for Kant. Precisely due to the role of intuition in mathematics and the pure principles of the understanding, such knowledge goes essentially beyond the fully abstractive notion of form of pure general logic, which "abstracts from all content of knowledge" (B 79). Synthetic *a priori* knowledge does abstract from both the particularities of empirical intuition and the empirical concepts that we derive therefrom. But it keeps all the conditions of objective judgment at hand and, thus, presents not merely the forms of thought in general, but the forms of thought of an object of intuition in general (B 79–80).

Pure logic for Kant does not, therefore, exhaust the forms of thought required for the acquisition of objective knowledge; he, in this way,

The synthetic a priori

lacks *our* understanding of the distinction between the form and content of knowledge. Both intuition and the understanding have forms peculiar to them. Moreover, the pure forms of intuition are presupposed in our pure thought of objects and, hence, provide, in a sense, the content of the principles of the understanding (B 80). Thus, the sense in which the synthetic *a priori* is "contentful" is the sense in which it is not totally abstractive, as logic is, but rather must keep the manifold of pure, *a priori* intuition to hand. The notion of the synthetic *a priori*, in this way, indicates the inability of pure logic to provide the principles of objective thought. The sense in which it is formal is just the sense in which its content is wholly *a priori* – imposed by the mind and not received in sensation.[20]

The second sense of the synthetic *a priori* also brings us back to the Kantian Copernican revolution. Kant explains the possibility of synthetic *a priori* knowledge through the framework of faculties of the mind. The forms at issue in the synthetic *a priori* are knowable to us because they are the forms imposed by us upon the material given in empirical intuition. Thus, Kant's transcendental idealism both reinterprets and explains the possibility of *a priori* knowledge.

It is possible to endorse this second notion of the synthetic *a priori* without endorsing the claim that, say, Euclidean geometry or Newtonian physics has this status. The systematic import is that there are nonlogical but *a priori* sources of knowledge – the forms of intuition. To take a famous example, Husserl endorsed such an idea in his notion of 'essential insight' (*Wesenserschauung*). It seems also that Poincaré endorsed such a claim in his dispute with the logicists. Poincaré argued that there were certain *a priori* principles (such as mathematical induction) the cognitive import of which could not be captured purely logically but only by reference to "mathematical intuition."[21] Clearly, neither of these authors would want to be committed to the synthetic *a priori* status of Newtonian physics or Euclidean geometry *simpliciter*.[22]

---

20 That Kant's understanding of the form–content distinction is not ours comes even more forcefully to the fore in his discussions of the 'categorical imperative' in his practical philosophy. The categorical imperative is purely formal, from a practical point of view, precisely because it does not presuppose an independently given object of the will as material for the principle. Here, we have clearly wandered quite far from "formal" as "purely logical."
21 For more on Poincaré's understanding of mathematical intuition see Folina (1992, 1995), and Goldfarb (1988). For Husserl's views, see Husserl (1913/1976).
22 Although, of course, both of these authors may well be happy to carve out a notion of

Of course, such a project threatens to sever the connection between pure intuition and the mathematical sciences of space and time, so much of the texture of Kant's project would be lost. On the one hand, for Poincaré, geometry moves into the realm of the conventional and, thus, not the synthetic *a priori*, on Poincaré's intuitive account of the synthetic *a priori*. On the other hand, Husserl's essential insight need not yield any metrical geometry as part of the primitive phenomenology of space perception.

The third notion of the synthetic *a priori* in Kant can be approached by suspending our earlier acceptance of the *a priori* status of mathematics and pure physics and asking how Kant can argue that they have this status. Claiming necessity or self-evidence directly for mathematics and pure physics amounts to little more than simply contradicting the strict empiricist. Kant's more telling line of argumentation involves pointing toward the unique status of mathematical and geometrical principles and Newton's laws of motion in constituting the framework of Newtonian physics, within which empirical judgments take on objective significance. Thus, the synthetic *a priori* principles constitute the framework within which objective, empirical enquiry first is possible.

This point can best be illustrated by an example.[23] One of the leading revolutions of early modern science was, of course, the transition from Ptolemaic to Copernican astronomy. However, if the theories of planetary motion remain strictly at a phenomenological and kinematic level, there is really nothing to choose between the two theories. Both theories have the resources to approximate observed planetary motions to any degree of precision desired. Thus, without a truly dynamical theory and the distinction between true and merely apparent motion, there is nothing beyond practical or aesthetic reasons to induce us to choose one theory over the other. With Newtonian dynamics, however, the question of the truth of the theories becomes serious, for, within Newtonian mechanics, the distinction between true and apparent motion is well founded. Thus, the issue can be interpreted as whether the sun undergoes a true revolution around the earth or vice versa.

---

a nonlogical, nonempirical source of mathematical knowledge that would ground the entire metageometrical project and, thus, the mathematical status of the theorems of Euclidean geometry.

23   The example is taken from Friedman (1993, chap. 3) and vastly simplified. Interested readers are directed to Friedman's book for a greatly more sophisticated and nuanced account of both the physical situation and Kant's philosophical understanding of it.

The synthetic a priori

The answer to this question can be given as a consequence of Newton's account of universal gravitation. Newton's famous "deduction from the phenomena" begins with the phenomenological regularities of observational astronomy and uses his laws of motion and mathematical and geometrical arguments to derive the force law for gravitation. With this in hand we can raise the question dividing Ptolemy and Copernicus as follows: Conceived of in a modern way, we can take Newton's laws of motion to define the notion of an inertial frame – that is, one within which the law of inertia and the canceling of impressed forces in accordance with the law of action and reaction are valid. The question then becomes, Which frame is (more nearly) an inertial frame – the frame at rest with respect to the earth, or the frame at rest with respect to the sun? Now, the law of universal gravitation, the values we can calculate for the mass of the earth and the mass of the sun, and the geometrical argument that the center-of-mass frame for an isolated system is an inertial system lead to the following result: Only the center-of-mass frame for the solar system is (essentially) inertial. The center of mass can be calculated from the respective masses of the heavenly bodies and their orbital trajectories. We then find that the center of mass lies very close to the center of mass of the sun itself. Thus, the question is resolved in favor of Copernicus; the sun is very nearly the point around which the solar system rotates.

The point of this example is the very particular role played in the Newtonian argument by those principles Kant designates as synthetic *a priori*. The "deduction from the phenomena" does not begin simply with the observed motions of the planets; rather, it also assumes the laws of motion, the Euclidean structure of physical space, and the applicability of mathematics through the calculus to objects in physical space. These principles comprise the framework that first makes a physical dynamics possible and that, therefore, renders objective and objectively decidable the issue between Copernicus and Ptolemy. It is in this sense that the laws of motion and the applied mathematical principles are "conditions of the possibility of the object of experience." Newtonian physics provides the framework within which putative physical issues first acquire a determinate sense: The issue between Copernicus and Ptolemy resolves itself into a question of calculating the center-of-mass frame of the solar system.

This is, then, a third strand in the account of the synthetic *a priori*. Synthetic *a priori* principles are those that must be assumed before objective knowledge in the empirical realm is possible. Thus, the sense of *a prioricity* of the synthetic *a priori* is here more methodological than straightforwardly epistemological; synthetic *a priori* status is grounded in the methodological role of constitutive principles rather than some independent epistemological notion of certainty, necessity, or self-evidence.

Thus, we have three notions of the synthetic *a priori* that are distinguishable in principle. The first is basically epistemological: Synthetic *a priori* principles are those contentful judgments knowable independently of experience. The second is representation theoretic, or "semantic":[24] Synthetic *a priori* principles express the formal principles of the dual types of representation needed for objective knowledge. The third is methodological: Synthetic *a priori* principles are principles that must be assumed before any objective knowledge is possible in the empirical realm; these principles are revealed in the methodological structure of the sciences that express such objective knowledge: mathematics, geometry, and the Newtonian laws of motion.

Of course, these various notions interact substantially within Kant's own philosophy. For example, the representation theoretic account yields the structure of the First Critique itself and, in particular, yields the need for the schematism of the categories. Moreover, from the transcendental standpoint, we explain the objectifying role of the principles of pure physics by deriving generalizations of them from the schematism of the categories under the pure intuition of time. Thus, the philosophical explanation of the status of physics (and the third notion of the synthetic *a priori*) proceed via the second notion and the general investigation of the conditions of the possibility of objective judgment.

Similarly, the rejection of metaphysics borrows from all three accounts of the synthetic *a priori*. The first account gives the epistemic status that metaphysics must have for the rationalist. The second provides the full account of the representations necessary for objectivity and can be used to show that the basic ideas of metaphysics (the soul, God, the totality of the world) cannot be captured in intuition and, hence, yield no synthetic *a priori* knowledge. Similarly, the third account is meant to show, against the strict empiricist, that *a priori* knowledge is requisite in the empirical realm, even as we reject any knowledge beyond the conditions of the sensibility. The interaction of these three

---

24 "Semantic" in the sense of J. Alberto Coffa's (1991) semantic tradition, not semantic in the post-Tarskian sense of dealing with word–world relations. Questions of linguistic semantics do not arise in any straightforward sense in Kantian philosophy. Indeed, the transference of the appropriate realm of form from mind to language is part of the story of twentieth-century analytic philosophy, as we shall see.

different strands in the account of the synthetic *a priori*, thus, is responsible for much of the richness of the Kantian argument against all earlier philosophy.

Moreover, the third strand of the account of the synthetic *a priori* can help us toward a reconciliation of the tension between the contentful first account and the formal second account. The methodological, constitutive role of the synthetic *a priori* indicates how it straddles modern accounts of contentful and purely formal judgments. The synthetic *a priori* judgments do not merely state further facts about the world in the manner of the synthetic *a posteriori*; rather they provide the conditions without which there would be no empirical facts at all. This role is not dissimilar to the role of logic, as it is sometimes explained today: Logic must be presupposed before any facts are possible. But, the constitutive principles for Kant are significantly different from ours – precisely because he lacks modern logic, which provides us with universal rules of inference and representation underlying all areas of knowledge. In particular, for Kant, a spatiotemporal framework and a particular physical structure for the objects within that framework are conditions for the possibility of objective judgment; objective thinking is inconceivable except through this physical structure. Kant's understanding of the formal poverty of his logic leads him to an account of representation and objectivity that builds into the conditions of objective judgment much that we would think of as simply empirical fact.

There is one further place where we can see the interaction of the various notions of the synthetic *a priori* in Kant. This is in the direct argument against (problematic) subjective idealism given in the section called the "Refutation of Idealism" in the second edition of the First Critique. Here Kant argues that the subjective idealist epistemological starting point is a determinate order of ideas in inner sense. From this starting point the subjective idealist inquires as to the possibility of acquiring concepts such as spatial structure, causality, and objective necessity. Regardless of the answer to this question, the question itself presupposes that there is a notion of temporally determinate inner experience that does not itself rely on the categories. Kant argues against this view. We can achieve a determinate temporal ordering of inner empirical intuition only by embedding the empirical cognizer and her experience into the fully law-governed natural world.

Thus, the principles of the understanding provide the framework for the objective ordering of inner intuition in time by providing the framework for a law-governed external world and, with it, an objective correlate of the pure time series within experience. The principles are also generalizations of the very principles of Newtonian physics for which the empiricist cannot account: the laws of motion and the principle of the conservation of matter. The special metaphysics of matter exposes how far the methodological structure of Newtonian science goes beyond empiricist methodology. The general metaphysics of the First Critique provides the framework of the principles of the understanding that exposes the unavailability of the subjective idealist's epistemological starting point. The connection between the structure of pure physics and the refutation of idealism is stressed by Kant in note 2 to the "Refutation of Idealism" (B 277–8):

Not only are we unable to perceive any determination of time save through change in outer relations (motion) relatively to the permanent in space (for instance, the motion of the sun relatively to objects on the earth), we have nothing permanent on which, as intuition, we can base the concept of substance, save only *matter*; and even this permanence is not obtained from outer experience, but is presupposed *a priori* as a necessary condition of determination in time, and therefore, also as a determination of inner sense in respect of [the determination of] our own existence through the existence of outer things.

Despite these clear connections within Kant's own system, his accounts of the synthetic *a priori* are separable. Indeed, in light of developments in logic, mathematics, and physics, certain aspects of the full Kantian account of the synthetic *a priori*, as well as his particular examples of such principles, became deeply problematic.

The first account of the synthetic *a priori* is the most obviously problematic in light of subsequent history. Certainly, it can scarcely be said today that the principles of Newtonian physics and the theorems of Euclidean geometry are necessary and contentful truths knowable independently of experience. At the very least, if a philosopher were to claim this after Bernhard Riemann, Albert Einstein, and their cohorts, the claim would no longer be taken for a deep insight into the structure of the exact sciences but viewed as reflecting philosophical commitments that directly oppose the historical development of those sciences.

Consider, for example, a neo-Kantian commitment to Euclidean geometry that devolved into a phenomenological "Euclidean spectacles" view – a view that says that non-Euclidean geometries are mathematically on a par with Euclidean geometry but that, due to our mental makeup, we must experience the world as Euclidean. On this view, Euclidean geometry is still, in a sense, necessary for us. This view is extremely problematic, however. First, such visual-geometry views typ-

The synthetic a priori

ically ignore the fact that for small portions of the world such as can be given in sensation, the differences between many geometrical structures are too slight to be noticed. Second, this account loses the sense in which constructions in intuition constitute the structure of space for Kant. Also, by acknowledging the mathematical parity of non-Euclidean geometry, it renders the status of the purely mathematical study of geometry and its relation to physical space very puzzling. In essence, on such an account, intuition simply plays the role of picking out the true geometry from among infinitely many possible geometries and so loses its constitutive role in thought. Finally, such a view would render the sense in which relativistic physics is based on non-Euclidean geometrical structure for physical space entirely opaque. Somehow it is supposed to be necessary for us to experience the world as Euclidean, but our best theories of the world say that it is not. This opens up a gap between scientific knowledge and the structure of experience that is antithetical to Kant's own views.

Ultimately, the development of mathematics and physics has rendered the whole problematic leading to the first notion of the synthetic *a priori* dubious. Thus, after the development of non-Euclidean geometries, we want to provide a philosophical account for the seemingly *a priori* study of all the various forms of geometry discovered in the nineteenth century. What is knowable *a priori* in mathematics seems to have increased beyond limit. But the things we seem to be able to know *a priori* in mathematics are mutually inconsistent. We can prove things with certainty in Euclidean geometry and also in non-Euclidean geometries, but these provable things are not straightforwardly combinable into a single system, since the theorems contradict one another. The notion of mathematical truth and, hence, the sense in which we have learned something about the world in doing mathematics has become very problematic. Thus, our *a priori* knowledge in mathematics no longer seems synthetic in the nominal sense.

Meanwhile, the history of physics has called into question whether any principle of physics deserves to be called *a priori*. The wholesale rejection, in the theory of relativity, of even the most basic principles of Newtonian physics makes doubtful that any contentful claim about the physical world from any theory of physics can lay claim to certainty or immunity to empirical refutation. (I shall have more to say, both later in this chapter and in Chapter Five, about the operative notion of immunity here, however.) Thus, the synthetic *a priori* in the nominal sense seems to have lost its argumentative force; indeed, any philosophy that insisted on it would seem to have been, on that ground, decisively refuted.[25]

Similarly, the second sense of the synthetic *a priori* does not survive unscathed. If the development of non-Euclidean geometries called Kant's specific candidates for synthetic *a priori* status into doubt, the work leading to the rigorization of analysis renders the notion of *a priori* intuition dubious, for this work was motivated by the attempt to establish the autonomy of analysis from spatiotemporal notions.[26] Thus, intuition in Kant's specific sense is called into question. The rigorization of analysis sought, for example, to purge the notion of continuity of spatiotemporal metaphors such as the metaphor of the continuous motion of a mathematical point. These heuristic remarks were to be dropped, within serious mathematical work, in favor of a definition of continuity that does not borrow from geometry or kinematics. Ultimately, the now standard definition of continuity as convergence to a limit and the existence of the limit was achieved. The general notion of a mathematical function and its values – not now tied to possible trajectories of points through space – became the foundational ones for analysis.

This mathematical development runs counter to what a good Kantian might hope but does not yet call the systematic point of Kant's intuition–concept distinction into question. For, unlike the mathematician, the philosopher finds the sum total of what could be conceptual knowledge given by the formal constraints of the general theory of concepts, that is, by formal logic. So, regardless of the mathematicians' reluctance to countenance geometrical explications of notions in analysis, the philosopher can still point out the poverty of Aristotelian logic to provide a basis for such knowledge. Thus, it is the development of a new formal logic that provides universally applicable inference rules and a system of conceptual representation adequate to capture all thought that provides the decisive response to Kant's second account of the synthetic *a priori*. It is with logicism that Kantian spatiotemporal intuition is finally banned from any role in the foundation of arithmetical concepts and mathematical inference.

---

25 This is not to say that we have a vindication of traditional empiricism. Traditional empiricism seems to have no better story about the multiplicity of geometries than does Kant (as was argued earlier in the chapter). Moreover, as we shall see, the rejection of this notion of the synthetic *a priori* does not settle the issue against neo-Kantian approaches that look to the other notions for lasting insight.
26 On this point, see, e.g., Demopoulos (1995).

The synthetic a priori

The rejection of the second sense of the synthetic *a priori* brings with it the collapse of much of the detail of the Kantian system. We have lost the dual nature of representation needed for objective knowledge, and, hence, there is no need for forms of intuition. Since there are no *a priori* forms of intuition, there is also no need for a transcendental deduction to answer the question of our right to the use of the categories in intuition. Similarly, the schematism simply drops out; there is no form of intuition under which the categories are schematized. Indeed, with the movement from Aristotelian to modern logic, we lose the key to the twelve Kantian categories; the table of forms of judgment that Kant uses to derive the twelve categories is simply inapplicable in modern logic. Thus, the whole structure of the transcendental philosophy must change with the rejection of pure intuition and the alteration of the categories required by modern logic.

This leaves the third notion of the synthetic *a priori:* principles constitutive of the object of experience. Again, of course, Kant's own examples of such principles cannot be maintained. Nevertheless, one might find this methodological understanding of the synthetic *a priori* compelling, insofar as one can point to such principles throughout the changes of theory that lead from classical physics to the Einsteinian universe. That is, one might find that there are principles in any theory that play the constitutive role played by the laws of motion and the principles of geometry, arithmetic, and the calculus in Newtonian physics. Thus, any theory of the world requires an *a priori* commitment to some form of constitutive principles – principles that induce a notion of objectivity within the empirical realm.

With the revolution in physics, it is, however, clear that no set of principles of the strength of Newton's laws of motion within any theoretical physics can play the role of the universal constitutive principles within the physical realm. Nevertheless, there are still two options open to someone who wants to preserve the methodological synthetic *a priori*. First, one could continue to conceive of a single set of principles that provides the conditions for objectification but where these principles are not strong enough to induce a single objective physical framework. Alternatively, one could see the principles of objectification as themselves changing across changes of theory – as the principles constituting objectivity for that theory.

The first option was taken by those who saw conservation principles as constitutive of physical concepts that must play a role in any physics. Thus, conservation of energy could be considered a universal methodologically synthetic *a priori* principle, if 'energy' is a concept requisite for any physics and if a conservation principle for it partially constitutes its physical significance. On the other hand, one could take a relativized stance with respect to conservation principles by viewing them as partially constitutive of particular theories in which they occur; thus, for example, one might claim that a particular conservation-of-mass principle partially constitutes the framework of Newtonian physics, whereas a conservation-of-mass-energy principle partially constitutes the framework of the theory of special relativity.

Each of these options has interesting consequences for understanding the methodology of objective, scientific knowledge. The first reformulation of the methodological synthetic *a priori* severs the connection between matter of fact and theoretically informed judgment. That is, this weak universal notion of the methodological synthetic *a priori* introduces a notion of matter of fact of experience, subject to some minimal formal but physical principles, that is not informed by any particular theoretical judgment, since the universal principles are retained across changes of theory. Thus, we arrive at a notion of matter of fact of experience that underdetermines the choice of theoretical framework. Physical theory becomes a superadded structure built on the matters of fact of experience, which are conditioned by synthetic *a priori* principles too weak to induce the substantial empirical constraints on those theories that Kant himself had envisioned. Epistemic probity now reaches to statements of experiential matters of fact uncontaminated by particular theoretical structure. This reintroduces something like a neutral empiricist epistemic starting point but differs from traditional empiricism by stressing the *formal conditions* that structure the matters of fact.

These formal conditions might now be conceived on the model of mathematics or logic – the remaining *a priori* disciplines. Thus, the formal conditions of objective thought were, by historical figures to be discussed in Chapter Five, variously understood on the model of the mathematical function, given the foundational importance of this notion within nineteenth-century analysis, or modern logic. Hence, the *a priori* status of mathematics and logic is construed not in terms of self-evidence or certainty, but via their continuing role as conditions with which any experiential judgment – including the statement of matters of fact of experience – must conform.

The second, theoretically relativized, account of the synthetic *a priori* still takes full mathematical and physical structure to be the objectifying condition of experience but no longer seeks a single set of such principles to serve across changes in theoretical structure. Each theory will have objectifying principles, but no set of principles is common to all

The synthetic a priori

theories. These objectifying principles take on the status of something closely akin to Poincaré's conventions. Indeed, conventionalism was one of the major sources of inspiration for the neo-Kantians in the first quarter of the twentieth century.

There is, of course, a notion of immunity to empirical confirmation that attends the methodological synthetic *a priori* in either of these non-Kantian guises. But this is not a notion of immunity that appeals to antecedent notion of certainty or necessity. Even in Kant's theory of the synthetic *a priori*, the main lines of philosophical connection go as follows: The nominal notion of the synthetic *a priori* trades in an undetermined notion of certainty and necessity that is exhibited by the methodological status of mathematical and physical principles and comprehended via the conditions of objective judgment in the second account and the full philosophical machinery of transcendental idealism. If we drop the second account of the synthetic *a priori* in its full Kantian expression, we are left with two remaining options: Either we simply explain the certainty and immunity to empirical refutation of the methodological synthetic *a priori* in terms of their constitutive role in objective science, or we give a new account of the conditions of objective judgment, perhaps now solely in terms of formal logic, within which intuition plays no role. At no point, however, will a primitive epistemological notion such as 'certainty' play any explanatory role or do any philosophical work. In other words, the primitive epistemological vocabulary of the first account of the synthetic *a priori* is first explicated and made sense of in some account that makes use of logical and methodological notions, which serve as the replacements for the full Kantian account.

This general distinction between a universal (but minimal) and a theoretically relativized (but stronger) notion of synthetic *a priori* principles in their methodological guise will be crucial in our account of the neo-Kantian scientific philosophy that formed the basis of Carnap's philosophical education at Jena. It is to this final flowering of neo-Kantianism with respect to scientific knowledge that we now turn.

CHAPTER FIVE

The fundamentals of neo-Kantian epistemology

ALL the creative Kantian reconstruction in Chapter Four was not simply make-believe, although it may well have been a bit of "leading" history. It was, indeed, designed to lead naturally into a discussion of the foremost neo-Kantian thinking on the exact sciences in the first quarter of the twentieth century. I have in mind neo-Kantian philosophy as articulated by authors such as Ernst Cassirer (1910, 1921), Bruno Bauch (1911, 1914), and Paul Natorp (1910a, 1910b). I shall consider only the works of these three philosophers in this chapter, because they are the neo-Kantians who most influenced Carnap's thinking. Bauch was Carnap's dissertation director and the philosopher from whom Carnap learned what he knew about Kant.[1] Cassirer's *Substanzbegriff und Funktionbegriff* (Substance and function) (1910) was clearly the most systematic discussion of the general neo-Kantian line on science and mathematics; as we have already seen in Chapter Two, Carnap's references to it in *Der logische Aufbau der Welt* show a deep appreciation of some of its central points. Moreover, Cassirer's (1921) monograph on the theory of relativity, *Zur einstein'schen Relativitätstheorie* (On Einstein's theory of relativity) was the most methodologically sophisticated and technically informed neo-Kantian discussion of the issues raised by relativity.[2] As for Natorp, Carnap, in a letter to the conventionalist physicist Hugo Dingler in 1920, indicated that Natorp was the neo-Kantian whose views on mathematics and physical methodology had most occupied his thinking during the writing of his dis-

---

1 Bauch was the author of a famous book on Kant, *Immanuel Kant* (1917), as well.
2 Quotations from these works are from the Swabey and Swabey translations of 1953.

sertation.³ Also, Natorp, earlier in his career (in the 1880s), was a central figure (with Otto Liebmann, Alois Riehl, and Hermann Cohen) in the reemergence of a self-consciously transcendental neo-Kantianism in opposition to the physiological approach of Hermann von Helmholtz. Thus, Natorp's writings contain clear statements of the motivations of this type of philosophy. The views of these philosophers do not by any means exhaust the neo-Kantian views in the air at the time when Carnap began his study of philosophy, but their views are the ones that Carnap was most occupied with and to which his ideas are most closely allied.⁴

Of course, even among these thinkers there were significant differences. Bauch, for example, was much more reluctant than Cassirer to countenance the epistemic possibility of non-Euclidean geometry. Similarly, Natorp was much more exercised to find a detailed epistemological account of mathematics than was Cassirer. I hope only to give a feel for the general project and an account of its influences on Carnap's early work. The full details of the project and, thus, an adequate articulation of the controversies among its practitioners cannot be adequately explored here.

TRANSCENDENTAL AND FORMAL LOGIC

Perhaps the most important aspect of the neo-Kantian project, especially for Cassirer, but also for Bauch, is in the lesson it took from the development of pure mathematics and mathematical physics in the

---

3 The letter is document RC 028–12–11 in the Rudolf Carnap Collection, Archives for Scientific Philosophy in the Twentieth Century, Hillman Library, University of Pittsburgh. Cited by Coffa (1991, p. 207).
4 A list of other important figures would include Hans Vaihinger, Richard Hönigswald, and Heinrich Rickert. Friedman (1992a) presents Carnap's views against the backdrop of some works of Bauch and Rickert. We have already seen that Rickert's views are at several points fundamentally at odds with those of the neo-Kantians I will discuss and that at these points Carnap clearly sides against Rickert. This is especially true of the controversy about concept formation in the natural and social sciences and, hence, the unity of science, already discussed in Chapter Two. The multifarious connections of the philosophies of all these folks and their relations to contemporaneous positivist (Ernst Mach, Theodor Ziehen, Josef Petzoldt) and phenomenological (Edmund Husserl, Hans Driesch) programs would take us well away from our primary goal of understanding the motivations of Carnap's philosophical program.

nineteenth century. For the neo-Kantians, this development exhibits a new type of concept formation that makes evident the functional nature of objective concepts and stands opposed to the traditional notion of concept formation via the process of abstraction. In the work in the foundations of analysis, the theory of the manifold, and the generalization of geometry in projective geometry and Hermann Grassmann's *Ausdehnungslehre*, Cassirer saw a consistent element in the understanding of the mathematical concept. This common element is the view that the form of the mathematical concept is the serial relation that gives the law of connection of the entire series and determines the transition from one element to the next. Thus, for example, Cassirer (1910/1953, p. 36) writes of Richard Dedekind's deduction of the concept of number that the

> "things," which are spoken of in the further deduction, are not assumed as independent existences present anterior to any relation, but gain their whole being, so far as it comes within the scope of the arithmetician, first in and with the relations which are predicated of them. Such "things" are terms of relations, and as such are never "given" in isolation but only in ideal community with each other.

That is, arithmetical objects are constructed from the forms of the relations in which they stand. These relations are considered as arbitrary mathematical functions that induce a systematic connection in the manifolds over which they are defined. This systematic connection, as given in the functional equations that provide the logical forms of the relations, allows us to claim objective understanding of the whole manifold and its elements. Indeed, it first allows the unique designation of individual elements of the manifold, for their individuality is to be found only in their unique place in the system of relations itself.

Cassirer emphasizes that this method of concept formation stands opposed to the traditional abstractive method which yields generic concepts. Such a traditional view of concept formation, he claims (1910/1953, p. 19), cannot begin to make sense of the logical structure of mathematics:

> When a mathematician makes his formula more general, this means not only that he is *to retain* all the more special cases, but also be able *to deduce* them from the universal formula. The possibility of deduction is not found in the case of the scholastic concepts, since these, according to the traditional formula, are

formed by neglecting the particular, and hence the reproduction of the particular moments of the concept seems excluded.

This new, functional understanding of the logic of concept formation is why the scientific neo-Kantians were happy to depart from Kant's own reliance on pure, *a priori* intuitions of space and time in accounting for the necessity of mathematical knowledge. The functional concepts of mathematics in themselves go beyond the syllogistic logic of Aristotle in precisely the important way that Kant recognized that mathematical and geometrical knowledge must go. Thus, Cassirer writes, in his review of Bertrand Russell's (1903) *Principles of Mathematics* and related work of Louis Couturat, entitled "Kant und die moderne Mathematik" (Kant and modern mathematics) (1907, p. 32), that the "division of understanding and sensibility is, in the way it is introduced in the transcendental aesthetic, in the first instance thoroughly convincing: because here it is a matter only of distinguishing mathematical concepts from the general *species-concepts*, which are defined by genus and difference, of traditional logic." That is, Kant's insight into the formal poverty of Aristotelian logic is preserved in the movement to the new, functional account of the logic of objective concepts. But, the new analytic account of functional dependency and the logic of relations is accepted as an adequate tool for such reasoning without the invocation of pure intuition and is accepted as such by the neo-Kantians. Thus, they (at least in part) were happy to see a new logic at work in mathematics that allowed them to dispense with pure intuition as a separate origin of mathematical knowledge.

This acknowledgment of one of the fundamental philosophical points of logicism is, however, in stark contrast to the assessment Cassirer gives to logicism as an epistemological program. Cassirer seeks to show in *Substance and Function* that the same logical function played by the concepts of pure mathematics is played by the concepts of any truly objective empirical science. Thus, Cassirer sees in the nature of energism in mathematical physics the correlate of the type of mathematical thinking exhibited by Bernhard Riemann, Dedekind, Georg Cantor, and others. Of the fundamental importance of energism in physics he (1910/1953, p. 190) writes:

The structure of mathematical physics is in principle complete when we have arranged the members of the individual series [e.g., quantity of heat, motion, electrical charge, etc.] according to an exact numerical scale, and when we discover a constant numerical relation governing the transition from one series to the others . . . Only then it becomes clear how all the threads of the mathematical system of phenomena are connected on all sides, so that no element remains without connection.

Here Cassirer is concerned to show that the type of concept formation that is operative in pure mathematics can be extended to the empirical realm. The application to the empirical realm guarantees the objectivity of both the empirical laws and the applied mathematical principles. This role for the logical principles underlying mathematics is missing in the logicism of Gottlob Frege and Russell, according to Cassirer. As he writes in his review of Russell (1903) (Cassirer 1907, pp. 44f.):

Thus there begins a new task at the point where logistic ends. What the critical philosophy seeks and what it must demand [fordern] is a *logic of objective knowledge* . . . Only when we have understood that the same foundational syntheses [Grundsynthesen] on which logic and mathematics rest also govern [beherrschen] the scientific construction of experiential knowledge, that they first make it possible for us to speak of a strict, lawful ordering among appearances and therewith of their objective meaning: only then is the true justification of the principles attained.

For Cassirer, it is this requirement that the principles of logic and mathematics receive their justification through the way in which they ground the objectivity of empirical science that captures what is of lasting importance in Kant's critical approach to philosophy. It is this demand that grants these principles synthetic *a priori* status in the methodological sense. The propositions of pure mathematics are the guarantors of objectivity within empirical science, for they provide the formal syntheses needed for the individuation of empirical objects via their strict and lawful interconnections – interconnections comprehended only through mathematical, functional equations.

Cassirer (1907, p. 43) sees, on the other hand, a radical separation of epistemic tasks in Russell's logicism:

According to the fundamental view of logistics the task of thought has ended when it has succeeded in making a strict deductive connection among its structures [Gebilden] and creations [Erzeugungen]. The problem of the lawfulness of the world of objects, on the other hand, is left completely to direct observation, which alone within its own, very narrow limits is able to teach us whether there are also here certain regularities or whether pure chaos reigns.

Cassirer (1907, p. 48) thus presents the logicist with the challenge that he give an account of "the role that [mathematical principles] play in the construction of our concept of an 'objective' reality." Failing that, the logicist has not even addressed the central issue raised by transcendental philosophy and the critique of knowledge.[5]

In the next section, we shall examine more closely Cassirer's reasons for so indicting logicism. First, however, we ought to note some of the consequences that the view of philosophy as the logic of objective knowledge has for the program of neo-Kantianism. These consequences are, first, the reinterpretation of the notion of transcendental logic, entailed by the rejection of pure intuition and Aristotelian logic, and second, the subservience of ontological questions to questions of logic. The latter leads to a rejection of both ontological realism and ontological idealism and, hence, to a type of ontological neutrality.

The rejection of pure intuition and the reinterpretation of logic to a logic of functional relations led to a reevaluation of the notion of transcendental logic. Kant's (B 80f.) own formulation of transcendental logic as a logic that does not abstract entirely from content but applies to the manifold of pure intuition to yield the principles of the pure thought of an object of intuition in general obviously cannot survive. Transcendental logic is converted into Cassirer's logic of objective knowledge – into the insistence on the mathematical structure of objective theoretical knowledge in the empirical realm and the demand for an account of pure mathematics that shows how it plays this role.

The latter account is given in the logic of the relational concept considered as arbitrary mathematical functional coordination. Such coordination is the fundamental moment of conceptual thought. The ubiquity of this conceptual function in knowledge grounds the unity of science and the applicability of mathematics to the manifold of experience. Natorp expresses the point as follows (1910b, p. 9):

In particular, the unity of the sciences is to be grounded in the unity of their logical basis [Fundament], i.e., not merely in the use of the same thought process, but rather in that the basic plan according to which their common object is constructed [sich aufbaut] is prescribed by the basic lawfulness of objective knowledge in general, which is expounded [darlegen] by logic. Every special science constitutes [konstituiert] its particular object in particular laws of thought; that these special objectifications [Gegenständlichkeiten], however, unite in one objectivity [Gegenständlichkeit] (so that for example the object of mathematics does not create for itself one world, the object of natural science a

---

5 Compare here the remarks about Cassirer and logicism in Sauer (1989, §2).

The fundamentals of neo-Kantian epistemology

second, and so forth, but rather the object of natural science must from its origin onward be constructed in mathematical form [Gestalt] and so on without exception) finds its ground in the original lawfulness of knowledge, which creates [erzeugt] them all in necessary inner connection with one another.[6]

The "original lawfulness of knowledge" is just formal logic, conceived as the form of conceptual thought in general.

The central philosophical role of logical form and the new understanding of the logical construction of concepts allow, indeed require, the neo-Kantians to claim that there is neither an ontological nor a psychological foundation to logic. Both of these attempts to ground logic in some other discipline, according to Cassirer, rely on the old mistaken understanding of the concept as abstractive. Once we go beyond the species-concepts (which classify objects according to their qualities) to consider the fundamental importance of the coordinative concepts of pure mathematics and mathematical science, all attempts to ground logic in an ontological notion of 'substance' or a psychological notion of 'idea' are ridiculous. Abstraction can yield concepts suitable for science only on the supposition that abstraction uncovers essences of substances (or ideas) that condition their causal interactions.[7] But this makes sense of neither the structure of pure mathematics nor, therefore, the mathematical form of scientific theories.

The new understanding of concept formation removes the priority of ontological substance or psychological idea and replaces them with the logico-mathematical notion of function. Logic now no longer must find completion in ontology or psychology; rather, it is both exhibited by and conditions the possibility of all conceptual developments in the mathematical sciences. Cassirer (1910/1953, p. 26) writes:

> The totality and order of pure "serial forms" lies before us in the system of the sciences, especially in the structure of exact science. Here, therefore, the theory [i.e., the critical theory of knowledge – AR] finds a rich and fruitful field, which can be investigated with respect to its logical import independently of any metaphysical or psychological presuppositions about the "nature" of the concept.

Indeed, any attempt to ground logic in some other discipline must misfire. For one has only succeeded in so grounding logic to the extent

---

6 For greater legibility, I have altered Natorp's punctuation in this quotation by setting off the example toward the end in parentheses rather than commas.
7 Cf. Cassirer (1910, chap. 1).

that such a metaphysical or psychological story is a true and objective story. But in order to be true or objective it must presuppose the very logical functions it is meant to justify. The neo-Kantians, unlike Russell with his notion of 'acquaintance,' have no further, independent epistemological constraints that condition the philosophical foundation of logic itself. Thus, we see here a convergence with Carnap's own radicalized adherence to "logic as the essence of philosophy" as the perspective from which metaphysical issues are subverted.

The role of relations in grounding objectivity indicates that the neo-Kantians do not abide by either the doctrines of naive realism or those of subjective idealism. Objects do not simply exist as such outside of their logical relations to one another, nor are they collections of sensory representations. Objective knowledge is found not in pure experience but in the laws of the mathematical sciences of nature, which require mathematized concepts and individuate objects through the ways in which they mutually condition one another in the system. Bauch (1915, p. 101) expresses this idea in discussing the formal conditions of space:

> The objectivity of the "things outside us" is lost in any case, as long as one does not cognize an objective mathematical law [Gesetzlichkeit] in space itself, but sees rather either a mere appearance or also an *absolute* reality . . . The reality of the "things outside us" with reference to the conception of space can only be secured if space is understood mathematico-lawfully as a "systema relationum," as a system of relations.

Here Bauch is echoing in the realm of the geometrical the view of scientific objects as individuated via their relations to one another that we saw Cassirer express for mathematical objects and physical objects under the methodological requirements of energism.

This view clearly contrasts with any naive realism that speaks of objective knowledge as objective not because of the systematic interrelations of the objects in the system but by relations to transcendent objects outside the system. Similarly, it is inconsistent with any idealism that founds objectivity in the subjective experience of any one individual, or that denies objectivity to knowledge in general. Thus, the neo-Kantians' version of transcendental or formal idealism seeks to deny both transcendent realism and subjective idealism. Bauch (1915, p. 102) says that it is precisely the hypothesis that these two views "are contradictory [and hence one must be right] . . . that the critical idealist combats." The critical or, in Cassirer's term, logical idealist does not deny the reality of scientific objects or seek to legitimate them via reduc-

The fundamentals of neo-Kantian epistemology

tion to pure experience. On the contrary, he stresses that objects are not given in experience but require a formal, conceptual element for their constitution out of experience and their full objective, scientific status. Ontological questions about the existence of objects presuppose a structured framework of relations in which logical form has already discharged its epistemological function. In this sense, all existential questions must be interpreted as internal to the system of the sciences itself.

CONVENTIONALISM AND THE LOGIC OF OBJECTIVE KNOWLEDGE

But what is the task of this logic of objective knowledge? Consideration of this question will indicate the importance of conventionalist themes in neo-Kantianism as well as sharpen the distinctions that the neo-Kantians saw between their project and empiricism, on the one hand, and logicism, on the other. The neo-Kantians saw themselves as able to tell a more convincing methodological story about the relation of mathematized scientific theories than the empiricists or, indeed, the strict conventionalists. But, as foreshadowed in my discussion of Kant, the lessons of conventionalism that the neo-Kantians must take on board lead to significant modification in central Kantian doctrines.

The principal example of conventionalism since the arguments of Henri Poincaré in *Science and Hypothesis* (1902/1952, chaps. 3–5) has been the metrical structure of physical space. Poincaré's arguments are meant to persuade us that no empirical experiment can ever establish whether physical space is Euclidean or not. This being the case, the metrical structure can be assigned according to free choice, though perhaps constrained for practical reasons by considerations such as simplicity. Thus, Poincaré uses his arguments to claim that practical considerations will always induce us to impute Euclidean structure to physical space and that these practical considerations will never be overridden by empirical ones.

Poincaré's arguments can be seen as proceeding in four steps.[8] First, he points out that non-Euclidean geometries are, from a mathematical point of view, at least possible structures of physical space, since they

---

8 I rely quite heavily on Sklar's (1973, pp. 88ff.) outstanding discussion of Poincaré's arguments here. New interpretations are now being developed that rather oppose my discussion; see, for example, Friedman (1995). My account is sufficiently close to the understanding of Poincaré that informs Carnap and the neo-Kantians that I shall rely upon it for these purposes, leaving ultimate questions of Poincaré's own philosophical intentions aside.

can be shown to be consistent relative to Euclidean geometry. Second, he argues that non-Euclidean geometries cannot be ruled out as physically impossible by some type of phenomenological examination of sensation; our sensory experiences do not require an *a priori* commitment to Euclidean spatial structure. Third, he seeks to show that the metrical structure of space is not experimentally determinable, because its determination would require independent access to physical law. That is, if we knew the laws of physics that obtained in abstraction from all knowledge of physical geometry we could use these to discover the metrical structure of physical space, but we cannot approach the world with this neatly separated notion of physical law and metrical structure. Thus, the metrical structure of space is not experientially determinable. To show this, Poincaré presents a thought experiment in which we are given the metrical structure of a two-dimensional world and we introduce certain physical peculiarities into that world that affect such things as the length of objects as they move and the paths of light rays. He then argues that this situation is describable in a different way: The physical peculiarities can be systematically absorbed into the geometry, thereby leaving us with a different metric (especially, a different measure of length and a different conception of straightness) and a different physics. The same type of argument goes over in analogous fashion to our case – but without the argumentative conceit that there is an external perspective from which we could tell which of these experimentally identical theories was a true description of the facts. Having shown that metrical structure is thus underdetermined by any possible evidence, Poincaré concludes that we can choose any metrical structure we like. As I have recently mentioned, Poincaré argues that simplicity and other practical concerns will induce us to choose Euclidean structure in all cases.[9]

Poincaré's arguments received a great deal of attention right from the time of their publication (1902), but with the Einsteinian revolution in physics the issues he raised were placed at the heart of philosophical thought about physical methodology. Among the consequences that the special and general theories of relativity were seen to have for the general issues of conventionalism were the following. First, given that a

---

9   The curious aspect of this argument is that it relies on a holism of empirical and mathematical knowledge in the argument against empiricism but then cleanly separates the two by making geometry, but not physics, the realm of the conventional. Poincaré's motivation seems to have to do with his understanding of the hierarchy of the sciences. See, again, Friedman (1995).

univocal stipulation of simultaneity for spatially noncontiguous events is a prerequisite for a well-defined global space-time structure, Einstein's argument that Newtonian physics lacked any such univocal stipulation underscored the lesson that precise definitions are methodologically of the first importance in the construction of mathematically expressed physical theories. Second, the Lorentzian electrodynamic rival to special relativity seemed a plausible case of theoretical underdetermination in high-level physics; the theories were arguably empirically equivalent but quite different in the metrical structure they attributed to space-time and in the physical processes they took to be real features of the world. Third, the non-Euclidean structure of space-time in the theory of general relativity brought the whole question of the metrical structure of space(-time) to the forefront of the debate. Moreover, it seemed that Poincaré's conventionalism was wrong with respect to general relativity in its insistence that practical considerations of a requirement such as simplicity would induce a continued commitment to Euclidean geometry, but not in its insistence that the choice was ultimately a matter of convention.[10]

What is devastating to empiricism in all of this, however? It seems to be open to the empiricist to interpret the conventionalist argument as follows. The underdetermination argument shows that no empirical facts determine the metrical structure of physical space. So, an empiricist will conclude simply that there is no fact of the matter about the metrical structure of space, which seems to be the conventionalist conclusion as well. Moreover, she will take all these "different theories" that different conventional choices of metrical structure impose merely to be different formulations of the same theory: They all say the same thing about the genuine empirical facts. Lastly, she will choose among these formulations by reference not to some *a priori* objective principle of simplicity but by reference to a self-consciously subjective principle such as Ernst Mach's "principle of the economy of thought." Mach's principle states that simplicity is a practical human matter and, thus, brackets any suggestion that the formulation of the theory that we choose to work with in any sense reflects the way things really are that the other formulations do not. This is, it seems, quite compatible with

---

10 At least some of these putative relations between relativity and conventionalism may well have been mistaken. See Friedman (1983a, 1994), Howard (1994), and Ryckman (1992, 1996) on this score. For our purposes, what is important is that these were relations that put conventionalism quite at the forefront of methodological thought in the first quarter of the twentieth century.

Poincaré's invocation of the principle of simplicity, which is more a pragmatic, even calculational, principle than an *a priori* principle governing theoretical knowledge.

That response, despite its attractiveness, misses the methodological lesson the neo-Kantian finds in the conventionalist argument, however. The empiricist sees the ability of scientific theories to describe and predict experiential findings to be the hallmark of the epistemic content of those theories. The point that the neo-Kantian insists on is that scientific theories that allow the finite description and prediction of the potentially infinite relations of experience must be expressed in mathematical form. This in turn requires the imposition upon experience of mathematical form not derived from experience itself. Thus, the formulation of scientific theories that perform even the minimal epistemic function that the empiricists insist on requires conventions that are neither statements of experiential fact nor themselves assimilable to a subjective principle of the economy of thought. That is, for the neo-Kantians, it is the methodological necessity of the conventions themselves for the formulation of any theory (not the methodological role of the principle of simplicity, as a principle of selection among various candidate conventions) that is the important point of conventionalism.

Here is where the neo-Kantians find the decisive advantage of the critical philosophy over pure empiricism. The conventional coordination of pure mathematical manifolds with the manifold of experience provides the objectifying element in scientific theorizing and reflects the *a priori* formal conditions of objective experience stressed by Kant. This is the principal application of the "logic of objective knowledge." Thus, in *Substance and Function* (1910/1953) and also in his monograph *On Einstein's Theory of Relativity* (1921), the principal problem Cassirer sees in extending logical and mathematical principles to the empirical realm – thereby grounding the objectivity of the empirical knowledge – is to give content to the Planckian dictum that in physics everything that can be measured exists. Cassirer's problem becomes one of finding "the logical conditions of the operation of measurement itself" (1910/1953, p. 361) and the role that such conditions play in scientific knowledge and its empirical basis. In his discussion of the theory of relativity, he puts the puzzle this way (1910/1953, p. 363): "If not only place but the velocity of a material system is to signify a magnitude that entirely depends on the choice of a reference body and is thus infinitely variable and infinitely ambiguous, there seems no possibility of an exact determination of magnitude and thus no possibility of an exact objective determination of the state of physical reality." This problem

The fundamentals of neo-Kantian epistemology

leads to the search for a *non plus ultra* that grounds the objective validity of empirical knowledge.

As Cassirer sees it, empiricism is utterly unable to help with this problem. Empiricism grounds the objectivity of scientific knowledge through a "simple registration of facts" of experience, which are then conceptually worked up into scientific theories. Logical idealism, on the other hand, sees a conceptual element in experience itself, that is, that only by virtue of having certain logical forms does experience first yield matters of fact. Thus Cassirer's answer to his own question of the objective determination of physical reality is this (1910/1953, p. 365):

> In the multiplicity and mutability of natural phenomena, thought *possesses* a relatively fixed standpoint only by *taking* it. In the choice of this standpoint, however, it is not absolutely determined by the phenomena, but the choice remains its own deed for which it alone is responsible. The decision is made with reference to experience, i.e., to the connection of observations according to law, but it is not prescribed in a definite way by the mere sum of observations. For these in themselves can always be expressed by a number of intellectual approaches between which a choice is possible only with reference to logical "simplicity," more exactly, to systematic unity and completeness of scientific exposition.

In other words, the metrical conventions are imposed upon the manifold of the experience. This first allows the matters of fact of experience to be expressed in the form of the precise value of physical quantities. That, in turn, allows the construction of mathematized physical laws that express the systematic interconnections among such matters of fact in general. Conventions are thus the means by which physical laws gain both their mathematical form and their relation to experience; the imposition of form induces the thoroughly lawful connection of empirical objects *and* connects physical law to experiential content. The empiricist, on the other hand, leaves entirely unexplained the relation between the theories of mathematical physics and the matters of fact of experience that these theories are meant to describe and have as their whole epistemic content.

It is precisely this point that Cassirer urges against Bertrand Russell's logico-empiricism when he complains that it fails to address the fundamental question of transcendental epistemology. In claiming that Russell's logicism offers no account of the application of mathematics to experience, Cassirer is not simply confusing logicism with a formalist doctrine that completely separates mathematical judgments from empirical judgments. Cassirer's primary target is Russell's account of geometry in *Principles of Mathematics* (1903). There Russell thinks he can give a logicist reduction of topology to logic but despairs over the possibility of reducing metrical geometry to logic – the metrical concepts go beyond the purely logical and contain an empirical element; as Cassirer writes (1907, p. 43): "Thus, according to Russell the general concept of magnitude already falls outside the domain of pure mathematics and logic; it contains an empirical element that can only be given to us through sense perception."

But Russell's view has two related and important problems. First, it leaves us with a notion of logic and mathematics too impoverished for it to provide precisely what the neo-Kantians want to understand: the sense in which it is the fully mathematized, quantitative theories of physics that are our paradigms of the application of mathematics to experience and, hence, of objective knowledge. It leaves to pure experience itself the very metrical concepts whose application to experience makes objective theoretical knowledge possible. Second, it simply cannot account for the methodological lessons of conventionalism. For, the standard conclusion of conventionalist argumentation is precisely that such metrical concepts are what cannot be univocally given in or derived from experience – that, in Poincaré's famous maxim, "Empiricism with respect to metrical geometry is senseless." Thus, this logicist view leaves us with no account of the methodological role of conventions in the movement from pure experience to scientific knowledge.

There is, however, an important ambiguity in Cassirer's account. There are passages in *Substance and Function* that suggest a somewhat different account of the relation among experience, conventions, and the synthetic *a priori*. In one such passage, Cassirer calls the theory of experience as given in logical idealism "the universal invariant theory of experience" (p. 268). Likening the procedure to that of a geometer investigating the invariants of figures under transformations, Cassirer (pp. 268f.) claims that in critical philosophy "the attempt is made to discover those universal elements of form, that persist through all changes in the particular material content of experience." He gives a preliminary list that includes space, time, magnitude, and the functional dependency of magnitudes. These play the role of Kantian categories – they are *a priori* conditions for objective knowledge in the empirical realm in general:

The goal of critical analysis would be reached, if we succeeded in isolating in this way the ultimate common element of all possible forms of scientific experience [i.e., facts of experience as conceptually comprehended from within some scientific theory – AR]; i.e., if we succeeded in conceptually defining those elements which persist in the advance from theory to theory because they are conditions of any theory . . . Only those ultimate logical invariants can be called *a priori*, which lie at the basis of any determination of a connection according to natural law. (p. 269)

Although it is not obvious that Cassirer was completely clear about this, these two notions of the conceptual element of objective experience amount to closely related but importantly different views. These are precisely the two views on the methodological synthetic *a priori* that we canvased at the end of the discussion of Kant in Chapter Four. On Cassirer's first account, the important conceptual element in experience is the imposition of particular metrical stipulations to yield mathematically expressible laws of physics. The matters of fact of experience can, then, be expressed within that mathematical language. Such matters of fact are antecedent to the conventions, however – they form "the phenomena." Here, the synthetic *a priori* element is in the conventional choice that conditions the construction of some particular physical theory. The conventions are not determined by experience; rather, experience is objectified, codified, and rendered predictable when the mathematical physics constructed on the basis of those conventions is in hand.

On the second view, the universal invariant theory of experience, the important formal moment in empirical knowledge is the minimal form that experience must have to guarantee the possibility of any such conventions. Moreover, this formal element in experience must yield the result that this minimally ordered experience allows various systems of physics to be formulated by differing sets of conventions. The *a priori* element in empirical knowledge is not now imposed upon matters of fact and, hence, "with reference to" an independent notion of experience. Rather, it is to be found in the minimal form inherent in the matters of fact of experience themselves.

On the first view, the synthetic *a priori* conventions are principles of objectification through mathematization from within a particular theoretical framework and, hence, they change with a change of framework. They form, therefore, an example of our *relativized* notion of the synthetic *a priori*. The second view entails a notion of a universal *a priori* formal element in experience which grounds the possibility that such conventions can be imposed. It is a universal synthetic *a priori*.

As we noted in Chapter Four, for Kant the synthetic *a priori* conditions imposed by the forms of sensibility and understanding were of sufficient strength to impose one particular physics and physical geometry, that is, Newtonian physics and Euclidean geometry, upon the manifold of experience. Thus, his methodological synthetic *a priori* conjoined two aspects that must be rendered distinct in neo-Kantianism: The synthetic *a priori* was considered both as the conditions of the possibility of experience and as the conditions of the possibility of theoretical understanding of experience. In this sense, experience was already a type of theoretically informed knowledge for Kant; objective experience was already of physical objects governed by the laws of Euclidean geometry and Newtonian physics and must be strictly separated from the mere play of sensations.

A twentieth-century neo-Kantian who has absorbed the lessons of Poincaré and Einstein, however, wants to maintain the following: First, with Kant, he will maintain that real objective knowledge is found within mathematical physics, not simple, theoretically uninformed experience. Second, with Poincaré, he will insist that mathematical physics relies on conventions in a way that requires that alternative conventions are equally experientially possible (and hence a multiplicity of experientially equivalent systems of physics is possible). Third, and the crucial methodological point for the neo-Kantians, these conventions go beyond mere experience to provide the mathematical structure that is necessary for objectivity. This leads to two distinct resolutions to the problem of the formal components of knowledge. Each of these requires, however, that we make a distinction between conditions of experience and conditions of objective (theoretical) knowledge.

First, one could – as in the relativized understanding of the synthetic *a priori* we have gleaned from Cassirer – decide that the conventions underlying any one particular system of physics form the synthetic *a priori* component of knowledge for that system. This is done because those conventions allow the mathematization of the manifold of experience and hence the formulation of the mathematically expressed natural laws that are the hallmark of objective understanding. Since systems of alternative conventions are possible, this notion of the synthetic *a priori* is then relativized to particular systems of physics constructible from those conventions. This, of course, was Hans Reichenbach's reorientation of Kantian doctrine in his first book, *Relativitätstheorie und Erkenntnis A Priori* (The theory of relativity and *a priori* knowledge) (1920). Reichenbach was led to understand synthetic *a priori* principles as conditions of the possibility of objects of knowledge but to deny Kant's claims that they are apodictically necessary principles.[11] Moreover, they cannot be conditions of the possibility of experience if we want to consider the possibility that alternative conventions are possible on the same experiential basis. Nevertheless, one could consider them conditions of the objectification of experience. For, without such conventions, mathematical principles are inapplicable to experience, and, hence, facts of experience are not expressible in the mathematical language of the theories that are the paradigms of objective knowledge. In other words, but for the conventions, matters of fact of experience are not of objects – for the notion of object is first given in the lawful structure of relational manifolds comprehended by mathematics.

Alternatively, one could decide that the synthetic *a priori* lies in the conditions of the possibility of the conventions themselves and construe such conditions, then, as conditions of the possibility of (objectifiable) experience. Since these conditions underlie any possible conventions and, hence, any possible objectifying mathematical physics (but do not limit us to any one physics), these principles are universal and necessary, but they are not sufficient to be conditions of the possibility of objective knowledge. This idea lies behind Cassirer's "universal invariant" theory of experience. This seems to be unambiguously Paul Natorp's view of the situation as codified in his maxim describing the object of empirical knowledge as an "endless task."[12] If we have no independently specifiable notion of the minimal form of experience but must wait and see what forms do in fact persist through all changes of theory, then clearly this task can never be known to be at an end. Thus, Natorp thinks that we will never know the objects of experience in their minimal form; in this sense, empirical objects are not given (*gegeben*) but only pursued (*aufgegeben*) for Natorp.

The point against empiricism is, correspondingly, different according to these two views. In the relativized account, the point is that full mathematical structure is not available in experience but is necessary for objectivity. Thus, there is a formal impoverishment to experience that makes it insufficient to serve as the sole epistemic basis for empirical knowledge. Metrical conventions are necessary for the construction

---

11 Reichenbach's relativized *a priori* is discussed illuminatingly in Friedman (1983a, chap. 1, 1983b, 1991, 1994). See also Coffa's (1991, chap. 10) discussion of Schlick, Cassirer, and Reichenbach.
12 Compare Natorp (1910a, chap. 2) and (1910b, §3), where he says: "Facts are not given, nor in an absolute sense even achievable in empirical knowledge."

of the mathematized theories that codify our empirical knowledge. Empiricism cannot account for the requirement of this conventional element for the comprehension of experience. Nor can empiricism explain how matters of fact of experience can serve as evidence for theories couched in mathematical terms. On the universal account, the objection is that the minimal form of experiential judgments indicates that they are themselves subject to the forms of the mind. Thus, they are unavailable except via the framework of the synthetic *a priori,* that is, not available as a starting point for the strict empiricist.

Both of these views have similarities to Kant's "Refutation of Idealism." On the relativized account, the neo-Kantians follow Kant in arguing that the principles of the possibility of theoretical knowledge in mathematical physics (namely, the conventions) are also the principles by virtue of which matters of fact of experience become evidence for physics. But, to preserve the possibility of a plurality of objectifying conventional frameworks, the neo-Kantians need to introduce a more impoverished notion of matter of fact of experience, not yet subject to objectifying form. Thus, they grant the empiricist her epistemological starting point – experiential matters of fact – and draw closer to a direct disagreement with her about the relation of scientific theory to empirical evidence.

On the universal account, the neo-Kantians weaken the notion of objective form. Thus, they subsume the minimal form of experience under the notion of objective form. In this way, they can argue with Kant that the empiricists' starting point cannot call the formal framework imposed by the mind into question, for that framework is presupposed in the very notion of experiential matter of fact. Thus, if Cassirer accepts Poincaré's claim that topological structure is the structure of matters of fact of experience, then he can claim that at least the topological structure of space and time is a formal condition of the possibility of experience. But, the neo-Kantians have lost the independent access to the formal conditions of experience that Kant had in the formal conditions of intuition and the categories. Having no antecedent specification of such conditions, subjective idealism cannot be "refuted" in Kant's way. Rather, the locus of the disagreement between the subjective idealist and the neo-Kantian, on the universal invariant theory, is wholly within their conceptions of experience. Thus, the disagreement becomes quite tenuous, and the neo-Kantian looks to be dangerously close simply to begging the question against the subjective idealist attack.

Of course, on both the relativized (conventional) and the universal

The fundamentals of neo-Kantian epistemology

invariant understanding of the *a priori* element of experiential knowledge, the logico-mathematical principles that underlie the possibility of the mathematical expression of the laws of natural science are absolute, pure *a priori* principles. As we have seen, however, Cassirer and the other neo-Kantians consider these also to be synthetic *a priori* because mathematics is not justified in abstraction from, but rather only by virtue of, the role it plays in theoretical, empirical knowledge and the individuation of objects in the empirical realm.

PROBLEMS FOR THE NEO-KANTIANS

The neo-Kantian project makes some important observations about scientific methodology. From the point of view of constructing physical theories in mathematical form, the need for – rather than multiplicity of – principles that induce such form is of primary importance. Moreover, the conventionalist argument that such form is not derivable from experience but is necessary for the scientific comprehension of it is clearly an anti-empiricist point. Nonetheless, it is surely a sign of philosophical tension within the neo-Kantian project for there to be two distinct accounts of the synthetic *a priori* in physical knowledge. The conventionalist argument ultimately belies any possibility of capturing even the methodological synthetic *a priori* in the fullest Kantian sense. The bifurcation of principles of objective experience and the principles of objective theoretical knowledge pulls apart the tight connection between theoretical – mathematical and physical – form and objectivity in judgment found in Kant.

Moreover, a diagnosis of the tensions that lead the neo-Kantians to two resolutions of the relation of conventionalism to the methodological synthetic *a priori* points to some general tensions in the whole project. The neo-Kantians want to provide a compelling epistemological response to empiricism, a methodological account of mathematical physics, and a transcendental explanation of objectivity. Moreover, although they make no particularly compelling attempt to discharge this obligation, their account requires a detailed exposition of logico-mathematical form. These aspects of their philosophical situation form an uneasy tandem, however.

It is clear that the relativized account of the synthetic *a priori* provides the more compelling response to the empiricist. Recall, for example, the conclusion of the "Refutation of Idealism" in Kant: The subjective idealists want to start with a determinate temporal ordering of ideas in inner sense, but this is available only by locating the subject in the full structure of the Newtonian world. That is, the structural features of the empiricist starting point derive from the more robust features of the categorical framework. Compare this with the corresponding point in the universal invariant theory of experience: The minimal structure of matters of fact of experience already exhibits a formal, conceptual moment of thought in experience itself. Kant could grant the empiricists a desire to have certain structure to their epistemic starting point, but argue that this structure required the full categorical structure. The neo-Kantians, through their insistence on seeing form as *ipso facto* indicating the structure of the mind, must view the empiricist as either covertly relying on the synthetic *a priori* or requiring a wholly amorphous epistemological starting point.

On this issue the relativized notion does the empiricist more justice. The relativized account offers a notion of matter of fact common to both the neo-Kantian and the empiricist and makes the methodological point that such a notion of 'matter of fact' is insufficient for scientific theory construction. This does not simply amount to a difference in paradigms of knowledge, since the neo-Kantian has the methodological trump card: The empiricist cannot rest content with this notion of matter of fact if he wants to maintain the ineliminable epistemological value of theories through their role in predicting future experience. Staying solely with matters of fact requires that we give up even the practical use of scientific theory as a predictive device. The relativized account succeeds in raising an objection to strict empiricism in terms that are compelling for the empiricist himself.

On the other hand, the universal account is more closely connected to the starting point of the conventionalist argument in Poincaré. The methodological story begins with the physicist's more robust sense of the observable basis of science. That is, local topological features of the spatiotemporal world are the presumed observable basis in the conventionalist argument. Thus, a good deal of structure is presumed at the start. Moreover, this structure is not tied to subjective experience. On the contrary, it serves as the intersubjective basis of science.

The neo-Kantians also want to preserve Kant's transcendental explanation of the way form yields objectivity via its connection to the mind. Transcendental idealism continues to be the philosophical explanation of the possibility of objective knowledge. This provides the principal motive for the universalist account: The minimal structure of the matters of fact is, after all, structure. Structure is, moreover, the hallmark of the forms of the mind. Anything subject to the forms of the mind is objective. Thus, objectivity is found even in matters of fact of experience.

The basic problem is this. The neo-Kantians want to preserve transcendental philosophy's place as a genuine alternative to empiricism, that is, as an alternative account of the relation of subjective experience to objective knowledge. Moreover, they want to exploit conventionalist arguments in presenting this alternative. But, conventionalism points not to a movement from the subjective to the objective, but to a distinction within the objective between minimal and metrical form. This distinction, in turn, points to an unclarity in the very subjective–objective distinction that is guiding the story. The latter is variously construed as an "unformed–subject-to-form" distinction, in accordance with transcendental idealism; or a private–intersubjective distinction, in accordance with the empiricist problematic; or as a minimal–mathematical form distinction, in accordance with the methodological lessons of conventionalism. Not knowing what they mean to account for, the neo-Kantians end up with a plurality of inconsistent accounts.

This tension is augmented by the inchoate account of logic found in the neo-Kantian literature. Despite calling their project "the logic of objective knowledge" and investigating "the logical conditions of measurement," there is very little by way of delimiting the principles of logic. Cassirer adopts no framework that begins to match the detail of Frege's conceptual notation or Russell's type theory. It would seem that the neo-Kantian account of logic must be strong enough to include all of classical mathematics; this is requisite for the account of objectivity in terms of theories in mathematical form. Presumably the fundamental coordinative nature of thought is meant to ground the strength of logic also. But none of this is spelled out.

This being the case, the obscurities in the relations of the minimal form of experience to the mathematical form of physical theory become intolerable. Without more detail in the account of logic, it is very hard to see how this structural difference can be maintained. Thus, Cassirer's list of the formal conditions necessary for any theory contains not merely the (topological?) structure of space and time, but also magnitude and the functional dependency of magnitudes. But this would seem to be enough to guarantee a full metrical structure. The universal account would then regain the strength of Kant's original account and be at odds with conventionalism, however.

Alternatively, Cassirer could maintain the distinction by explicitly following the conventionalists in maintaining that topological form is the form of experiential matters of fact and metrical form is the form of physical theory. But then, topological form, by virtue of being form, is sufficient for objectivity. And, the transcendental account of the mind plays no role in the methodological argument against the sufficiency of this notion of form to provide predictive laws of experience. This difference is wholly a matter of mathematical structure.

There is one final, very general question that relates to the neo-Kantian transcendental perspective. The appellation "logical idealism" is meant to underscore the methodological role of logic in providing the form of objective judgment. Logic grounds the only notion of existence for objects within the sphere of empirical knowledge itself. Nevertheless, as we have seen, the neo-Kantians feel called upon to explain how logic is meant to perform this role. Thus, the logical idealists find themselves on the horns of a dilemma that indicates that their view has not found adequate expression in their own work. For, when pressed, they seem to inevitably slide into an account of the ideality of logic and mathematics that commits them to either a Platonic idealism of pure forms or a more robust story of transcendental psychology that compromises their antipsychologism and rejection of subjective idealism.[13]

The first horn is exhibited in Cassirer's account of the structuralism in mathematics he takes over from Dedekind. The easiest way to make sense of the idea that the objects of mathematics exist "in ideal community" with one another in such functionally connected manifolds is to view this as a commitment to the Platonic existence of the manifolds of pure mathematics. Read in this way, the neo-Kantian account of the primacy of logic is hollow; ultimately, logic itself requires an ontological foundation, albeit not in an Aristotelian ontology of substance.[14]

To counteract this reading and stress the epistemological import of logic, the neo-Kantians prefer to speak of logic in terms of "the basic logical syntheses" or "the formal elements of thought." This, however,

---

13 I am indebted in the rest of this section to concerns about neo-Kantianism raised by Friedman (1992a). I present the difficulties somewhat differently than does Friedman, who in his discussion of Rickert's views sees both a Platonic ontology grounding logic and a continuing psychological element in the account of the application of logic to experience. I present the problem as a dilemma, since I do not think that Cassirer's, Bauch's, or Natorp's views on these issues are the same as Rickert's. In particular, the *Geltung–Sein* dichotomy is only very problematically attributed to Cassirer, Natorp, and the young Bauch.
14 I am indebted here to Geoffrey Hellman, who has quite rightly emphasized to me that this ontological way of understanding structuralism is the standard way we post-Quineans read Cassirer's account.

leads to the second horn of the dilemma. For, if this transcendental idealist perspective is necessary to understand the methodological role of logic, it seems that an ontology of transcendental minds is presupposed. This compromises both the alleged universal primacy of logic and the nonontological foundations to logical idealism. In any case, the neo-Kantians have not made the commitments of transcendental idealism either more comprehensible or more palatable. Indeed, transcendental idealism is perhaps made less palatable. The transcendental perspective loses explanatory power as it loses its variegated form and antecedently understandable structure.

THE TRANSITION TO CARNAP

So far, I have only sketched some of the general themes of the neo-Kantian project. I hope that certain affinities between it and the philosophical themes we found in the *Aufbau* are obvious: the central role of logic, the attempt at ontological neutrality, the connection with exact science, and, especially, the epistemological distinction between the objective and the subjective. Moreover, certain problems with the neo-Kantian position have been outlined. Now we shall take up the historical development of Carnap's work from his dissertation (1921) until the publication of the *Der logische Aufbau der Welt* in 1928. This survey will exhibit much closer relations between Carnap and neo-Kantianism than my thumbnail sketch has allowed. Carnap began as a neo-Kantian in his dissertation, and all his pre-*Aufbau* writing was concerned with logic and/or conventionalist physical methodology. The project of the 1928 book began from a philosophical position quite close to the one I have outlined.

Of course, there are some crucial differences. From the start, Carnap was a logicist with respect to mathematical geometry and was in possession of a precise and powerful logical tool in type theory. Moreover, he was better versed than the neo-Kantians I have discussed in the details of the methodological situation in physics. In the end, also, we see an expression of Carnap's philosophical genius as he pushes neo-Kantian ontological neutrality to its ultimate conclusion – a general metaphysical neutrality that rejects the neo-Kantians' own transcendental idealism.

CHAPTER SIX

Carnap's neo-Kantian origins: *Der Raum*

The neo-Kantian themes uncovered in Chapter Five provide an entry point to Carnap's thinking about epistemological and methodological issues throughout the 1920s.[1] Carnap's dissertation, *Der Raum* (Space; hereafter *Raum*), written and defended in 1921 and published in 1922, shows him to be an unabashed, if unorthodox, neo-Kantian about space. His views show many similarities to the account of physical methodology we saw in Cassirer, especially as regards the distinction between the universal and relativized synthetic *a priori*. There are, of course, differences, which stem largely from Carnap's commitment to Russellian logicism and from his more detailed understanding of the technical physical and mathematical issues. In this chapter and the next, our goal is to use the framework for thinking about neo-Kantianism to investigate Carnap's evolving thought in his pre-*Aufbau* period. We shall see that in Carnap's work, also, there is an attempt to tie the methodological synthetic *a priori* to a logic of objective knowledge. Conventionalism in mathematical physics, combined with a desire to have a scientific understanding of philosophy itself, leads ultimately to the problems Carnap finds in explaining the relation among objectivity, intersubjectivity, and logical form in the *Aufbau*.

This chapter is given over entirely to an outline of the theories about space and geometry that Carnap presents in his dissertation. Chapter Seven provides a brief examination of the main themes of the essays on the methodology of physics that he published during the years (1922–6) when he was writing the *Aufbau*. At no point in any of these essays does Carnap endorse anything that looks like strict empiricism. Indeed, Car-

---

[1] The best English-language introduction to Carnap's pre-*Aufbau* publications remains Edmund Runggaldier's *Carnap's Early Conventionalism* (1984). I stress the neo-Kantian interpretative framework for thinking about conventionalism much more than does Runggaldier, however.

nap's favored term for his view is "critical conventionalism," a term that clearly suggests a generally Kantian approach to the understanding of conventionalist methodology.

LOGIC AND CONVENTION: MATHEMATICAL AND PHYSICAL SPACE

Carnap's researches into the epistemological, methodological, and metaphysical questions about space in his dissertation were, in the first instance, directed at a metaphilosophical goal. His goal was to clarify the philosophical controversies surrounding (Raum, p. 5) "the cognitive source, the nature of the object, and the domain of validity of the theory of space." According to *Der Raum* (p. 5), confusion had arisen in the philosophical disputes over space because the various participants were discussing "very different objects . . . from very different points of view." Carnap sought to bring clarity to the debate by untangling three distinct meanings of the concept of space that were being confused. Thus, already in his dissertation Carnap embarked on a characteristic philosophical task: He sought to bring clarity to a philosophical discussion by uncovering what the various participants were talking about. In the end, the disputes, by his account, turned out to be largely verbal, rather than substantive.

The three concepts of space that Carnap distinguishes are *formal space, intuitive space,* and *physical space*. The first is the province of the mathematician, the second that of the philosopher, and the third that of the physicist. Carnap endorsed logicism with respect to the first and was a conventionalist with respect to the metrical structure of the third. His account of intuitive space was meant to mediate between the other two, and here he was influenced by Kantianism generally and, especially, Husserlian phenomenology.

Carnap introduces his three meanings of space in the introduction to *Der Raum*. *Formal space*, which we shall, following Carnap but transliterating into English, abbreviate as S rather than R, is (Raum, pp. 5f.) "a structure of relations, not between determinate objects of a sensible or non-sensible domain, but rather between completely undetermined relational terms of which we know only that from a connection of a certain kind we may infer a connection of another kind in the same domain." He follows Bertrand Russell in claiming that all such relational structures can be captured in the logic described by Whitehead and Russell in *Principia Mathematica*. Thus, the study of formal space falls within the purview of the mathematician and the logician.

Intuitive space, S', is (Raum, p. 6)

the structure of relations between "spatial" forms in the customary sense, namely the linear, planar, and spatial elements whose individuality we grasp on an occasion of sense perception or even mere imagination. However, we are not thereby dealing with the spatial facts present in experiential reality, but only with the "essence" of these forms themselves, which can be discerned in any representative of the type whatsoever.

Physical space (S'') is, finally, the space that forms the domain of the particular spatial facts given in experience. It is the space investigated by the physicist.

Further complicating this tripartite division is the fact that all of these meanings of space have an infinite variety of subcategories. Depending on how much structure one takes the relations definitive of the space in question to have, one will arrive at spatial structures of varying degrees of complexity. This distinction gives rise to the familiar types of geometry. The types of geometry that Carnap considers are *topology*, *projective geometry*, and *metrical geometry*. Similarly, at least in principle, any of the three meanings of space allows an infinite variety of dimensional variants. I shall follow Carnap and designate these subcases with subscripts. The first subscript is the dimension number and is, hence, either a numeral or n, which stands for arbitrary dimensionality. The second subscript is either t, p, or m, standing, respectively, for "topological," "projective," and "metrical" space. Thus, for example, S'_{4t} designates four-dimensional topological intuitive space, and S_{np} designates projective formal space of arbitrarily many dimensions.

In what sense can we say that Carnap was a neo-Kantian in *Der Raum*? He does claim (p. 63) that the axioms for intuitive space are "synthetic *a priori* propositions whose existence was asserted by Kant," but this is more straightforwardly Kantian than neo-Kantian, given the rejection of intuition and the representation theoretic synthetic *a priori* by the neo-Kantians.[2] More directly connected to the neo-Kantian methodological synthetic *a priori* are two other claims that Carnap makes. First, he claims that one can uncover a type of spatial structure that serves as a condition of any possible objective experience (Raum, p. 67):

2   That is, the neo-Kantians we are considering. The nature and role of intuition was one of the vexed issues that divided the neo-Kantians into distinguishable and hostile camps.

Der Raum

It has already been explained more than once, from both mathematical and philosophical points of view, that Kant's contention concerning the significance of space for experience is not shaken by the theory of non-Euclidean spaces, but must be transferred from the three dimensional Euclidean structure, which was alone known to him, to a more general structure . . . The Kantian conception must be accepted. And, indeed, the spatial structure possessing experience-constituting significance (in the place of that supposed by Kant) can be precisely specified as topological intuitive space with indefinitely many dimensions . . . We thereby declare, not only the determinations of this structure, but at the same time those of its form of order [topological formal space with indefinitely many dimensions], to be conditions of the possibility of any object of experience whatsoever.

Thus, both a particular type of intuitive space and that part of logic that exhibits its formal structure are, for Carnap in 1922, conditions of the possibility of objective experience.

Second, and more generally, Carnap argues that the whole epistemological point of both intuitive and formal space lies in this relation they have to the physical space of experience (p. 61):

It can now also be seen why the different types of S' – especially the sub-types of S'_{3m} – and the corresponding types of S are constructed. The point and purpose of these constructions lies in S". The spatial relations of experience are to be brought into a consistent structure S", for this the general form S' is constructed, and for this in turn the still more general conceptual form S.

This remark relates the *a priori* nature of these formal disciplines to their role in constituting the structure of physical space. Indeed, an endnote to this section ties the Kantian conception of intuitive space directly to this methodological role of constituting the framework for spatial judgments in experience:[3] "The purest expression of this relationship appears to be the Kantian conception of S' (perhaps also of S, where a few declarations can be indicated . . .) as the synthetic lawfulness of the order of experience and thus of S"."[4] So, although Carnap does endorse

---

3 Moreover, the endnote under discussion is one place where Carnap wholeheartedly endorses the Marburg neo-Kantians' interpretation of Kant and their understanding of the functional nature of the synthetic lawfulness of the order of experience. In it he refers to Bauch (1914, 1917) and to Cassirer's *Substance and Function*.

4 It is, of course, highly dubious that there is a distinction between S and S' in Kant. Kant lacks any notion of logical structure that permits multiple-dimensional manifolds, and this is precisely why he requires intuition in his account of space. But, the role of

Mathematical and physical space

intuition as a separate cognitive source, ultimately the justification of any knowledge claims stemming from intuition – and from the logical derivation of formal geometry – lies in their methodological role in constituting the framework of objective, physical space. Thus, Carnap endorses the methodological account of the synthetic *a priori* rather than the nominal account. He also explicitly extends this constitutive role to that portion of formal logic that gives the abstract structure of intuitive space.[5]

Our interest is in the various roles that each of these concepts of space is meant to play in Carnap's account of our knowledge of space. We shall adopt a somewhat different order for consideration of them than does Carnap. We shall begin, as he does, with formal space. Then we shall go directly to a consideration of physical space, in order to uncover from Carnap's arguments there the mediational role that intuitive space is meant to play between formal and physical space. (Carnap presents these two concepts of space in the reverse order, but our way has certain expository advantages.)

Carnap's exposition of formal space is very brief. In it he endorses the line adopted by Whitehead and Russell in *Principia Mathematica* that all the various branches of mathematical geometry can be reduced to logic. The basic idea is to build on the theory of "order types" that is exploited in the reduction of real number theory to logic. Carnap's formal geometry is the mathematical investigation of continuous series of more than one dimension. It can be shown that all continuous series without end points based on a single relation are similar. One can then define the "real numbers" as the abstraction class of these series. Formal geometry is the study of series of such series. Thus, S_{nt} is the *n*th cross-product of the real number series with itself, and formal topology becomes the arithmetic of n-tuples of real numbers.

Projective and metrical versions of formal space then are formed by placing further conditions on the relations that generate the series. For example, suppose we have a three-dimensional topological formal

---

mathematics in constituting the framework for physical judgments about space is what is at stake in what Carnap writes, and in this his view coincides with Marburger interpretations of Kant (and with my own).

5 Carnap also calls formal geometry "analytic," due to its derivability from logic. But his willingness to view formal structures as playing a constitutive role in accordance with the methodological synthetic *a priori* indicates that his notions of the analytic and synthetic are not really in conflict. We shall return to these issues at the end of this chapter.

space, generated by three distinct continuous betweenness relations; we can convert this into a three-dimensional Euclidean metrical formal space by defining a distance function in the usual Pythagorean way. This distance function can be understood as a further condition on the betweenness relations. That is, rather than just any betweenness relation, we investigate only those that fulfill the Pythagorean requirement. Other metrical spaces can be investigated by defining other metrics with other properties.

Carnap's own account of formal space is scarcely less sketchy than this. There are a couple of points to remark before moving on to the other concepts of space. First, Cassirer's explicit complaint – noted in Chapter Five – against Russell's 1903 logicism with respect to geometry does not apply to Carnap's version (nor to the *Principia Mathematica* of 1910). For now metrical geometry is also reduced to logic. Thus, there is no worry that the logicist leaves to experience the very same formal element that, according to the relativized neo-Kantian, objectifies experience: the metrical conventions. Thus, Carnap's logicism is consistent with conventionalism; it does not seek the concept of spatial distance in experience itself.

Second, Carnap explicitly contrasts his view with David Hilbert's view of implicit definition via axioms. Carnap notes that if one is particularly interested in a particular geometrical system, say, three-dimensional Euclidean geometry, one can give axioms directly in the manner of Hilbert. This is not the procedure that he undertakes in his own account of formal geometry, though. The constraints imposed by logicism are not fulfilled by laying down certain disinterpreted axioms and claiming that these implicitly define the properties and relations that appear in them. Rather, the spaces studied by formal geometry must be shown to be themselves logical objects, that is, definable in terms of logic alone. Hilbert's procedure takes mathematical geometry to be the study of the relational features of any objects so structured as to make the axioms under consideration true. Carnap, following Whitehead and Russell, defines the spaces of the various formal geometries directly in terms of number theory and, hence, logic. The spaces are themselves type theoretic objects that are explicitly defined in the type theoretical hierarchy. The axioms can then be shown to be logical truths about such well-defined objects.

Nonetheless, Carnap does note that for certain purposes one can view a particular formal space as the abstraction class of the properties and relations in its axiomatization. This underscores one aspect of Carnap's logical geometries that they have in common with Hilbert's formalist versions: They are multiply, indeed infinitely, applicable. Any objects having properties and standing in relations to one another, where these properties and relations themselves stand in the logical relations given in the axioms, fulfill the theorems as well. Indeed, on Carnap's account, these relational structures are members of the formal space. Thus, formal space subsumes (and formal geometry describes) structures that are not themselves physically spatial. For example, one might think of the space of color tones, ordered by hue, saturation, and brightness, as forming a structure described by three-dimensional topological formal space. Also, formal geometry is multiply applicable to spatial objects. Thus, at the end of his discussion of formal space, Carnap shows how the formal version of Desargues's theorem applies not only to points and lines, but also to circles and pencils of circles, provided these fulfill the conditions of the theorem. The very formality of the structures means that formal geometry is applicable in principle to any objects whatsoever.

Let us now turn to Carnap's discussion of physical space. This begins with a consideration of the question (Raum, p. 33) "whether and in what way a *straight line in physical space* can be established." Even leaving aside questions of precision (i.e., Is this exactly straight or only approximately so?), Carnap argues that this cannot be done purely on the basis of experience. Our ordinary procedures for determining whether any given three points lie on a straight line in physical space presuppose a testing procedure or measuring instrument that is itself antecedently taken to yield a straight line – say, a light ray or a ruler. This just pushes the question back to the measuring procedures. One is quickly led to the view that (p. 33)

It is in principle impossible to establish such things if one relies only on what proceeds unequivocally from experience, without coming upon freely chosen stipulations about the objects of experience. Such stipulations . . . are set up by postulation without any possibility of confirmation or refutation by experience, and . . . make it possible to test physical lines for straightness (more precisely: for whether they should count [gelten] as straight).

Carnap then notes that such stipulations can be either direct stipulations of a class of physical objects that are to count as straight or a metrical stipulation that defines a notion of spatial distance and from which straightness is defined on the basis of well-known geodesy principles.[6] Carnap's own interest is in metrical geometry, so he considers only the latter in depth. We shall follow Carnap in this.

There seems to be an obvious lacuna in the argument just sketched: Independent of an account of what *is* given in experience, we cannot tell whether we need to stipulate an affine or metrical structure for physical space or not. Carnap's account of the given in experience makes crucial use of a distinction between necessary and optional form (Raum, p. 39):

> Let matter which is certainly not unformed, but appears only in *necessary* form, be called "matter of fact" [Tatbestand] of experience. This can be subjected to a still further formation in terms of optional form. In order to test an experiential statement for whether it is a statement of matter of fact or not . . . we have to investigate whether the experiential statement remains valid for all possible formations, which means, for our investigation, for all possible types of spatial structure. Mathematically expressed, this will be the case if the content of the experiential statement is unchangeable (invariant) under one-to-one, continuous spatial transformations. Now this holds for all *topological* statements and only these.

Carnap's account here may seem to beg any interesting question in the area. We wanted to know why we should think that metrical relations are not simply found in experience, and Carnap has responded by making exactly the topological properties of space the ones definitive of the notion of 'matter of fact of experience.' We were pressing for a reason to believe that the structure of acquaintance does not itself guarantee that a particular metric holds for physical space, and Carnap offers a definition that simply rules that possibility out.

But, in a sense, this is precisely the point. Carnap seeks to uncover the minimal form that experience must have in order for the knowledge of physical space that we in fact have to be possible. If he can tell a conventionalist story in which topological facts and conventions – with an admixture of *a priori* intuitive knowledge – suffice to explain the knowledge of physical spatial structure we have, then this story gets highest marks on all epistemological questions. Moreover, this story is most consistent with the methodology of physics since the advent of conventionalist arguments and the relativistic revolution. This is not simply to accept conventionalism as given, but it does ask us to take the

---

6   Actually the situation is more complicated, since we can, according to Carnap, stipulate a global metrical structure for space directly and then read off the local metrical and affine relations from that, as we shall see presently.

methodological situation of the physical sciences as the explanandum of the theory of our knowledge of physical space. The distinction Carnap makes is, therefore, not meant to answer questions raised from some independent epistemological perspective, but to clarify the methodological structure of physics itself. To this end, his purely mathematical distinction between necessary and optional form for spatial judgments provides a precise and compelling account; it is consistent with (his understanding of) the methodological situation in physics and slots nicely into his general account of geometrical knowledge.

His account, moreover, exhibits his characteristic difference from Russell. A Russellian account (circa 1914) would rely on acquaintance and either directly attempt to show that we are not acquainted with a notion such as 'straightness' or 'distance' in our sensibilia or argue that the fallibility of metrical judgments shows metrical notions to be incomplete symbols to be defined away. Carnap's response does not rely on any primitive epistemological notion like acquaintance but moves directly to the physicist's understanding of the methodological situation. Additionally, Carnap's worry is not that we are fallible in our metrical judgments, but we lack the requisite concepts even to formulate them, if we stay only with what is given in experience. Conventional stipulations import structure *not antecedently available in experience itself* and hence go beyond Russellian constructions.

Carnap's distinction between necessary and optional form recalls Cassirer's universal invariant theory of the synthetic *a priori*. Topological form plays the role of the minimal form that any spatial facts must have in order for any outer experience to be possible at all. Physical theories arise, then, via the metrical stipulations that are superadded to this topological structure of physical matters of spatial fact. These stipulations first provide the conditions of mathematization – for example, a definition of spatial distance. Moreover, in contradistinction to Cassirer, Carnap has an account of topological space available within his logic; thus, he has a clear notion of topological form and one that ties it to logic alone. He can, therefore, give a more fully precise account of the minimal form of experience in a way not available to Cassirer and Natorp. Thus, Carnap can eschew their insistence that objects are never known in their minimal form. In this sense, Carnap's *formal* logic provides him with something that Kant's *transcendental* logic had but that Cassirer's logic of objective knowledge lacks: Within Carnap's formal logic, the philosopher can give a precise account of the formal aspects of experience antecedent to the course of experience (indeed, to the course of the history of science) itself. This is because Carnap's logic had been fully and explicitly worked out by Whitehead and Russell in *Principia Mathematica*.

Moreover, Carnap has a precise distinction between topological and metrical form within his logic. Therefore, he can redeem the vague distinctions between minimal and metrical form found in Cassirer. The connection between necessary form of spatial experience and the synthetic *a priori* is made particularly strongly at the end of the dissertation (Raum, p. 65):

> According to Kant, space is the condition of the possibility of every (outer) experience as such. Is this true for the spatial determinations of all the structures we have distinguished? To decide this we must consider which spatial determinations are necessarily to be met with in *every* (outer) experience, and thus also when that experience has not yet been brought, on the basis of freely chosen determinations, into a *special* form that goes beyond the necessary form. Now, we have called experience, in so far as it is presented only in that univocal necessary form that contains no arbitrary stipulation whatsoever, "matter of fact." Therefore, only the spatial determinations contained in matters of fact can be conditions for the possibility of experience. And these, as we have seen, are only the topological, but not the projective and above all not the metrical relations.

In adopting this universal invariant synthetic *a priori*, Carnap must, of course, adopt its consequences. The matters of fact of experience are independent of any particular theory of mathematical physics – indeed, they are exactly what is capturable prior to and independently of the metrical concepts used in such theories. Hence, objectification occurs independently of theoretical structure. Just as for the neo-Kantians, the distinction between matter of fact and theoretical judgment is a distinction within the realm of the objective. But Carnap spends no effort in the chapter on physical space tying the objectifying structure of necessary form to the transcendental mind. It seems that the objective status of matters of fact is due to their being subject to necessary form, and that is the end of the story. The topological and, hence, logical form they are subject to is not explained via its relations to the objectifying structure of the mind. Indeed, it is not *explained:* It is explicated mathematically and nothing more.

Carnap's physical interests lie in *metrical* physical space, however. Metrical structure is necessary if one is to have well-defined notions such as 'distance' and, hence, 'velocity' and 'acceleration.' Thus, the most basic notions of mathematical physics require a metric. In accordance with his conventionalism, Carnap thinks of metrical structure as added to the physical topological space of experience by stipulating a measure or by stipulating a global metrical structure immediately. Either of these paths will allow a quantitative physics to be set up. This physics has the ability to express the individual facts of experience in equations and, thus, to systematize our physical beliefs and render prediction of future experience possible through derivation from physical law. Insofar as any genuine theoretical knowledge requires systematization and not the mere stringing together of empirical facts, this quantitative physics is what we are striving to attain in our knowledge of the physical world.

There are two principal methodological points that Carnap wants to make about metrical physical space. First, he wants to establish the following functional dependencies: Call the sum of particular matters of local topological fact of experience F. Call the metrical stipulation M and the global metrical structure thereby induced S.[7] Then F and M uniquely determine S; F and S uniquely determine M; and M and S uniquely determine F. That is, any two of these notions (the total class of matters of fact, the metrical stipulation, and the global metrical structure of physical space) uniquely determine the third. Second, he argues against the simple conventionalist view according to which, given the various conventional options, one will always choose to induce the most simple possible S, that is, choose Euclidean metrical structure for S.

A metrical stipulation consists of the adoption of a measure body, two points on that body that never coincide, and a positive definite function which is taken to define the distance between those two points at any time. (Note that this makes a metric for time antecedent to a metric for space.) This function could be a simple, constant function that proclaims the interval between those two points as a constant distance, or it could be a much more complicated function that takes temperature, electrical charge, or what have you into account. All that matters is that we can use the measure body to measure distances between other points, and for this only certain formal features need be met; we are constrained to give zero distance to coincident points and to give a distance greater than zero to noncoincident points. Having made this stipulation, the question of whether any three points lie on a straight line is answerable univocally, since straightness is determined when a metric is determined.

---

7 This notation is Carnap's but it is a departure from Carnap's earlier notational conventions, that is, S here refers to physical, not formal, space.

With this metrical stipulation in hand, the heretofore merely topological facts of experience can now be expressed in metrical terms. Thus, one can experimentally determine the degree of curvature of physical space at any given spatial point. Carnap outlines a procedure for doing this based on the angle-sum property of a triangle. Given that different curvatures in the neighborhood of a point will induce different angle-sum properties for triangles in a neighborhood around it, Carnap proposes to test the curvature by fitting six equilateral triangles together to form a regular hexagon. If they fit exactly, then we have a zero curvature. If they do not fit together exactly, we have a divergence from zero curvature that can be measured via the extent to which they overlap or leave a gap. This procedure can, in principle, be done at any point in space, so the full global metric of space can be discovered point by point, experimentally, on the basis of M and F. This is the first of Carnap's functional relations.

Carnap then argues in the second direction. We can stipulate that physical space has a certain global metrical structure and then use that structure and the facts of experience to induce the appropriate metrical stipulation. Carnap again argues via example. We could choose to consider the earth's surface as a spherical plane in a three-dimensional spherical space – rather than as a sphere in a three-dimensional Euclidean space. This will induce certain peculiarities when compared to our standard view. Measuring rods will behave differently depending on whether they measure along the earth's surface or above or beneath it.[8] Similarly, light rays move in circular paths going through the zenith point antipodal to the point at the center of the earth, and so on. This vastly different metrical structure requires a complete reworking of the laws of physics also. But such laws – agreeing with the matters of fact of experience – can be found. Hence, this situation is describable without contradiction and can generalize to any global metrical structure we want. Thus, S and F determine M.

The final functional dependency, that M and S determine F, is presented as an aspect of scientific representation in a hypothetico-deductive vein (Raum, p. 54):

This, in fact, is the basis on which the spatial matters of fact of experience are presented in scientific theory: it is asserted that physico-spatial forms are or-

---

8   Carnap notes that since the spherical space is bifurcated by any plane, the total volume of the earth is equal to the total volume external to the earth, given this metric.

dered in a particular metric structure S according to a certain M; and by this statement the matters of fact of experience F are completely described with respect to spatial relations. Still this third case is quite essentially different from the others in that, while S or M may indeed be freely chosen, F may not: the matters of fact are uniquely given.

Thus, the global metrical structure and particular metrical stipulation are presumed in the scientific representation of physical space. This determines what spatial facts are in accord with this physical theory. If we presume the empirical adequacy of the theory, then we can deduce the actual matters of fact of experience from it. We are not, of course, in the position of being assured of the empirical adequacy of any given physics, but without this possibility of representing spatial facts in accordance with the theory, the whole issue of its empirical adequacy could not be raised. The global metric and the metrical stipulation first allow the finite representation and derivation of the infinite class of matters of fact of experience, including those which have not been (and might never be) observed.

Carnap's second methodological point was directed against the conventionalists themselves. Poincaré and Hugo Dingler argued that once the conventionality of the metric was admitted, practical considerations would always induce us to choose the simplest possible global metric, that is, Euclidean geometry. Carnap grants the claim that Euclidean geometry is the simplest global metric. His tripartite account leads him to claim that the conventionalist is mistaken about how the principle of simplicity applies to this situation, however. The principle could be directed toward three distinct things. We could opt for the simplest global metrical structure, a la Poincaré and Dingler. Or we could opt for the simplest metrical stipulation. Finally, we could opt for the simplest overall physics (spatial and temporal structure and contentful physical laws) for systematizing and predicting facts of experience.

Choosing to direct the principle of simplicity to the global metric yields the conventionalist conclusion of the practical indispensability of Euclidean geometry. Choosing to direct the principle to the metrical stipulation will yield any of a variety of global metrical structures for physical space, depending on what material one chooses for the measurement body. This is because the simplest metrical stipulation would merely declare two points on some body as the unit distance and use that metric to determine the metrical structure of space and to formulate the laws of nature. Obviously, depending on whether one chooses

Der Raum

an iron, wooden, rubber, or some other measuring rod, one will get various different results for the metrical structure and, hence, various different laws of nature.

Carnap selects the third option. Although we recognize the freedom of choice we have in principle with regard to the global metrical structure or the metrical stipulation, we actually choose them with an eye toward the matters of fact of experience. That is, we choose so that the system of physical space and laws of nature present the matters of fact in the simplest way (Raum, p. 56):

A middle way, as it were, is to be followed, that proceeds neither from the simplest S nor from the simplest M, but receives its justification only by virtue of its goal, in that it leads to the simplest structure [Aufbau] constituted from our current knowledge . . .

If we take the principle of simplicity as belonging to the definition of science, then the relation between S and F might be expressed as follows: conceptually [denkmässig] it is a matter of free choice and independent of experience, but determined by F scientifically; or better: is to be determined, in order thereby to make clear that a particular S does not already lie implicit in the matters of fact F, but has first *to be set up* on the basis of that postulate.

Carnap's conventionalism, thus, approaches the relativized account of the synthetic *a priori* but ultimately does not endorse it. The conventions play the role of principles that make mathematical physics possible and, of course, there is a plurality of choices. So, the conventions have the same role as relativized synthetic *a priori* principles. But Carnap does not use the term "synthetic *a priori*" with respect to the conventions; in fact, when he lists the spatial judgments the conventions are left out of the list altogether (Raum, p. 64): "Therefore, apart from the determinations added by means of freely chosen stipulations, the propositions governing formal, physical, and intuitive space are analytic *a priori*, synthetic *a posteriori*, and synthetic *a priori*, respectively." It seems that the conventions lack any epistemological status whatsoever; they are not judgments at all. They coordinate the matters of fact with the physical theory that presents and predicts them, but they express neither matters of fact nor formal conditions of experience.

Thus, Carnap accepts a view of the methodological situation quite like the one that led Cassirer and Hans Reichenbach (1920) to the idea of the relativized synthetic *a priori*. But Carnap does not endorse their way of presenting the situation; rather, he simply adds the new methodological category of convention. Thus, given his endorsement of the universalist *a priori*, he avoids the terminological confusion we found in

Cassirer. Conventions coordinate manifolds of greater formal structure with the formally impoverished structure of the matters of fact of experience. Thus, they take us from the minimal, intersubjective starting point for science to the scientific theories that systematize this starting point. But these conventions themselves do not have the status of either logical truths or synthetic *a priori* judgments.

INTUITION AND SPATIAL KNOWLEDGE

So far, I have said little about intuition and intuitive space. It may be unclear why Carnap needs to have any such notion as intuition at all, especially given its absence in the work of Cassirer. There are two reasons why Carnap introduces the notion into his account. First, his notion of formal space is wholly general and so cannot itself ground the idea that geometry, appropriately so called, is about space. Carnap is concerned to provide an *a priori* content to geometry that gives it its "properly spatial" character. Second, intuition is meant to provide the *a priori* guarantee that the topological matters of fact of experience can be ordered into a univocal global metrical structure. Intuition is meant to guarantee the metrizability of physical space. In these ways, intuition is an ineliminable intermediary between formal space, conceived of as part of logic, and physical space.

The absolute generality and, thus, multiple applicability of formal space was, as we have noted earlier in the chapter, stressed by Carnap. At the end of the chapter on formal space, Carnap gives examples of how Desargues's theorem, conceived of as a theorem of formal projective geometry, can be instantiated by all manner of spatial and non-spatial objects and relations. He gives examples drawing from colors, judgments, points and lines, and circles and pencils of circles. A formal geometry is about all the structures that satisfy it. How, then, can we account for the peculiarly spatial relations and objects that were the historical *raison d'être* for the study of geometry? This is a role for intuition.

Carnap introduces intuition with the following words:

Intuitive space is an order structure whose formal type we can certainly delimit conceptually but, like everything intuitable, not its particular nature. Here we can only point to contents of experience, namely to intuitively spatial forms and relations: points, linear segments, surface-elements, volume-elements, the lying of a point on a line or in a volume, the intersection of two lines, etc . . . [As] Husserl has shown, we are certainly not dealing with facts in the sense of experiential reality, but rather with the essence ("Eidos") of certain data which can already be grasped in its particular nature by being given in a single instance. Thus, just as I can establish in only a single perception – or even imagination – of three particular colors, dark green, blue, and red, that the first is by its nature more akin to the second than to the third, so, I find by imagining spatial forms that several lines pass through two points, that on each such line still more points lie, that a simple line segment, but not a surface-element, is divided in two pieces by any point lying on it, and so on.

This mode of apprehension is called "intuition" or, following Husserl, "essential insight."

This intuition, thus, has a properly spatial component. One can intuit some properties of spatial forms directly. It also clearly has other elements: Carnap's color example indicates that certain essential features of colors are known directly by essential insight. Nevertheless, it is this intuitive apprehension of spatial objects and their properties and relations that grounds the possibility of properly spatial judgments and makes this available as a domain for the application of logical structure. Thus, there is a primitive *a priori* mode of apprehension that distinguishes spatial features from color features, auditory features, and any other feature of the intuition of objects. This spatial *eidos* connects the purely formal logical structures of mathematical geometry to the experience of spatial relations.

Carnap argues that there are severe restrictions on what can be known about spatial forms through intuition, however. The primary investigation of the chapter on intuitive space is, therefore, directed at uncovering exactly what can be known in spatial intuition. The primary tool for this investigation is Carnap's claim that (Raum, p. 23)

Intuition always relates only to a limited spatial region. Therefore, it can only yield cognitions about spatial forms of limited magnitude. On the other hand, we have complete freedom with respect to the total structure we construct from these basic forms. If, for example, a form is of such a kind as to permit a second form of the same kind to be added to it in a certain way, then we can postulate that this process of addition should be possible without end.

In this way, intuition as such yields only knowledge about small regions. The postulated iteration then allows these forms to be connected in an unbounded way. The unboundedness of the operation does not, however, entail actual infinitude and cannot, therefore, decide between finite but unbounded spaces and infinite spaces.

Armed with this understanding of intuition and its postulated extensions, Carnap sets about discovering the structure of intuitive space in two stages. First, he searches through Hilbert's axioms for Euclidean geometry to find which of these "arise from the intuition of a *limited region*" (Raum, p. 24). Next, he investigates the postulates that can and must be added to these to determine a global structure for intuitive space. In essence, Carnap attempts to impose the weakest postulates consistent with some form of global structure for intuitive space.

There is no need to detail Carnap's deliberations here. Let us, rather, cut directly to the resulting structure for intuitive space. The axioms directly given in intuition guarantee the infinitesimally Euclidean structure of intuitive space. The postulates then bind these regions together in a smooth way. The resulting structure is that of a general class of three-dimensional metrizable Riemannian manifolds. Thus, it generalizes the notion of a metrical manifold; it is a class of three-dimensional manifolds that allow a metric but have none defined on them. Because of its connection with the metric, Carnap dubs it "three-dimensional metrical intuitive space" (S'_{3m}), although it has no determinate metrical structure in itself.

This solves a problem not raised by Cassirer about the metrical conventions. Not all topological spaces are metrizable. So, even if the matters of fact of experience gave us a fairly complete knowledge of the topological structure of physical space, there would be no guarantee that a metrical convention could be univocally set up for physical space. The structure of intuitive space provides, then, an *a priori* guarantee that such a metric can be set up, since the structure of intuition is imposed on physical space. (Indeed, the connection with spatial, as opposed to, say, auditory, intuition is what makes physical space *space*, whereas the manifold of auditory tones is not spatial.) The metrical conventions are guaranteed to be able to play the systematizing role they are meant to only if we augment the matters of fact of experience with the *a priori* structure of intuitive space. Only then can we be sure that we can fulfill the strictures of the conventionalist argument.

There is one last aspect to Carnap's discussion of intuitive space. Carnap uses the tools of formal space to generalize the knowledge given in intuitive space to more comprehensive structures. Ultimately, he arrives at S'_{nt}, "the *most comprehensive intuitive space*, which contains all other possible intuitive spaces – some as parts and some as particularizations (specializations) by means of further forms and relations" (Raum, p. 31). This is the intuitive space that he called a condition of the possibility of any object of experience.

Carnap's use of intuitive space is instructive. His need to introduce it as the source of the peculiarly spatial character of spatial judgments indicates two aspects of his early thought. First, his epistemological perspective finds room for raising questions concerning the source of the phenomenological feel of the difference between spatial relations and color relations, for example. Second, his logicism with respect to formal geometry is in principle unable to provide answers to such epistemological questions. Once one raises such phenomenological questions about spatial judgments, one can do no better than to offer primitive phenomenological moments of thought, such as the essential insight that guides our knowledge of spatial objects, colors, and their differences.

In this way, Carnap's logicism still does not provide an answer to Cassirer's challenge. We do not yet have an account of logic and mathematics that shows how logic can play the objectifying role it must assume in the critical theory of knowledge. For, the essential natures of various modalities of phenomenological life are provided not by logic, which generalizes over any such contents, but by a primitive epistemological notion of essential insight. Moreover, within the domain of spatial judgments themselves, only such insight provides the notion of a truly spatial topology that underpins the notion of necessary form, on the one hand, and the *a priori* guarantee of univocal metrical conventions, on the other. Intuition is ineliminably implicated in both the universal synthetic *a priori* that grounds the notion of matter of fact and the conventionalism that provides the added form requisite for the systematic representation of such facts in mathematized theories of physics.

Moreover, the uses of intuition indicate that Carnap himself is subject to a kind of confusion about the *a priori* moments of thought, much as the neo-Kantians were. For, intuition discharges its role in guaranteeing univocal conventions only if it yields the full structure of S'_{3m}. S'_{nt} surely provides no assurance of the metrizability of physical space. On the other hand, what is univocally *given* in intuition, and not added by postulation, does not even provide the global topological structure that is needed to provide an *a priori* ground for the notion of necessary form and matter of fact of experience. S'_{nt} itself relies on postulation to take us beyond the local structure given in intuition. Thus, taken in itself, intuition does not provide enough peculiarly spatial form to guarantee global topology for physical space. But, when augmented by postulation, it yields a structure that undermines rather than supports Carnap's methodological argument for necessary form as topological form. For in this case we have an *a priori* intuitive structure that yields a notion of form that outstrips local topological form for spatial matters of fact. Intuition is, then, variously thought of as providing both of the two characteristic features of the synthetic *a priori:* On the one hand, it is meant to guarantee the possibility of mathematical physics, and on the other it is meant only to provide the form necessary to have matters of fact of experience at all. Carnap purchases logicism with respect to formal space at the cost of pushing the confusions of the neo-Kantians about the objectifying structure of logico-mathematical form into similar confusions now located in intuition.

The problems of reconciling the conventionalist methodology with the universal synthetic *a priori* remain, then, in Carnap's dissertation. He does not use the term "synthetic *a priori*" gladly anywhere, but, when called upon to use it, reserves it only for the necessary form requisite for matters of fact of experience. Conventions, playing the role of the relativized synthetic *a priori,* are then given a separate category in the methodological story and have no independent epistemological status at all. Intuition reenters the story as a way to link the purely formal structures of mathematical geometry to physical space and to solve a technical problem in linking topological matters of experiential fact with metrical conventions.

Here and there, however, Carnap's technical sophistication (as in the details of the examples in the physical space chapter) and philosophical reorientation show through. The latter is more important and appears especially in the argument for topological form as necessary form. This argument proceeds from the methodological situation of physics, as then conceived, and clarifies the situation via a purely mathematical distinction between necessary and optional form. Moreover, although it is form that is crucial for the objective status of matters of fact so distinguished, no attempt at a transcendental explanation over and above the mathematical distinction is offered. Topological form is not revealed as the structure of the transcendental mind. Carnap's neo-Kantianism takes over the importance of form for objectivity but weakens the transcendental perspective even more than the neo-Kantians did.

Having thus weakened the hold of the transcendental conception, Carnap does go some distance toward giving a logic of objective knowledge that places logico-mathematical form at the center of epistemology and eschews any metaphysical, including transcendental, interpretation of such form. Two problems remained, however. First, logic by itself seemed unable to distinguish spatial relations from relations of other phenomenological modalities (such as colors, tones, and temporal relations) and unable to guarantee to space its global metrizability. These were the two – rather contrary – roles for intuition. Second, by adopting the universal synthetic *a priori* in the way he did, Carnap surely was distancing himself from empiricism, but, just like the neo-Kantians before him, not presenting an epistemological alternative that the empiricists could find compelling. Carnap takes up these two tasks in the next phase of his philosophy, his "critical conventionalism" of 1923–6.

CHAPTER SEVEN

Critical conventionalism

ON THE TASK OF PHYSICS

Carnap's first postdissertation publication, his 1923 *Kant-Studien* essay, "Über die Aufgabe der Physik und die Anwendung des Grundsatzes der Einfachstheit" (On the task of physics and the use of the axiom of simplicity; hereafter *UAP*), brings with it many divergences from the view put forward in the dissertation. Carnap makes no mention of intuition and presents a more general framework for physical conventionalism. His one reference to the Kantian synthetic *a priori*, a half-hearted nod in the direction of the relativized *a priori*, reveals his reluctance to engage Kantian terminology or to wear a neo-Kantian mantle. Nonetheless, the essay begins with a clear rejection of strict empiricism, worth quoting in full (UAP, p. 90):

After a long time period during which the question of the sources of physical knowledge has been strenuously debated, perhaps it may be said already today that pure empiricism has lost its dominance [Herrschaft]. That the construction of physics cannot be founded on experimental results alone, but rather must employ nonempirical axioms, has already been proclaimed for a long time by philosophy. However, only after representatives of the exact sciences had begun to investigate the particular nature of physical methodology, and had in so doing been led to a nonempiricist conception, were solutions produced that could satisfy even the physicists.[1]

Carnap backs this rejection of pure empiricism up with an argument against reductionism that makes clear that the conventional choices underlying mathematical physics are not to be viewed as logical definitions on the basis of experiential primitives in the manner of Russell.

---

1 Carnap has in mind the work of Poincaré and Dingler here, as is evident from the immediately following sentences.

Critical conventionalism

Methodologically, Carnap moves much closer to the relativized synthetic *a priori* here. His crucial methodological distinction is between the objective structure of mathematical physics and subjective experience. Carnap, thus, moves the minimal structure of experience from the realm of intersubjective matters of fact like those that form the basis of physics in *Der Raum* into the individual subjective experience of epistemic agents. Nevertheless he continues to think of this experience as having a minimal structure. He can do this only by severing the inherent connection between structure and objectivity that is the hallmark of neo-Kantianism. This is a decisive break with the neo-Kantian project that stems from Carnap's willingness to give up transcendental explanations of the objectifying role of form.

Carnap's main focus in "Über die Aufgabe" is the thesis that there are three distinct conventional aspects to the construction of a complete physics. Moreover, he again makes the methodological point, directed at Henri Poincaré and Hugo Dingler, that there are two distinct ways in which conventionalism can employ the axiom of simplicity.[2] The three places where conventional choices arise in physics, he argues, are in the construction of the spatial system, the temporal system, and the force law (*Wirkungsgesetz*). Carnap takes the idea that the systems of space and time require conventional choices and cannot be read off directly from experience to be relatively well known and uncontroversial.[3] What is more controversial, and more fundamental to the essay, is the idea that the force law requires a further conventional choice. Carnap writes (UAP, pp. 92f.):

That, however, when [the conventions for space and time] already are fixed, the laws of nature cannot be deduced from mere experiential findings requires a new deliberation, which Dingler undertook. In the laws of nature there appear magnitudes whose measurement is not immediately possible but is reduced to space-time measurements (e.g., mass, force of gravity, electric charge, electrostatic field, etc.). This reduction, however, presupposes a general force law.[4]

---

2 This is, indeed, foreshadowed in the second part of the title of the essay, "the use of the axiom of simplicity." There were, of course, three ways to employ the axiom of simplicity in the dissertation, but, as we shall see, within the broader conventionalist framework there is nothing that quite corresponds to the choice of simplest metrical stipulation.
3 He refers the reader to the work of Dingler and Poincaré and to *Der Raum* (UAP, p. 91).
4 Carnap refers the reader to Dingler for the origin of such considerations.

Carnap has in mind the idea that, to take his example (UAP, p. 93), if mass is defined as the quotient of force and acceleration, we cannot measure mass without presupposing a general force law. This is because, absent such a law, force cannot be determined without knowing mass. Carnap refers us to the fact that the mass of a heavenly body is determined, in classical mechanics, by the use of the Newtonian inverse square law for gravitational force. He claims that clearly another, non-Newtonian, force law could be used for this purpose without contradicting experience.

It is important to note that Carnap is not here worried about empiricist problems that we generally associate with Hume regarding the inductive justification of general laws.[5] Rather, he is concerned with the fact that in mathematically expressible laws of nature there occur concepts of physical magnitude whose numerical values and mathematical relations cannot in principle be established without some form of conventional choice of force law. The problem that Carnap sees in grounding laws of nature solely in experience is not that they might conflict with future experience and, hence, are subject to inductive uncertainty. That is inescapable. The problem is rather that they cannot even be formulated, for they employ concepts whose identity and values are radically underdetermined by experience alone. In this he is guided by his view of the laws of nature as functional (typically differential) equations among quantitative concepts and by the conventionalist claim that no such quantitative concepts are given in experience. Force laws such as the Newtonian inverse square law, then, constrain the possible assignments of magnitudes of force to physical objects and thereby render other magnitudes, such as mass, capable of being measured univocally.

Having accepted this much of conventionalist methodology, Carnap is concerned once again to distance himself from the radical conventionalist conclusions of Dingler and Poincaré. The axiom of simplicity can, he once again urges, be directed either to the system of laws (metrical geometry, force laws) themselves or to the description of the world that these laws allow. Since the role of a force law in physics is Carnap's primary focus, he considers how this bifurcation of possible employment of the axiom of simplicity affects the choice of force laws for an imagined complete and fully empirically adequate physics. His imag-

---

5 This is not to say that the problem Carnap is raising is not a problem that empiricists might consider. Carnap clearly thinks, however, that naive empiricism cannot solve it: It requires a notion of convention.

ined physics exhibits both his quarrel with conventionalism and his distance from radical empiricism.

For Carnap, such a completed physics must fulfill the requirement of a "Laplacean spirit," which "can calculate every future or past event" (UAP, p. 96). Carnap thinks that such a completed physics consists of three distinct types of knowledge, so he considers it as being contained in three volumes (UAP, p. 97):

> The first proceeds *more geometrico*: it lays down a few *axioms* and derives arbitrarily many sentences purely logically from them . . . The derivations are only to save work in the calculations . . . The entire knowledge content of the first volume lies already in the axioms alone. These consist of the basic laws of spatial determination, temporal determination, and of the dependence of processes on one another, in short: spatial law, temporal law, force law.

This volume, which provides the formal axiom system for physics, contains, according to Carnap, synthetic *a priori* knowledge (UAP, p. 97). That is because the natural laws derived from the axioms are not justified by appeal to experience; rather, the logical connection of these laws to the conventional axioms first permits the scientific description of experience. This constitutive role in scientific understanding of experience connects the first volume to the synthetic *a priori* in Kant's methodological sense. Carnap, however, stresses the free choice available in the axiom systems and, thus, the relativized notion of the synthetic *a priori* here (UAP, p. 97):

> The first volume contains, therefore, synthetic *a priori* judgments [Sätze], but not exactly in Kant's transcendental-critical sense. Because that would mean that they expressed necessary conditions of the object of experience, conditioned themselves by the forms of intuition and thought. But then there would be only one possible form for the content of this volume. Actually, its construction [*Aufbau*] is in many ways a matter of our choice.

Carnap (UAP, pp. 97ff.) illustrates this freedom of choice by describing eight distinct formulations of physics that he finds in current literature. Ultimately, he suggests (UAP, p. 97) that "hypothetico-deductive system" might be a better term than "synthetic *a priori*" to describe the methodological role of the axiom system.[6]

The second volume of the completed physics contains a kind of dictionary that correlates the concepts found in the axioms of the first

---

6 He takes the term "hypothetico-deductive system" from "the Peano school" (UAP, p. 97).

volume with the observable realm. Carnap's distance from radical empiricism is found in his comments on volume 2 (UAP, p. 99):

> The second volume establishes the mediation between the realm of perception and the realm that forms the object of physical theory. That these two regions exclude one another completely cannot be emphasized strongly enough. The first contains the contents of perception: colors, tones, smells, pressures, sensations of warmth, etc., which, strictly speaking, are not discussed at all in theoretical physics.

Despite Carnap's claim that volume 2 presents a dictionary that mediates between these two realms, he explicitly rejects reductionism. Carnap states (UAP, p. 100): "The dictionary is usable in both directions: It serves just as well for the translation of a phenomenal matter of fact into the corresponding physical one as the reverse. It is to be noted, however, that *only in the second case is the coordination univocal*" (emphasis added). For, as Carnap notes, a vast variety of physically distinguishable situations gives rise to the same phenomenal qualities.[7] Thus, whereas a complete knowledge of the physical state of a system allows one to describe the phenomenal qualities of it completely, one cannot univocally determine the physical state of the system from even a complete account of its phenomenal qualities. Unlike Russell, Carnap is claiming that there is no way to solve the physical equations in terms of sense data.

This antireductionism contrasts, of course, with the received view of the epistemology of *Der logische Aufbau der Welt*. It has obvious relations to the procedure Carnap employs for the construction of the physical world there, however. Indeed, but for a few changes in the conception of the starting point of the construction, Carnap's account in the 1928 book is just the same as his view in "Über die Aufgabe der Physik" in 1923. There is a striking difference between the epistemological starting points of the essay and the 1921 dissertation, however. It is clear that in the 1923 essay Carnap is taking subjective sensation to be the experiential starting point. This drives the notion of 'matter of fact of experience' from intersubjectively available facts (such as the topological facts of *Der Raum*) into subjective, personal experience. The added structure that yields the mathematical form of the axioms of volume 1 belies empiricist reductionism and shows how physics can go beyond the

---

7   Carnap also notes that a large number of physical situations have no perceptual effects. For example, there are any number of distinct sound waves that are imperceptible to us because of pitch that is too high or low or volume that is too low.

subjective starting point of knowledge to yield an objective physical structure common to all. Carnap, thereby, raises again the neo-Kantian concern with the movement to objectivity from subjectivity. He is, however, granting a crucial point to the empiricist, for now the experiential starting point is subjective in the sense of private and qualitative, but not subjective in the sense of wholly without form or structure.

Volume 3 contains a complete description of the physical state of the world for two arbitrary points of time. Clearly the vocabulary of this volume is that of volume 1, not the vocabulary of sensation. Volumes 1 and 3 together allow the derivation of the physical state of the world for any point of time whatever, given the Laplacean dictates of the system. Such a state then can be translated (univocally in this direction), via the dictionary of volume 2, into the vocabulary of sensation. Thus, this complete physics can tell us what to expect in experience at any spatiotemporal point. It is the need for precise, deterministic physical laws for the prediction of future phenomenal experience that Carnap, like the neo-Kantians, stresses against the pure empiricist. Thus, the distinction between minimal and objectifying structure does double duty in this essay. It marks the distinction between private sensation and public matters of scientific fact and provides the locus of the methodological criticism of empiricism.

The two ways of employing the axiom of simplicity are explicated with respect to this imagined completed physics as follows. If one feels that the first volume is the most important part of physics, then one should employ the axiom of simplicity in such a manner as to maximize the simplicity of the axiom system of the first volume. That is, one should choose whatever consistent axiom system for physics is simplest in itself. If, on the other hand, one is interested in choosing the system of physics that allows of the simplest representation of the matters of fact of experience, then one must take into account the second and third volumes of the completed physics also. Carnap argues in favor of the second option and, indeed, stresses the preeminent import of the second volume (UAP, p. 104):

Since, however, the testing of the simplicity of the physical processes that correspond to the individual contents of sensation is easier than that of the simplicity of the (in practice never known) state of the entire world, the criterion is more usefully related to the second volume, and the claim is expressed thus: The physical axioms are to be chosen such that the physical processes that are coordinated with individual contents of sensation and complexes of such contents are the simplest possible; and among the axiom systems that satisfy this claim to the same extent, the one that is in itself simplest is to be chosen.

This second way of employing the axiom of simplicity is directed against Poincaré and Dingler, for although Carnap agrees with them about the role of convention in physical theorizing, he wants to make room for acceptance of the lessons of relativity. In contrast to the privileged role given to Euclidean geometry in radical conventionalism, Carnap's second method allows for the choice of a different metric if such a metric leads to a simpler coordination between the geometrical structure and the facts of experience. Similar considerations hold for the choice of a force law.

Carnap's sympathy for the second method notwithstanding, he claims that his proposals in the essay are meant only to aid in formulating the appropriate questions in deciding among various possible physical theories, not to provide answers to those questions. If one decides that the first method of employing the axiom of simplicity is the correct way, one then needs to formulate criteria by which to measure the simplicity of axiom systems regardless of their application to the actual physical world. Carnap's point is to stress the need for the conventionalists to provide criteria for simplicity of axiom systems that justify their insistence on the privileged position of Euclidean geometry.[8]

The situation is more complicated if one chooses the second way of employing the axiom of simplicity. For, in this case, one must determine the simplicity of the dictionaries between the physical and the phenomenal vocabulary of each theory. This amounts to posing a question concerning the simplicity of a *coordination relation* between perceptual processes and purely formal axiom systems. That, in turn, entails establishing a criterion for the simplicity of the coordination relation and also (since after the coordination each psychological process is an instance of some physical process) a criterion for the simplicity of physical processes. Of the latter, Carnap writes (UAP, p. 107):

One must lay down standards to be able to determine the *degree of simplicity of the structure of physical processes*. The difficulty of the nonarbitrary laying down

---

8   Thus he is less willing here to grant Poincaré the claim that Euclidean geometry *is* the simplest than he was in the dissertation. Carnap now sees Poincaré's claim as a logical hypothesis about axiom systems that needs to be justified. Poincaré, no doubt, did not conceive of his endorsement of the simplicity of Euclidean geometry as a logical point, however.

of these standards is, by the way, not as large as it perhaps appears at first glance. Because by "physical processes" we understand here purely formal complexes ("order structures" of the theory of relations). Absolutely no other characteristics are to be taken into consideration in the judgment of the simplicity of their structure, therefore, than those exhibited by, e.g., the figures [Gebilde] of (formal) geometry.

Simplicity measures are, then, just to be defined over classes of purely formal structures.

This is a stunning logicization of the physical world. Moreover, it is one that illuminates the displacement of intuition in Carnap's critical conventionalist framework. In *Der Raum,* intuition was meant to provide the connection between the formal structures of pure logic and the phenomenologically spatial structures in physics. Now, physics has itself been absorbed into logic; the mathematically expressed physics is a type theoretical object in its own right. Its only contact with phenomenal content is just the coordination relations expressed in volume 2 of the completed physics. All basic phenomenological distinctions (e.g., the distinction between colors and auditory tones) are relegated to the merely subjective, which does not form part of the subject matter of physics at all. Hence, the capturing of such phenomenological moments is no longer a constraint on the appropriate understanding of the epistemological project with respect to science.

Logico-mathematical form correspondingly plays a much greater role in epistemology on this view. Physics is wholly devoid of spatial, temporal, or any other qualities; physical processes simply are mathematical relationships. There is the many-to-one connection between physical states of affairs and phenomenal states, given the volume 2 of the completed physics, but even here the connection is considered as a (UAP, p. 100) "purely formal relation of coordination." Logico-mathematical form constitutes the law-governed world of physics and its relation to experience.

Moreover, Carnap's refusal to tell any transcendental story meant to explain how form plays these roles is here, for the first time in Carnap's published writings, connected to the rejection of metaphysical issues. Carnap rejects any metaphysical interpretation of the relation between the physical domain and the phenomenal world that constitutes the content of volume 2 of the completed physics. The passage (UAP, p. 100) is worth quoting in full:

The epistemological (or actually metaphysical) question as to the existential import [Seinsbedeutung] of the two domains shall be left aside entirely here.

The three-dimensionality of space and causality

The answer matters not at all for the solution to our task. For (in opposition to a widely held view) it is without meaning for physics whether one, in the phenomenalist-realistic sense calls the contents of the first domain (e.g., the perceived blue color) "mere appearances" and those of the second (e.g., the corresponding electromagnetic waves) "reality," or, on the contrary, in the positivist sense designates the first as "the actually [wirklich] given" and the second as "mere conceptual complexes of those experiential contents." For it is not [expressed that] "where this blue appears, there is in reality such an electron process" nor "in the place of this blue we create [fingieren], in order to make calculation possible, such an electron process"; rather, physics expresses itself neutrally with the aid of the purely formal coordination relation and leaves aside those interpretations of a nonphysical investigation.

The realists, on the one hand, and the positivists, on the other, import metaphysical issues into physics by insisting on some further interpretation of the coordination between the physical and the experiential realms. Carnap, on the contrary, insists on noting only its formal properties, such as its many-to-one nature and its methodological role in the construction of physics. The same centrality for logic that eschews any transcendental explanation of the objectifying role of form brings with it the complete separation of metaphysical issues from the methodological ones with which Carnap is concerned.

THE THREE-DIMENSIONALITY OF SPACE AND CAUSALITY

Carnap's next published work, which appeared in 1924, was entitled "Drei Dimensionalität des Raumes und Kausalität" (The three-dimensionality of space and causality; hereafter, *DRK*).[9] This essay clarifies three crucial aspects of Carnap's critical conventionalism: his disagreement with both empiricism and the "universal invariant" version of neo-Kantianism; his antimetaphysical stance; and the sense in which mathematical physics is for him the locus of objectivity. It does this through an examination of a distinction between two levels of experience. The first is "the immediately given in its original order" (*DRK*, p. 105). The second is experience subject to "further formation" (*DRK*, p. 107); that is, experience as expressed in either the language of everyday physical objects or the language of mathematical physics. The distinc-

---

[9] It had the subtitle "An Investigation of the Logical Connection of Two Fictions." It appeared in volume 4 of Hans Vaihinger's *Annalen der Philosophie*, which was the house organ of Vaihinger's fictionalist "Philosophie des Als-Ob."

tion between these two levels is that the first is not – whereas the second, especially when conceived of in the form of physics rather than that of everyday life, is – subject to lawful connections. Moreover, it is this notion of being subject to law that gives us our purchase on the notion of an object, and hence on the notion of the objectivity of knowledge. Again, however, Carnap explicitly claims to be investigating only the relations between these domains and their contribution to knowledge; all metaphysical questions about the preeminent reality of one of these domains as regards the other are left out of account.

Carnap introduces the distinction between the primary world of experience and the secondary world of experience with these words (DRK, pp. 106f.):

The criticism that has been urged especially from the side of the positivists against the Kantian concept of experience has taught that not all the formal factors to which Kant ascribed necessity apply [zukommen] as such to it. Sensible experience shows indeed a certain spatial and temporal order and furthermore certain qualitative relations of likeness [Gleichheit] and nonlikeness. But the combination of certain experiential elements into "things" with "attributes," or further the coordination of experiential elements with others as their "causes," is not at all necessary, i.e., a condition of every possible experience. Rather, it is a matter of free choice whether this synthesis happens and also, in large measure, how it happens. We designate experience that bears only necessary formation [Formung], as "experience of the first level," the further synthesized as "experience of the second level."

Carnap's principal examples of experience of the second level are the "ordinary" formation of everyday life in terms of substance and causality and the various conventional choices that underlie systems of mathematical physics.

Carnap assimilates the primary world to the "given" in experience, as understood by epistemologists such as Johannes Rehmke and Theodor Ziehen, with the proviso that (DRK, p. 108) the primary world "has in part quite different attributes from those ascribed to it by those theories." The chief characteristic of this primary world of experience is that it is *not* a "chaos of sensation" to which the synthetic functions of thought are applied to induce order. Rather, it stands in an order already (DRK, pp. 108f.):

It is not here a question of the origin of experience but rather of the consideration of the attributes it has if it is in hand as "experience," and that means: as content of knowledge . . . The elements of such experience already always stand in particular relations to one another (e.g., spatial contact of two simulta-

The three-dimensionality of space and causality

neous color sensations in the visual field). The minimal number of these relations, i.e., the set of those that never are missing when such experience is in hand, forms the order of experience of the first level.

Thus the primary world of experience is experience in the minimal necessary form for it to count as the content of knowledge at all.

Carnap's view of the given in experience now contrasts with the view of the given in both empiricism and neo-Kantianism. Against empiricism, Carnap continues to stress that the given is only the content of knowledge by virtue of its formal structure. Against the neo-Kantians, Carnap now locates that form fully within qualitative, subjective experience. Indeed, his arguments that there is such experience at all cite as examples such things as optical illusions and the manner in which painters are trained to see color patches (rather than objects) – psychological data about "quite uninterpreted impressions" (DRK, p. 109). This severs the inherent connection between form and objectivity. Even the subjective – the private and qualitative – is subject to form. Objectivity comes in the movement from minimal form to the fully law-governed form of physical knowledge. Carnap writes (DRK, p. 108):

> The neo-Kantian philosophy does not know [kennen] the primary world, since its conception, according to which the forms of experience of the secondary world are necessary and unique [eindeutig], hinders it from recognizing [erkennen] the difference between the primary and the secondary world. Their actual achievement, that is, the proof of the object-creating function of thought, however, remains and lies also at the foundation of our conception of the secondary world.

There is, of course, an inaccuracy in this claim. As we have seen, some of the neo-Kantians had made a similar distinction themselves. Moreover, Carnap's own position in *Der Raum* was both neo-Kantian and also made out such a distinction. But, two points of difference between the position of the 1924 essay and the neo-Kantian work are crucial. First, the primary world of experience here is, as we have noted, wholly subjective in the sense of traditional empiricism, the psychological experiences of a given agent. Thus, for the first time, the distinction between the primary and secondary worlds takes on a crucially unequivocal role as the distinction between the subjective and the objective. Even in *Der Raum*, as we noted, the matters of fact of experience were physical facts whose topological form guaranteed their intersubjective status. By breaking the neo-Kantians' inherent link between minimal form and objectivity, Carnap crystallizes the issue between critical conventionalism and empiricism. His position differs from strict empiricism on the question of the role of added mathematical form that takes us from the subjective starting point of knowledge to objective, intersubjective knowledge in physics. The distinction between the formal structure of the primary and secondary worlds, which is necessary in order to engage with empiricism on this issue, is confused, for example, in Cassirer's list of formal components of knowledge in *Substance and Function:* space, time, magnitude, and the functional dependencies of magnitude. As we have noted in Chapter Five, this list leaves the relation of minimal form to full mathematical form wholly unclarified. Moreover, such a list would not enable Carnap to make the distinction between the primary and secondary worlds in the way he does here, as we shall now see.

Throughout the essay Carnap is interested only in the relations between the primary world of experience and the secondary world of mathematical physics, not the world of everyday life. As opposed to the everyday world, which is based on the superadded and secondary forms of substance and causality, the world of physics is to be thought of purely mathematically (DRK, p. 108):

> The "physical" transformation, on the other hand, knows no causal relation in the sense of an [active] force [Wirkung], and in its purest form also no substance. It constitutes [konstruiert] a world free of sensible qualities, in which there are only spatial, temporal, and certain nonsensible state magnitudes. In the purest form these three types of magnitude also have no character similar to spatiality, temporality, or sensible qualities but are, rather, mere number determinations, that is terms of relations . . . The relation between this type of experience of the second level and that of the first level is set up through a coordination . . . The processes of the physical world do not act [wirken] on one another; rather there holds for them a dependency, which is to be viewed as a purely mathematical-functional relation.

From this it is clear that the mathematical functionality of the form of physics is to be contrasted to the minimal order found in the primary world. Thus, Cassirer's functional relations among magnitudes are of the essence of objective knowledge in physics but are not part of the necessary form of experience. Necessary form of experience is for Carnap now the hallmark of the subjective. Of course, in another sense, functional dependency is necessary for objective knowledge – necessary precisely for distinguishing merely subjective experience from genuine scientific knowledge.

This discussion of the secondary world of physics also points to the importance of Carnap's rejection of Husserlian intuition after *Der Raum.* The phenomenological role that intuition was supposed to play by picking out of the "properly spatial" in physical geometry is here set aside, as in "Über die Aufgabe der Physik." Whether and how certain order structures are phenomenologically spatial and others are qualitative (visual, auditory) is now seen to be completely immaterial for epistemological investigations, because mathematical physics is once again conceived of as a purely mathematical structure.

Carnap urges two principal distinctions between the primary and secondary worlds. First, the primary world of experience has two spatial dimensions, and the physical world has three. Second, the primary world is not subject to any deterministic laws, whereas the physical world is constructed explicitly to have Laplacean deterministic structure. That is, as noted in "Über die Aufgabe der Physik," a complete tally of the physical state magnitudes (including their derivatives) at any one point of time determines their values at all points of time by virtue of the laws of physics. Carnap argues that the first distinction follows from the second.

Employing the topological definition of dimensionality, Carnap argues (DRK, pp. 113ff.) on empirical, psychological grounds that the number of spatial dimensions in the primary world is two. He claims that (DRK, p. 117) "no one doubts" the three-dimensionality of physical space, but adds (ibid.): "Occasionally the attempt is made to deduce the three-dimensionality of space *a priori*. Occasionally it is viewed as an empirical finding, but of course of a higher degree of certainty than other empirical facts. But it is known neither *a priori* nor *a posteriori*, because it is not known at all but rather agreed on, chosen." What determines the choice is the methodological imperative that the laws of physics have the Laplacean character just noted. That is, the three-dimensionality of physical space is determined by the constraints on the mathematical functions that express physical laws, constraints induced by the need for these to be deterministic laws. This need is itself only a conventional choice, in the following sense: We could give it up and insist only on weaker conditions for physical knowledge. But once Laplacean determinism is required, the three-dimensionality of physical space is ensured.

The argument that the dimension number of physical space follows from the Laplacean determinism that we require of a complete physical theory is somewhat complicated and, fortunately, tangential to our concerns. Rather than go into this argument, let us simply note a few aspects of the view Carnap is offering. First, Carnap thinks of physical theory as mathematical functional relations of nonsensible physical magnitudes. Second, he claims as a methodological imperative that these functional relations allow a Laplacean determinism. Only on the Laplacean condition do the functions univocally determine the physical state magnitudes of the world at any given time. Third, this methodological drive is a conventional choice and leads beyond the necessary form of experience to full mathematical form. Finally, experience itself, nevertheless, plays a role in knowledge, because and only because its necessary form allows the conventional coordination of physical magnitudes to experiential qualities.

The crucial formal impoverishment of pure experience is that it exhibits no lawful structure. Carnap (DRK, pp. 123ff.) takes it to be an empirical fact that the experiential qualities of any portion of the two-dimensional space of the primary world do not determine or substantially constrain their values in any other part. For example, no amount of knowledge of the color qualities of any portion of the visual sense determines the color qualities of some point not in that portion. Nor does the complete knowledge of experiential qualities at any point in time determine or constrain their values at any prior or subsequent time. Moreover, he maintains that this is not changed by the availability of a Laplacean deterministic physics, for precisely the same reason that he argued against reductionism in the 1923 essay. The many-to-one nature of the relation between physical state magnitudes and experiential qualities leads to the conclusion that determinist laws of physics do not translate into determinist laws of primary experience. To take a simple, fictional example suggested by Carnap (DRK, p. 126): Suppose that we have a functional relation between the wavelength of electromagnetic rays and their energy and that energy is phenomenally expressed by a feeling of heat and wavelength by color. The physical functional relation still cannot be transformed into a functional relation between feelings of heat and color sensations. This is because the many-to-one character of the coordination collapses, at the level of color sensation, many different wavelength combinations that give rise to very different energies and, hence, feelings of heat. Thus, the many-to-one relation between physical state magnitudes and phenomenal qualities leads us from one-to-one functions of physical state magnitudes to many-to-many relations among phenomenal qualities. No predictive power accrues to the purely phenomenal, even with physics secretly mediating the relations.

THE TEMPORAL DETERMINATION OF SPACE

Carnap's next essay (1925), "Über die Abhängigkeit der Eigenschaften des Raumes von denen der Zeit" (On the dependence of the attributes of space on those of time; hereafter, *ERZ*), is concerned to show a result regarding the axiomatization of physics itself. Carnap argues that the topological properties of physical space can be deduced from the topological properties of physical time – in particular, from a system of temporal topology that takes only proper time order within world lines and coincidence of points of space-time as primitives. It presents the beginnings of a physical constitutional system that is meant to show the power of logical definition in physics. The constitutional system of spatiotemporal topology was, as Carnap notes in his "Intellectual Autobiography" (hereafter, *IA*), the topic about which he had wanted to write his dissertation (IA, p. 11); in the early 1920s he wrote a lengthy manuscript on it that was never published, although the basics of the system were presented in his 1929 *Abriss der Logistik* (Outline of logistic; hereafter *Abriss*) (§36).[10]

One point from this rather technical 1925 essay on space and time bears mention. Carnap's concern is to show that spatial topology is deducible from temporal topology, that is, its concepts are definable from the primitives that I have mentioned earlier, and its theorems are provable from the axioms holding for those primitives. Carnap notes that we need, therefore, a criterion for telling whether a putative axiom of the system is "properly" (*echt*) temporal, that is, involves only the primitives. This criterion is provided by symbolic logic (cf. ERZ, pp. 335ff.). Logic provides a stock of purely structural properties, and the criterion we use to make sure that we have not smuggled in any other empirical relations beyond the primitives is that we can express the axioms in terms of the primitives and logic alone.

Now, of course, classes have no ordinal properties in themselves, so it is very important that the primitives are relations, indeed the serial relations that have been exploited by Carnap since the dissertation. The axioms, then, capture the ordinal features of the primitive relation using the resources of the theory of relations. Carnap ties this feature explicitly to Cassirer in an unpublished manuscript as follows (RC 081–02–07, p. 25):

10 This manuscript, dated 1924, was entitled "Topologie der Raum-Zeit-Welt: Axiomatisch dargestellt mit den Mitteln der symbolischen Relationstheorie" (Topology of the space-time world: Presented axiomatically by means of the symbolic theory of relations), now manuscript 081–02–07 in the Rudolf Carnap Collection in the Archives for Scientific Philosophy in the Twentieth Century at Hillman Library of the University of Pittsburgh. A reference to this manuscript in "Über die Abhängigkeit" (p. 345) indicates that Carnap still thought of it as "forthcoming" in 1926. It may well have been part of the proposed alternative *Aufbau* with physical basis that is suggested in §62 of *Der logische Aufbau der Welt*.

The circumstance that both of the basic concepts, of which alone in the end all the axioms and theorems treat, are not attributes (class concepts) but relations (concepts of coordination) deserves special attention. Insofar as things are spoken of at all within the system, they are understood only as terms of these coordinations (as "terms of relations") without any further attributes. In this way, in the domain in question a methodological development, which has been investigated most deeply by Cassirer, has reached its goal, namely the transition from "substance concepts" to "function concepts."

In a footnote to this passage Carnap refers to *Substance and Function*. This indicates a rather different interpretation of Cassirer than in the essay on three-dimensionality. There, the neo-Kantians' insistence on conceptual functionality was taken by Carnap as mathematical functionality and taken to indicate that they did not have room for the primary world. Now it is seen that functionality can be cashed out in terms of logical structure of relations, which is capable of expressing even the minimal form of experience. Any merely ordinal properties of relations can be expressed in the theory of relations.

In order to show that spatial topology is a "branch" (ERZ, p. 334) of temporal topology, Carnap begins with the formal axioms of temporal topology and explicitly defines (ERZ, p. 338) spatial topological notions from them. He sketches the definitions of these concepts through the crucial concept of 'spatial neighborhood' (*Umgebung*) (ERZ, p. 341). Once he has this concept, he can give the topological definition of dimensionality (ERZ, p. 342) and express the claim that space is three-dimensional. Explicit definition is requisite, because we have to show that claims such as this are themselves equivalent to properly temporal claims. Carnap writes (ERZ, p. 343):

It is to be noted here that the change of form through substitution of the defining expressions does not bring any diminution of content [Inhaltsverlust] . . . The original sentence – in the example, the sentence about the three-dimensionality [of space] – is therefore not richer in content than the one that is gotten from it via the change of form; it is of the same logical value [logisch gleichwertig] as this, therefore a formal statement about K [coincidence] and Z [proper time] like this one.

Two things should be noted about this procedure, however. First, such formal statements about K and Z are not, of course, themselves logical truths. The formal properties of the primitive relations are known only empirically. Second, the definitions may allow sentences with other concept signs to be translated into formal statements about the primitive relations without it being the case that such complicated formal statements about K and Z are deducible from more primitive

Physikalische Begriffsbildung

axioms. That is, for example, the claim that physical space is three-dimensional may translate into a purely formal statement about K and Z, but one not deducible from simpler formal statements such as the fact that K is an equivalence relation or Z is a partial ordering. If one knew the sum total of formal features of the system of K and Z, one would know whether the three-dimensionality claim is true. But there is certainly no guarantee that there is any less detailed account of the formal features of K and Z (such as is given in the axioms) that will determine whether space is one-, two-, or three- (or more) dimensional. Moreover, being formal features of an empirically known relation, the dimensionality of physical space is not a matter for logic alone.

THE GENERAL CONVENTIONALISM OF *PHYSIKALISCHE BEGRIFFSBILDUNG*

Carnap's final work on physical methodology in his pre-*Aufbau* period was his 1927 monograph, *Physikalische Begriffsbildung* (Physical concept formation; hereafter, *PB*). This work generalizes the conventionalist themes in his work from simply the metrical properties of physical space to *all* quantitative concepts. He gives a general account of how one moves from subjective and qualitative concepts to precise, quantitative concepts in mathematical physics. The procedure relies only on the logical form of the qualitative relations and certain conventions imposed upon them.

He begins the work by stating what he takes to be the task of science (PB, p. 1): "Science has the task of collecting and ordering cognitions in order to achieve an ever greater degree of mastery over reality." He distinguishes between an intellectual mastery of nature that comes with understanding the connections of events even if those events remain unalterable for us (weather, movement of the heavenly bodies) and a practical mastery of nature in which we can bring about events that we want to occur. Either sense of mastery over nature requires precise, predictive laws of nature. Formulating these laws is "the second phase of scientific activity," in which "the forms supplied by the formal sciences are used as frames or schemata to synthesize [verarbeiten] [the results of observation and experiment], to assemble it into an organized structure" (PB, p. 2).[11] This process yields quantitative concepts connected by mathematical laws.

---

11 The first stage of scientific activity is the accumulation of experimental results. Carnap stresses that this distinction into stages is not meant to capture actual temporal stages of enquiry but logically separable tasks.

A 'concept,' for Carnap, is anything designated by a nonarbitrarily employed symbol. Carnap's main order of business in *Physikalische Begriffsbildung* is to show how concepts are introduced in science. About this he says (PB, p. 3):

> A sign is introduced or, if it is already in use, legitimated, when those conditions in the representation of states of affairs in which the sign is to be used are stated. The introduction or legitimation of the word "horse," for example, occurs when those conditions which must be in hand for us to call something a horse are stated, hence through the statement of the *characteristics* of a horse (or the definition of the word "horse").

Thus he states (PB, p. 4): "*The formation of a concept consists of the statement of a law about the employment of a symbol* (e.g., a word) in the representation of states of affairs."

In the course of everyday life, concepts are typically designated by words of ordinary language. But already here, as Carnap notes (PB, p. 14), at certain times and for certain purposes, quantitative statements and, hence, the use of number terms for the designation of concepts are very useful. More than this, though, he claims (PB, p. 14) that "the use of quantitative statements, indeed ultimately the reduction of *all* qualitative statements to quantitative ones, proves itself to be necessary to a still higher degree in the scientific, hence methodical, investigation of natural processes." He presents his reasons for this in a section entitled "The Superiority of the Quantitative Method in Relation to the Qualitative" (PB, p. 51). The first reason is the simple and purely practical one that the way in which numerals are formed presents us with an inexhaustible collection of symbols with which to designate concepts. The second reason is that the order in which elements stand in relation to one another can be mirrored in their designations with numerals. That is, the physical relations of objects can be transformed into mathematical relations among the numbers assigned to them. Moreover, any order properties among objects can ultimately be captured within number theory. Thus, (PB, p. 51)

> the designation by numbers makes it possible to collect general laws into *one* expression (that is, through the mathematical relations between the numbers, the "functions"); with word designation thousands of individual sentences would have to appear in the place of a single mathematical identity; practically said: with a word designation one would not express at all what the identity expresses, but rather would satisfy oneself with the assertion of vague relations.

In the third and final section of the monograph, Carnap returns again to the idea that physical laws can be conceived of as purely formal.

Physikalische Begriffsbildung

Taking the four-dimensional space-time account given by H. Minkowski and the idea that ten state magnitudes are necessary for the complete physical description of each space-time point,[12] one can view physical states as 14-tuples. Then one can view the physical processes governed by the laws of physics as mathematical relations among the various components of the 14-tuples that form the state of each world point. In this way, physics can be conceived as being "transformed into the *arithmetical consideration* of a certain number system" (PB, p. 59).

Carnap's account leaves him with the following problem, however. The statement of precise predictive laws of nature requires the mathematical, quantitative treatment of physical concepts, and this allows us to view physics purely mathematically. But pure mathematics does not have any particular and determinate connection with experience or any predictive value for the world of perception. It seems that the selfsame move toward mathematics necessary to give physical laws the requisite precision deprives them of the purpose of that precision: their application to future experience. Carnap puts the question this way (PB, p. 59): "Is the indicated, most abstract form of physics, then, still to be called physics? Does it still say something about nature, and does it teach us to predict later perceptions from ones already had?" Clearly the answer had better be yes, and Carnap's account of the manner in which quantitative concepts in physics relate to experience is to indicate how this is so.

This account is the "generalized conventionalism" that I mentioned earlier. Carnap bases the formation of all quantitative physical relations on certain experiential "topological" (ordering) relations. If such relations have the appropriate logical form, they can provide the basis upon which quantitative concepts are formed. That requires the imposition of three metrical conventions. The conventional aspects and ineliminability of metrical concepts in science indicate that this is still a nonreductionist account of the relation of theoretical to experiential concepts.

Carnap's view of the situation is indicated in the following example. How do we proceed from our own vague and private feelings of warmth or cold to a precise, lawful, and intersubjectively available temperature scale, such as the Celsius scale? A simplified account of

---

12 The idea of ten primitive state magnitudes expressed here (p. 58) might be derived from the Mie–Hilbert interpretation of general relativity that Carnap outlines in UAP (p. 98). The ten state magnitudes are the electrical density and the three components each of the vector potential and the electrical and magnetic displacements. But, in any case, it is only a suggestion for the purposes of framing the discussion, not an essential part of his methodological view.

Critical conventionalism

Carnap's deliberations of this case (see PB, pp. 16ff.) goes as follows. The formation of a quantitative concept of temperature is occasioned in our experiences of objects that yield different thermal sensations in us, either simultaneously or over time. Now certain formal aspects of this thermal experience give us the opportunity to construct a temperature scale.

Two formal aspects of the experience of warmth are requisite for the formation of a temperature scale. First, we need a transitive, symmetric, reflexive relation that sorts heated bodies into equivalence classes.[13] This can be done via the property of thermal equilibrium; we put two bodies in the same equivalence class in case they undergo no thermal change on contact.[14] Second, we need a transitive, asymmetric relation that orders these equivalence classes into a linear order. We can use the fact that (except in cases of chemical reaction) two bodies not in thermal equilibrium will move toward equilibrium when brought into contact: One will typically warm up and one cool down. We can then order their (prior) thermal properties accordingly. These are the "topological" properties of thermal sense that ground the temperature scale.

Already one could use the ordering properties and assign numbers to the ordered equivalence classes and, hence, to the thermal properties of the objects in those classes. But we do not yet have a measurable temperature scale – for, there is no guarantee that the mathematical properties of the numbers we assign to the classes have any physical significance. The assignment is arbitrary, as long as it gets the order correct. Moreover, because it is arbitrary, there is no reason why any two scientists would agree to what the numerical assignment is. As Carnap says (PB, p. 19), "Beyond this we want to now establish that [any] two [physicists] assign the same number as the temperatures of any body; we say: Their temperature assertions should agree not only topologically, but also *'metrically.'*"

To do this we must apply certain metrical conventions. First, we must decide on a "scale form"; that is, we must decide when two

---

13 Throughout, Carnap does not make the reflexivity requirement explicit. Perhaps he thought that the need for reflexivity in such experiential relations is obvious.

14 This seems to be a physical fact not statable antecedent to the establishment of a temperature scale. But Carnap thinks that we can begin with the experiential ersatz of assigning two objects to the same equivalence class if they undergo no perceptible change of warmth on contact. This convention can be modified as we go along (just as Carnap calls for modifications of the metrical conventions for space if they prove unwieldy for expressing physical law). It is not clear that such an experiential relation is transitive, however. It seems that if one begins with experiential relations, one has to rely solely on similarity relations and, correspondingly, lose transitivity. This is, of course, precisely what Carnap does in the *Aufbau*.

differences in temperature are to be considered equal. Second, we must decide on a null point for the temperature scale. Third, we must decide on a unit for the scale. For temperature, one can, for example, fulfill these requirements by, first, stipulating that (PB, p. 35) "two temperature differences [be] set as equal if mercury experiences the same increase in volume in both the corresponding heatings."[15] Second, one can choose a natural point, such as the melting point of ice, as the zero point. Finally, one can choose a certain fraction of the difference between two natural processes, such as melting of ice and the boiling of water, as the unit. In this way, a temperature scale, indeed the Celsius scale, can be developed, and temperature can be measured in the same way by various different agents. Thus, we achieve both precision and intersubjectivity of concepts as the result of this one process of concept formation.

Concept formation depends, then, on five conditions: two topological determinations (*Bestimmungen*) and three metrical conventions (*Festsetzungen*). The topological determinations amount to certain formal conditions of experiential relations. Carnap puts the point this way (PB, p. 22):

The prerequisite and occasion for the introduction of a type of magnitude is an empirical finding of the type that among the objects (bodies, processes) of a domain two relations obtain: one transitive and symmetric and one transitive and asymmetric. The first relation gives the occasion for the formation of a particular concept of identity, the second for the formation of the concept of a particular type of magnitude, and indeed chiefly (that is, if that relation has a certain sequentiality) a one-dimensional ("scalar") magnitude.

Having fixed the ordinal properties, we then set up a metrical scale through the conventions. The conventions coordinate the quantitative concepts of science to the topological determinations given in experience. This is how mathematical physics ultimately relates its quantitative, formal objects to experience and allows the prediction of future experience from the laws of physics.

Note the difference between this conception and that put forward in *Der Raum*. In *Der Raum*, Carnap claimed that the possibility of metrical relations (for space, anyway) was given an *a priori* guarantee through the role of intuition. In *Physikalische Begriffsbildung*, on the other hand,

---

15 This clearly requires antecedent metrical conventions for spatial magnitude. Indeed, the spatial and temporal conventions are the methodologically first conventions, because all other magnitudes can be measured only after these are set up.

there no longer is an *a priori* guarantee that metrical relations and, hence, mathematical laws for science are possible. Rather, such metrical relations are due to conventions that are grounded solely on the availability of empirical topological facts. Whether such conventions can be set up depends solely on the structure of experiential relations. Moreover, the notion of topology just is the logical form of experiential relations, which these experiential relations have for each epistemic agent. This agreement is required and presumed, but neither guaranteed by intuition nor explained transcendentally.

The laws of physics require, however, the complete formation of quantitative concepts and, hence, they require metrical conventions. These conventions go beyond experience and express stipulations whereby individual objects are coordinated with numbers in a way that allows intersubjective agreement and disagreement. Only on the basis of such stipulations can quantitative laws of nature be formulated. Moreover, only quantitative relations allow prediction and control. Hence, the conventionalist aspect of Carnap's thinking persists.

CRITICAL CONVENTIONALISM AND THE *AUFBAU*

If we collect together the most important aspects of Carnap's critical conventionalism, we get the following list:

It is anti-empiricist, in the sense that it rejects the idea that objective knowledge is reducible to or identical with sensory experience. Objective knowledge is found in mathematical natural science, which requires conventions that take us beyond experience to the mathematical structure described by scientific law. Only this structure is subject to lawful regularities. These regularities allow the prediction and control over the future course of experience.

The requisite conventions serve the purpose of coordinating richer mathematical structures with the formally impoverished structure of experience. Pure qualitative experience has a certain amount and type of structure but no mathematically expressible law-governed regularities. Experience serves as the starting point of objective knowledge but is not sufficient in itself. The methodological imperative to understand the world through scientific law requires going beyond the purely qualitative notions available within experience.

Carnap's view is also in some respects quite different from neo-Kantianism. Carnap no longer seeks to assign logical form to the mind and, hence, finds no reason to equate that which is subject to form with the objective. Thus, he can opt for expressing the epistemological situation in accordance with the relativized account of the synthetic *a priori* while holding onto a minimal form of experience. Experience is subjective, although it has a certain formal structure. It is subjective in the sense that we view it as the sensory experience private to an individual agent. Such experience has qualitative relations that have certain logical properties (serial structure) allowing metrical conventions. But no such mathematical lawful relations occur within experience itself.

Carnap's view is also nonmetaphysical. Carnap continues to insist that we can investigate the methodological relations between experience and the world of physics without even raising, let alone answering, any questions of metaphysics. His differences with neo-Kantianism stem ultimately from his eschewal of the last remains of a transcendental explanation of the connection between form and objectivity and from a more rigorously maintained and formally understood logocentrism. His differences with empiricism are epistemological differences about the relation of experience to scientific knowledge, not a difference over what it is real or ontologically primary.

It might seem that by 1928, in the *Aufbau*, Carnap has changed his mind radically. The antireductionism seems to have been given up and this, one might assume, must bring in its wake the rejection of the difference between the form of experience and the form of objective knowledge. That, in turn, seems to require giving up the anti-empiricist view. Once we have phenomenalist reductionism, we might expect to have empiricism pure and simple, and we would be taking sides on the ontological priority issue as well.

This chain of inferences is, of course, the one that I have been maintaining must be resisted. Indeed, we have already seen that there is a significant sense in which the *Aufbau* exhibits the critical conventionalist methodology internal to the constitutional system. That methodology can be observed in the construction of the physical world and in the role that this construction plays in the construction of intersubjectivity. The movement from the perceptual to the physical world, in section 136, is precisely where we would expect to find the type of considerations Carnap gives when discussing the movement from the primary to the secondary world of experience in the critical conventionalist period. In fact, this is exactly what he does. There he stresses the need for conventions to choose the state magnitudes for which he is trying to construct values. Moreover, he explicitly maintains the many-to-one nature of the correlation between the values for the state magnitudes and the perceptual qualities of the perceptual world. He also stresses the need to go beyond perceptual qualities to numerical systems in order to allow the formulation of "mathematically expressible laws." That is particularly important because (§136) "only [the physical] world, but not the perceptual world, can be made intersubjective in an unequivocal, consistent manner." It seems, then, that the critical conventionalist methodology now finds a place inside the constitutional system itself.

This outcome is, of course, both curious and problematic. Carnap's claim to be engaged in a definitional project in the constitutional system does stand at odds with the methodology of critical conventionalism. There are significant philosophical tensions here. It is insufficient to see reductionism and radical empiricism as simply taking priority over the other aspects of Carnap's thought in the *Aufbau*. Carnap's construction of the intersubjective world does lay great stress on the mathematical structure of physical science – a structure not constituted out of experience but coordinated with it. Moreover, even the definitional project itself subserves the project of purely structural definition descriptions, which is at least as problematic from the empiricist point of view as is critical conventionalism.

In the *Aufbau*, Carnap edges closer to direct engagement with the empiricist perspective by endorsing the project of explicit definition on the basis of experience. Both of his accounts of objectivity – and indeed the stress on objectivity itself – belie, however, an endorsement of empiricism. Indeed, we now have the resources to see more clearly where the stress points lie in the project of the book and why they lead to two distinct accounts of the objectivity of knowledge. Carnap has maintained the neo-Kantian understanding of the general epistemological project but has lost the neo-Kantian transcendental perspective that motivates that project. Within his general epistemology, formal logic itself takes on the burdens of the philosophical language of neo-Kantianism. But this leaves Carnap in an unstable position. In the end, there is a crucial mismatch between Carnap's formal logical resources in philosophy and the very distinction between objective knowledge and subjective experience that he takes over from neo-Kantianism to motivate his project. Carnap's general epistemology cannot find room for its own crucial distinctions in a scientific world view.

CHAPTER EIGHT

Epistemology between logic and science: The essential tension

THE look back at neo-Kantian epistemology and Carnap's own work in the 1920s leading to *Der logische Aufbau der Welt* has served to highlight important themes that we shall examine in this chapter in relation to the 1928 book itself. First, the point of view of the epistemological project of the *Aufbau* is in some respects closer to, for example, Ernst Cassirer's general epistemology in *Substance and Function* than to Carnap's own conventionalist methodology of science. Three aspects of the *Aufbau* are particularly noteworthy in this regard: First, the stress on the epistemological centrality of objectivity is more pronounced than it was in Carnap's methodological work; second, the role of logic is much greater here than it had been previously in Carnap's work; third, simply as a general epistemology, the *Aufbau* has the broad scope of Cassirer's logic of objective knowledge, rather than the more narrow scope of Carnap's work on physics. These connections, of course, give rise ultimately to great divergences between the project of the *Aufbau* and Cassirer's logical idealism. The principal reason for this is that Carnap's formal logic allows him to present a technical project that Cassirer had never attempted. This technical project no longer allows the expression of Carnap's earlier rejection of strict empiricism. But this does not mean that he now endorses strict empiricism; it means, rather, that he can no longer distinguish the genuinely epistemological aspects of the project of empiricism from the epistemological aspects of neo-Kantianism.

Beyond this, however, we now have all the pieces we need to understand the circumstance that has driven our curiosity. We can now see the tensions that led Carnap to have two separate accounts of the objectivity of scientific knowledge. There are two driving factors in this, neither one a newfound commitment to strict empiricism. The first factor is epistemological: In the *Aufbau* Carnap is concerned to give an account of the objectivity of *all* of the sciences. Physics no longer has ultimate epistemological privilege as the one objective science. A unified account of scientific knowledge requires that there be no sharp line between the objectivity of mathematized science and the subjectivity of less formal sciences. The point is not to find a division within the sciences but to find a demarcation that separates them from subjective experience, on the one hand, and metaphysics, on the other. This demarcation provides the content of the thesis of unified science. The second factor is meta-epistemological: Carnap is, for the first time, at pains to explain the objective meaning of epistemological notions, such as 'objectivity,' themselves. These notions must find a place either within the realm of empirical concepts of the objective sciences or within the formal concepts of logic. It is precisely the inability of the objective–subjective divide to be captured comfortably in either realm that lends it its problematic status here.

THE UNITY OF SCIENCE AND LOGICAL CONVENTION

The unity of science is a major theme of the *Aufbau*. The principal point of the epistemology here is not to draw a distinction of epistemic value among the sciences. There is no attempt to trumpet a general superiority of natural science over social science, for example. Objectivity inheres, rather, in all the sciences. Thus, the general epistemology of the book attempts not so much to privilege mathematized physics as to carve out a general epistemological status that applies to all the sciences.

This is not easily reconciled with the way that critical conventionalism locates objectivity in the mathematized sciences. According to critical conventionalism, the metrical conventions of mathematized science do provide the extra structure that first permits deterministic laws and, hence, predictable experience. Carnap, therefore, must recast certain of his principal doctrines in order to make them fit into the scheme of the book. This he does in the following manner. First, he assimilates all concept formation to convention (§107). Second, he maintains a privileged position for physics, not at the end point of objectivity but *within the dynamics of the construction of objectivity*, in the process of intersubjectivizing. Third, he reformulates the claimed advantages of objectivity over subjectivity.

Carnap endorses in this book, for the first time, a version of logical conventionalism.[1] If we view logical truths as conventions for the use of signs, then in particular we can view Carnap's constitutional definitions as conventional introductions of signs. They do not state facts, whether about experience or about physical objects. They simply grant new words meaning by defining them in terms of primitive, or already defined, words.

This way of thinking about convention is far removed from Carnap's use of that notion throughout his critical conventionalist period. Convention received its import within that program precisely to the extent that it differed from explicit definition. Conventions were crucial in the movement to objective science exactly because they provided additional structure that first allowed precise, predictive, functional relations among the mathematized, metrical concepts of physics. Conventionally introduced concepts were not those that simply collected prior facts into convenient expression; they first allowed the formulation of claims that were literally inexpressible in terms of primitive sensation. The arbitrariness of explicit definition is just the arbitrariness of the sign, that is, the arbitrariness in, for example, calling *this* color "chartreuse." Metrical conventions went well beyond this. They were arbitrary in the sense that all the facts expressible in the language of sensation underdetermined even the general structural relations of the metrical concepts, let alone their values at any point. Explicit definitions, by contrast, are required to be conservative extensions of the language: They add nothing to the expressive power of the language.

Thus, although Carnap does assimilate logical truths and explicit definitions to conventions in the *Aufbau*, it would be a mistake to see this as a further generalization of his view along the lines of that in *Physikalische Begriffsbildung*. Rather, it is a radical change in his notion of what a 'convention' is. It provides Carnap the terminological wherewithal to bring together his conventionalism and his adherence to the methods of formal logic, but only at the expense of rendering his earlier epistemological and methodological points about conventions and their importance for scientific knowledge moot.

Of course, as I have been at pains to note, the procedure of critical conventionalism is still to be found in the constitution of the physical world in the *Aufbau*. Having constructed all of classical mathematics and assimilated all concept formation to conventionalism, Carnap does

---

1 Here I sharply differ from Runggaldier's (1984) interpretation of Carnap's early conventionalism.

not pause to consider the possibility that this is a change of constitutional method. But, of course, this is exactly where Quine raises his objections. The constitutional method *has* changed, but this is masked by the new fluidity of the word "convention." The "conventions" appealed to here are conventions in the old sense – conventions that impose structure on the world of the appearances in order to render them mathematically well behaved.

Why is Carnap so sanguine about this alteration of procedure? Well, on the one hand, all of mathematics is available already, having been constructed antecedent to the system under discussion. Thus, there is nothing mysterious about the end point of the constitution of the fully quantized world of physics. That world simply is a particular type theoretic object, the existence of which is guaranteed by the power of his logic. On the other hand, with the world of physics constructed, the constitution of the intersubjective world will show exactly how the elements of experience are coordinated with it. To stop to object to the procedure when it begins would be to object that the scientifically ineffable (the subjective qualities of the perceptual world) has been lost in the movement to the scientific realm. This is not an objection, but rather the whole point of the account. After intersubjectivizing, the very coordination sketched in the construction of the physical world can now be expressed in the language of science itself. Here, however, the relations of meaning and objectivity flow from the physical to the experiential. Thus, we locate the objective meaning of experience by finding how it is imbedded in the structure of the physical.[2]

But, Carnap cannot now rely on the old advantages he claimed for the objective over the subjective, given the looseness of the notion of convention in the *Aufbau*. In a certain sense, the predictable nature of experience is posited right at the outset of the procedure of the book, since the whole structure of experience is taken to be given. Objectivity is tied, rather, always to communicability and, hence, intersubjectivity. The problem is not that my experience is unpredictable unless embedded in the world of physics; rather, my experience is utterly private and inaccessible to anyone else. If this is where my knowledge begins, then we need to know how I can know anything that anyone else, who is starting from her own experience also, knows. The control offered to knowledge by Carnap's conventions and definitions is not predictive

---

2   This process is a formalized version of a general account of objectivity and subjectivity within scientific experience quite similar to the one sketched by Cassirer (1910/1953, chap. 9).

control as much as it is communicative control. The story has become one of how we can reason together about objects of knowledge we have in common. This has been a theme throughout the neo-Kantian writings and Carnap's own pre-*Aufbau* writings, but now it is the *only* remaining problem in the area of objectivity.

In the *Aufbau*, then, explicit definition and convention are no longer held separate. Moreover, the problem of the predictive control over experience is no longer raised as the motivation for concern with physical objectivity. Thus, Carnap has lost the vocabulary for rejecting strict empiricism that guided, for example, the beginning of "Über die Aufgabe der Physik." This is not to say that he has become a strict empiricist. It is to say, rather, that the very terms in which both the neo-Kantians and his earlier self rejected empiricism are no longer available to Carnap. Thus, the dispute between the two schools has become idle and plays no role in any genuine epistemological endeavor. This is at the heart of Carnap's new professed neutrality in epistemology.

EPISTEMOLOGY AS EMPIRICAL SCIENCE

The very neo-Kantian epistemology now enfolded into the neutral project of constitution theory reasserts itself at a higher level, though. This is the level at which Carnap's troubles with objectivity become manifest. Carnap has rejected all metaphysical or transcendental explanations of his project. Nonetheless, he wants both to provide a general epistemology of empirical science and to redeem epistemology itself as objectively acceptable. This means that he has two options. Either he must find a place for epistemology within the empirical sciences, or he must find a place for it in the formal sciences. His troubles with objectivity are ultimately expressions of the lack of fit between the epistemological question about science he seeks to answer and the ultimate end products of the project itself.

The project of intersubjectivizing is a project that takes place wholly internal to the constitutional system for unified science. At no level does Carnap construct a corresponding concept of objectivity. Nor does he ever construct the totality of the intersubjective objects at any level. Nonetheless, the project of intersubjectivizing provides a division within the constitutional system between the objective and the subjective. A crucial example is the way in which the intersubjectivizing function shows that each object in the various autopsychological worlds is subjective whereas the physical objects are objective. But, we must not get confused by this. There are private worlds of physics also; the physical world of each agent is constituted prior to the intersubjective world. Moreover, for each private, autopsychological object, there is a correlated object in the intersubjective world. This is how it must be, otherwise it would be impossible to discuss one another's experiences, just as it is impossible to have one another's experiences.

As epistemologists in Carnap's scheme, it is utterly essential that we can talk objectively about one another's experiences. This is because experience is part of the subject matter of the science of psychology and, as such, must make its way into the objectivized unified science. More than this, psychology is the very science to which the epistemologist must turn to uncover those general facts about human experience that form the basis of the constitutional system itself. Psychology reveals the sense in which experience is private precisely by expressing objective facts about experience as a publicly accessible object in the scientific world.

Carnap is at considerable pains to make sure that the basis of the autopsychological system relies on genuine facts, rather than philosophers' fantasies, about human cognition. We have had occasion to note the way in which Carnap stresses the connection between his starting point and the facts as revealed by Gestalt psychology. This both accords with and lends scientific value to his epistemological view that the structure of experience is the basis for knowledge, whereas its content is subjective and private. This nonfoundationalist and psychological understanding of the role of experience in epistemology is given voice particularly strongly in section 122, where Carnap writes:

> The concrete constitutions themselves here serve only to make more clearly known the task of constitution theory and to illustrate the method. The execution of them is dependent on the particular results of the empirical sciences; if the facts that lie at the basis of the given constitutions are not scientifically sound, then we must induct those that occur in the sciences in their place into the language of constitution and introduce them into the constitutional system.

Moreover, the constitutional system itself is to show how these psychological facts that lie at its foundation are objective. Of the very basis elements, Carnap says (§177): "It is . . . only as constructed objects that they become objects of cognition in the proper sense, in particular, objects of psychology." Within the project of intersubjectivizing, that means that the intersubjective objects that correspond to the private worlds of the autopsychological are the genuine objects of psychological research. Thus, the epistemological project contains a virtuous circle:

Epistemology as empirical science

It takes information from psychology in formulating its basis elements and, in return, redeems precisely that information (among other claims) as objective in a reconstructed science of psychology.

But, all is not well with the project of intersubjectivizing. The project is meant to indicate how the objective divides from the subjective. But consider the kinds of claim that Carnap wants to make about the subjective realm – for example,

(*) mb_N ["my body" as a perceptual object in N's constitutional system, that is, N's perceptual constitution of his own body] is subjective in N's system.

This sentence is meant to draw our attention to the distinction between this subjective object and the objective physical object that is N's body, which is an object in the intersubjective world of physics. But, it succeeds in so drawing our attention only by speaking about an object that it says we cannot speak about. That is to say, the project of intersubjectivizing does occupy a position external to the sciences precisely by rendering possible objective claims about the subjective. Epistemology must trade in a distinction that cannot be a distinction between sense and nonsense, but a distinction within the realm of sense. This distinction between the objective and the subjective is, however, not a distinction within the empirical sciences, since they deal only with the objective. Epistemology must comprehend both halves of a distinction in order to demarcate science from subjective experience, on the one hand, and metaphysics, on the other.

The project of intersubjectivizing, as a way of constructing the objective–subjective distinction internal to the constitutional system itself, is, then, unstable. As an internal distinction, the project invites us to assimilate the objective–subjective distinction to a straightforwardly scientific, empirical distinction. But it is manifestly not a distinction within any empirical science, since these are recognizable as such simply because they deal with the objective only. Perhaps we could view epistemology itself as the very most widely ranging empirical science – one that comprehends both the objective and the subjective realms?

This is not sufficient. It calls into question the very need for the motivating dichotomy. For epistemology would have to be a science of the subjective, not in the sense of empirical psychology, which deals only with the intersubjective objects corresponding to the subjective streams of experience, but in the sense of a genuine way of speaking about the subjective as subjective – of speaking, for example, about both the recollection of similarity relation and the intersubjective object corresponding to it, although the relation is itself subjective and the intersubjective object is objective. But if we can speak of the recollection of similarity relation in a science of epistemology, then it cannot play the role of the scientifically ineffable starting point that it is meant to play.

The project of intersubjectivizing seems to mislocate both the motivating distinction and the project of epistemology. As noted earlier, locating the objective–subjective distinction within the constitutional system seems to miss the point of giving a constitutional system. The constitutional system, it would seem, exhibits the objectivity of all of the concepts within it. The operative distinction is the one between all the concepts that find a place within the system and those pseudoconcepts that can find no place. This is the crucial idea, and a very slippery one. Carnap's inability to find a place for his epistemology comes from the inadequacy of his only two choices here.

The choice made in the project of intersubjectivizing deals with this crucial idea in the following way: All objective concepts must find a place in the constitutional system for unified science. Epistemology must be an objective discipline, for otherwise it is no discipline at all. Epistemology trades in the objective–subjective distinction. Thus, this distinction itself must be made within the system. If this can be done, the operative motivating distinction for the project can be expressed within the project itself and requires no external perspective.

But the attempt comes to grief. For the motivating distinction cannot simply be the same sort of distinction as, for example, the distinction between the psychological and the physical. This is a distinction that can be made within the system, for as such it will simply demarcate the subject matter of two distinct sciences of the objective. The motivating epistemological distinction cannot be one that grants epistemology a separate empirical subject matter of its own – the subjective and its relations to the objective – for the distinction itself indicates that there are no such objects. A subjective object is an absurdity and a science of the subjective an impossibility.

There is another way to understand the motivational distinction. Rather than thinking of epistemology as a separate science that yields objective knowledge of the subjective, we can view it as a different, nonempirical discipline. It is a discipline that has no separate subject matter but that, as it were, exhibits how the empirical sciences have a subject matter. It is an analytic science that provides the tools by which to make clear how science is objective. With the constitutional system in hand, the objective status of the sciences can be shown. Epistemology does not issue in claims about objectivity or subjectivity; it presents the objectivity of science in a fully general and explicit manner. Thus, epistemology provides a logical function for scientific knowledge; it becomes truly a *logic* of objective knowledge.

EPISTEMOLOGY AS FORMAL SCIENCE

The idea that epistemology is a purely formal, logical enterprise is, as we noted in the section entitled "Carnap's *Aufbau* and Russell's External World" in Chapter One, the heart of Carnap's philosophical project in the *Aufbau*. It figures prominently in three features of the work. First, it guides Carnap's logical reinterpretation of traditional epistemological vocabulary. Terms such as "reduction" and "constitution" are captured as logical notions without metaphysical import. Second, it shapes Carnap's understanding of the type of epistemological role the constitutional definitions of empirical, scientific terms should have. The definitions are assimilated to logical truths. Finally, it leads to Carnap's purely structural notion of objectivity and to the failed attempt to define away even the basis of the system.

Carnap's meta-epistemological ambitions in this project are of the first importance. He stresses throughout that the main point is less the constitutional system actually outlined and more the new, technical project for epistemology exhibited in the constitutional system. His own terms of epistemological art are given their definitions also. For example, "constitution in a system" itself is captured as the metalogical concept of "explicit definition in the language of *Principia Mathematica* and the basic relations of the system" (§36). Indeed, as we saw in Chapter One, it is just this reinterpretation of epistemological notions that plays the largest role in the rejection of metaphysics. The title of Carnap's monograph of the same era, *Scheinprobleme in der Philosophie* (Pseudoproblems in philosophy; hereafter *Scheinprobleme*), published in 1928, indicates that the elimination of metaphysics serves philosophy, not science. It is the traditional project of epistemology, not the traditional project of science, that invites metaphysical pseudoproblems and unclear concepts to infect the structures of knowledge. The reconstrual of the point of epistemology without reliance on the old, metaphysically loaded terminology of the traditional schools of epistemology deprives the metaphysicians of their entering wedge. Carnap expresses this view clearly in *Scheinprobleme* – a statement well worth repeating (§1):

Epistemology between logic and science

It has frequently been stressed that the epistemological question of the grounding or reduction of one cognition to others must be differentiated from the psychological question of the origin of the content of a cognition. But this is merely a negative determination. For those who do not want to rest content with the expressions "given," "reducible," "foundational" or the like, or those who do not want to use these concepts in their philosophy, the task of epistemology has not been formulated at all. The goal of the following considerations is to formulate this task precisely. It will be shown that we can formulate the definition of epistemological analysis without having to use these expressions of traditional philosophy; we only have to go back to the concept of implication, the condition relation (as it is expressed in if-then-sentences). This is, however, a fundamental concept of logic that cannot be rejected or even avoided by anyone: it is indispensable in any philosophy, in every branch of science.

This view indicates the centrality of logic for Carnap's epistemological project. As the discipline that presents the formal conditions for any judgment on any subject matter, logic is neither subject to epistemological doubt nor in need of further grounding. Thus, to show how to reinterpret the positive portions of epistemology in logical terms is to ground the discipline in the most effective possible way. In essence, it is to show that epistemological distinctions are built into the very possibility of judgment.[3]

Moreover, it is this centrality of logic, rather than an epistemological conversion to strict empiricism, that guides Carnap's endorsement of the project of explicit definition in the *Aufbau*. Only this notion of concept formation – not the conventionalism of his critical conventionalist period – is available to him, once he has endorsed the logical resources of *Principia Mathematica* as his formal framework. Thus, Carnap's commitment to the centrality of logic supports the change of the notion of objectivity from the predictable to the intersubjective and adds one additional element to Carnap's inability to make out any distinction between neo-Kantianism and empiricism. The epistemological point of his physical conventionalism is no longer expressible, even as its methodological tenets find continuing employment in the construction of the physical world.

This meta-epistemological point feeds into the epistemological project itself. Carnap now sees the introduction of empirical concepts in terms of the treatment of logical truths in logicism. Just as the logical

---

3 Here I give only the bare bones of my interpretation of the rejection of metaphysics in the *Aufbau*; cf. Richardson (1992b).

truths of *Principia Mathematica* condition the possibility of making any objective claim about any subject matter, so too does the objective status of empirical claims rest on those principles that supply the objective meanings of empirical terms. Only against the background of an antecedent logical delimitation of the meanings of empirical terms can any meaningful question be raised in the language of the sciences. This logically primary aim of empirical science – which is the sole aim of epistemology – is, according to Carnap (§179), done "by convention" – that is, convention in the sense in which he also is now willing to call a logical truth a convention: a specification of the meaning of a sign.

The assimilation of the constitutive definitions of empirical terms to logical truths is the key to the purely structuralist account of objectivity. Carnap wants to extend the notion of logical truth to include principles providing the meaning of empirical terms. This idea, like the meta-epistemological idea, is basically metalogical. It requires a genuine change in or extension to the notion of logical truth. The logical truths of *Principia Mathematica* will not suffice for the grounding of analytic claims that provide the meanings of empirical terms.

But Carnap's general understanding of logic, which he has taken over from Bertrand Russell and Gottlob Frege, is as a fully general language in which everything that can be said at all can be said. Thus, Carnap's two positive ideas for the use of logic in epistemology cannot be given adequate voice. Indeed, they cannot be untangled from the technically impossible project of purely structural definite descriptions for *all* empirical concepts. In the project of the pure formalization of empirical science, Carnap's understanding of the need to extend the notion of logical truth to cover the introduction of empirical concepts is confused with a project of trying to show these constitutive definitions to be logical truths *in the sense of Principia Mathematica*. If the constitutive definitions are taken to be logical truths in the sense of *Principia Mathematica*, then the language of science will, *ipso facto*, be the language of *Principia Mathematica*, and the dematerialization of science will be complete.

Why is this? It might seem that the language would be an applied language with a primitive predicate, recollection of similarity. But this is not right. If the definitions must be logical truths in the sense of *Principia Mathematica*, there can be no nonlogical operators in them. Thus, the very idea that the constitutive definitions must be considered as prior to and independent of meaningful empirical claims and, thus, as having the status of logical truths requires that we pursue the project of definition all the way down to the basis, as Carnap does in sections 153–6.

Only then will the definitions have the status they require. But even if this were technically possible, no contentful empirical claims would be forthcoming anyway. All the concepts of science would be logical concepts, and the distinction between logic and empirical science would be erased.

The first project for objectivity, in which it is drawn internal to the constitutional system, is, therefore, incoherent. The second project, however, does not locate the distinction within the system but, rather, between the sciences that are shown to be objective when the system is in hand and all other alleged knowledge-producing enterprises. This project is not incoherent *simpliciter*. With the notion of logic that Carnap has and the strength of the logic of *Principia Mathematica*, the second project is, however, both technically unmanageable and (ultimately) philosophically misleading. But, in retrospect, it is clear that this project is both the bold new idea for a general epistemology in the *Aufbau* and the one that Carnap continually revises in his post-*Aufbau* writing. There is one key notion that Carnap lacks here which he needs to give his new logic of objective knowledge a workable form: a notion of logical truth that includes principles that constitute the meanings of empirical terms but that does not erase the distinction between logical and empirical truth. In essence, he needs the notion of *analyticity* for a language for empirical science.

Both Carnap's vision of epistemology as a formal discipline and his requisite version of logical truth – analyticity in an empirical language – require a change in view about logic itself. The view of logic as the most general science that Carnap takes from Russell and Frege cannot support either of his key ideas. This view permits no metaperspective, since, as logic provides the fundamental universal language within which everything sayable can be said, there is no possible external perspective for discussion of the language of logic itself.[4] But Carnap's account of epistemology requires just such a perspective. First, in his account, epistemological notions such as 'constitution' are not defined in terms of the primitives of *Principia Mathematica*; they are metalogical notions such as 'definability' in the language of *Principia Mathematica*.

---

4 Of course, one could use a portion of the language of *Principia Mathematica* to speak of other portions – thus, one could use the resources at type N + 1 to speak of the language of type N. (I am grateful to Peter Clark for bringing this to my attention.) Carnap needs more than this. He needs to have a general perspective from which to speak about the whole of the language of *Principia Mathematica* and, more importantly, he needs a perspective from which to speak of the introduction of empirical terms into the language of that system.

Epistemology as formal science

There is no reduction of epistemology to logic along the lines of the logicist reduction of mathematics to logic. Epistemology is, so to speak, exhibited *in* the logicist reduction of mathematics; it is not a further discipline to be grounded in logic. The extension of the project of definition (and proof) to the empirical realm is the key idea of the logical epistemology that Carnap offers for our approval.

Moreover, if the logic of *Principia Mathematica* is the general logic that Russell and Carnap say it is, then it does not allow the superaddition of more logical truths – those about empirical concepts – on top of it. Logical truths are not about particular concepts at all. They constitute the formal framework for speaking about any subject matter, but they themselves have no particular subject matter. Carnap's desire to extend logic to a logic of empirical knowledge requires an extension of the notion of logical truth. If there are to be logical truths that constitute the meanings of empirical terms, then Russell's account of logical truth is not sufficient.

Beyond Carnap's need for new logical resources, his epistemological vocabulary has, in the purely structuralist project, a troublesome status. Unlike in the intersubjectivizing project, in the second account of objectivity Carnap's epistemological claims, such as the claim "Primitive experience is subjective," are not redeemed as objectively meaningful. We cannot speak of the subjective. Thus, Carnap's motivational vocabulary must be seen on the model of hints in the direction of a project or ways to conceive of a problem situation that will be dissolved through the technical project. Epistemology does not issue in genuine claims of its own but provides a system of tools and a goal of analysis in pure structure. Therefore, the epistemological vocabulary serves a rather Fregean or Wittgensteinian role of a misleading invitation into a project that will ultimately show how misleading the invitation was.[5]

In section 178, for example, Carnap writes the following:

> How cognition can attain to one object level from others, how it can construct the levels of a system of knowledge, in which order and with which form, this is contained in what has been indicated [that is, in the constitutional system, ordered in accordance with epistemic priority, as outlined in the *Aufbau*]. The theory of knowledge can ask no more.

The epistemological work, on this view, comes in the construction of the system itself and the examination of its order and form. The subjective

---

5 The understanding of Frege and his relation to Wittgenstein that most informs my thinking here is found in Ricketts (1985, 1986).

is not discussed anywhere; rather, it is noted by its absence within the limits of the objective. The first view of epistemology, in which the objective–subjective distinction is drawn in the system, leads to the ability to discuss the ineffable and, thus, contradicts the motivational distinction itself. This second view, on the contrary, invites us into a project through use of a motivational distinction that disappears as a genuine topic of discussion once we have completed the project. We may speak of the subjective as only a problematic concept in the Kantian sense – a concept that limits the pretensions of knowledge without being positively determinable.

There is another aspect to this situation that bears mention. If we revert to the distinction we noted between the universalist and relativized *a priori* when we discussed Cassirer and Carnap's pre-*Aufbau* work, then the intersubjectivizing notion of objectivity is relativized. A change in the conventionally adopted laws of physics and methodological precepts would lead to changes in what is intersubjectivizable and how. But, the guiding rhetoric of "the structure of experience" and the adoption of the logic of *Principia Mathematica* as the analytic tool for concept formation both militate in favor of a universalist approach. Thus, Carnap is caught in the very confusion over which approach to adopt in a general epistemology that we saw in Cassirer.

The situation is complicated by Carnap's official repudiation of the synthetic *a priori* in the *Aufbau*. Such a repudiation is not the end of the story, however. The epistemological role that Carnap assigns to the logical truths embodied in his constitutional definitions is the methodological role played in Kantian philosophy by synthetic *a priori* principles: They first make possible objective, empirical knowledge. Carnap's new use of the term "convention" for the logical principles is interesting in this context. It suggests a radicalized notion of the relativized synthetic *a priori* in which the conventional reaches all the way down to the level of logic, heretofore the preeminent locus of universalist principles. Although he is not a logical pluralist in the *Aufbau*, there are pressures leading Carnap toward this path.[6]

---

6 I am not repudiating my claims about the radical difference between logical and metrical conventions here. Logical truths cannot sustain the role metrical conventions had in critical conventionalism, and, thus, Carnap's notion of convention has changed. I am indicating here that thinking of logical truths as conventional opens up the possibility of viewing them as relative to a framework, in just the way he views metrical conventions. When conventions become logical, certain epistemological stories are no longer possible; when logic becomes conventional certain philosophical moves become possible.

LOGICAL EMPIRICISM

I have stressed the neo-Kantian aspects of the *Aufbau* throughout, for it is an essential strand in the story I have told. Now, however, we must note how attenuated the neo-Kantian aspects are. We have, of course, Carnap's official claim to be neutral with respect to the earlier schools of epistemology, including transcendental idealism. We have already seen reason to take Carnap at his word on this. His own earlier rejection of empiricism relied on an understanding of objectivity that he no longer retains in the *Aufbau*. Moreover, his endorsement of the project of giving explicit definitions in accordance with his understanding of the logical basis of concept formation renders him unable to express any distinction between the empiricist and neo-Kantian epistemological projects. He does, of course, maintain that their partisans are engaged in a pseudodispute at the metaphysical level. Therefore, in the final section (§183) of the *Aufbau*, Carnap (not disingenuously) endorses a formal version of empiricism.

Contained within his professed neutrality is Carnap's continuing refusal to engage in transcendental explanations of the manner in which form confers objectivity. Carnap exploits the logical form of experience and adopts the view that but for such form objectivity would be impossible. But there is no effort to locate logical form in the transcendental mind. Indeed, Carnap's use of psychological research to explicate his epistemological starting point suggests that the structure of experience is either passively received or structured by the empirical mind. But no stress is laid on this either. Logical form provides the locus of objectivity, and that is the end of the story. Carnap's thoroughgoing logocentrism obviates any need even to attempt to explain this role for logic. The epistemology of logic consists of nothing more than noting this role for logical principles; nothing else can be said.

Moreover, although his Kantian account of the problem of knowledge and its solution must be taken seriously, it also leads to the most serious trouble for the project. The epistemological distinction that gives shape to the project finds no happy place within it. Carnap's epistemology either undercuts the very distinction that motivates it or leaves this motivating distinction behind once we have taken up the project. The way out of this dilemma would have to consist in the adoption of a genuine metalogical perspective. If this were done, epistemological notions themselves could be explicated as clearly as the concepts of science, and a logic of science could be given that did not obviate the logical–empirical distinction. Moreover, the metalogical perspective should still be consistent with the general view motivating a logic of objective knowledge – the idea that a logical framework must be in place prior to any objective empirical claims and that, therefore, no empirical concerns can arise for that framework.

These are, of course, the themes for which Carnap's version of logical empiricism is notable. Carnap never wavers from his belief that a notion of analyticity for languages for empirical science is necessary if any questions of justification are to make sense at all. Moreover, Carnap's logical work is guided by the attempt to provide formal metalanguages, in order to make precise the syntactic or semantic notions in which his philosophy invests its coherence. Finally, his adoption of logical pluralism throughout his later work is meant to support, not call into question, the claim that no internal questions can be raised to bring a logical framework into doubt.

THE *AUFBAU* IN THE FORMAL MODE OF SPEECH

Our examination of the difficulties that the objective–subjective distinction presents for Carnap in the *Aufbau* can fruitfully be augmented through a consideration of the fate of epistemology within Carnap's work over the next few years. The most extended essay in general epistemology that Carnap published after 1928 was his long 1932 *Erkenntnis* article, "Die physikalische Sprache als Universalsprache der Wissenschaft" (The physical language as a universal language of science). Revised for publication in English in 1934 (under the altered title *The Unity of Science*; hereafter *Unity*), this is the last published work in which the notion of constitution theory finds a place in Carnap's writing. Despite the discussion of constitution theory and the general project of definition of scientific concepts in experiential terms here, nothing like an outline of a general constitutional system is even attempted.

The major philosophical distinction between the *Aufbau* and *The Unity of Science* is that Carnap now systematically employs a new philosophical perspective that endorses what he calls the "formal mode of speech" rather than the "material mode of speech." The formal mode of speech issues in sentences about language, whereas the material mode issues in sentences either about objects (events, processes) in the world or apparently about such things. Thus, an epistemological example of the move to the formal mode of speech is the following. The *Aufbau* frequently employs the material mode of speech in epistemology: Carnap sought there to define the concepts of science in terms of subjective experience. Subjective experience is a process in the empirical world. Carnap now expresses his epistemology wholly in the formal mode of speech. Carnap would now say something like: "The terms of a physicalist language must be defined in terms of a language of primitive experience." (A language of individual experience is, as is well known, called a "protocol language" by Carnap at this time.) The topic of discussion in epistemology for Carnap in 1932, then, is precisely the relation between the physicalist language and the protocol language, conceived as a language of sensation.[7]

The chief similarity between *The Unity of Science* and the *Aufbau* is the shared thesis that the physicalist language is both intersubjective and universal. In *The Unity of Science* the physicalist language is conceived along the lines of the language implicit in the construction of the world of physics in the *Aufbau*. It is a pure coordinate language, that is, a language in which a singular sentence is an equation that expresses the value of a function at a coordinate point. For example, "$m(3,5,8,45) = 12$" might be a singular sentence which states that the mass of the object found at space-time point $\langle 3,5,8,45 \rangle$ (in some coordinate system) has the value 12 kilograms. Similarly, the general sentences in the language express functional relations among the physical quantities; the famous Newtonian equation expressing the relation of force, mass, acceleration, "$F = ma$," is such a sentence. This mathematized language for science is, according to Carnap, intersubjective; we all can understand, and, in principle, even come to agree about the truth or falsity of, its sentences. He also claims it is universal, in the sense that any state of affairs expressible in any language can be expressed in it.

The hard case for the claim of universality comes in the relation between the protocol language of an individual and the physicalist language. In *The Unity of Science* the protocol language is conceived along the lines of the language of the autopsychological world of the *Aufbau*. One role of the protocol language is that it provides the language of the verification of claims in any language. (That is, the verification of, for example, a sentence in the physicalist language is achieved only through inferential relations to the protocol language.) But Carnap

---

[7] Each agent has her own protocol language that refers to her own experience. Nevertheless, given our cognitive similarities, there are certain formal analogies among the protocol languages. Thus, I shall follow Carnap, in sometimes clearly distinguishing among the private protocol languages and sometimes speaking of "the protocol language," in the hope that the context will make clear whether I am talking about the collection of protocol languages or about a single one. The relation of the various protocol languages to one another will be discussed later.

is not much concerned about the details of this and presents a rather Duhemian line on how it is to work (Unity, p. 49):

> Protocol statements can be deduced by applying the rules of inference to sufficiently extensive sets of singular statements (in the language of the scientific system) taken in conjunction with laws of nature . . . Scientific statements are not, in the strict sense, "verified" by this process. In establishing the scientific system there is therefore an element of convention, i.e. the form of the system is never completely settled by experience and is always partially determined by conventions.

Carnap's principal interest is not in this part of the story, however. He is much more interested in the question of the extent to which the protocol language can be translated into the physicalist language. This brings with it the larger issue of the role of subjective, private protocols within an intersubjective science.

Before passing to a closer examination of this matter, let us note some of the advantages of Carnap's switch to the formal mode of speech. One important advantage to casting the discussion wholly in linguistic terms is that the antimetaphysical stance is substantially simplified. In the *Aufbau*, Carnap had devoted considerable energy to the discussion of whether metaphysical notions such as 'essence' or 'reality' could be constituted in the epistemological system. Carnap can now take a more direct route toward the rejection of metaphysics. As putative *philosophical* claims about the essences and reality of things, metaphysical claims must be translatable into the formal mode of speech. Philosophy is about language, and language alone. But Carnap sees no possibility that metaphysical claims such as the claim that "numbers are essentially constructs of the human mind" or that "the natural numbers, but not the rational numbers, really exist" can be recast in linguistic terms. Metaphysical claims can, in this manner, be shown to lie outside of logic and, hence, outside of philosophy in general. Carnap's linguistic understanding of logical philosophy leads to a more compelling rejection of a self-proclaimed anti-empirical metaphysics. Similarly, the move to the formal mode of speech allows us to see more clearly that notions such as 'logical definability,' 'deducibility,' and the like are those that fall within the purview of an epistemology of empirical knowledge. The formal mode of speech itself heralds the distinction between a psychological and a philosophical (i.e., logical) concern with knowledge. This also allows us to see that a thesis such as the unity of science is not a metaphysical dogma resting ultimately on the idea that "everything is physical." It is not an ontological thesis at all – there are no significant ontological theses for Carnap – but simply a thesis about the representational capacity of the physicalist language.

Carnap's discussion of the individual protocol languages and their relation to the physicalist language still carries with it a concern to show how science reaches beyond the subjective to the objective. Thus, his epistemological view again combines the logical perspective we have been discussing with a concern about experience that fits uncomfortably between empirical psychology and a more traditional transcendental epistemology or transcendental psychology. The protocol languages are meant to capture the given in experience in its given form. Thus, Carnap claims that there is a fact of the matter, though not a settled fact at the time, about how the protocol languages are structured (cf. Unity, p. 45). We have seen that Carnap's account of the recollection of similarity relation in the *Aufbau* was based on material investigations drawing from the findings of Gestalt psychology. Although he does not engage in similar deliberations in *The Unity of Science,* his view that the structure of the protocol languages can be settled by future research still indicates a role for psychology in specifying the starting point of epistemology.

As a language that presents the given in experience for an agent, a protocol language is subjective. In *The Unity of Science* Carnap argues that there are three senses in which a protocol language is subjective. First, each agent has her own protocol language. Second, each protocol language is a distinct language from the physicalist language – each protocol language stands outside of the language of science. Third, after physicalizing, the protocol languages can be shown to be disjoint sub-languages of the physicalist language. No two protocol languages ever speak of the same things, therefore. Thus, Carnap writes (Unity, p. 88): "The protocol language is a sub-language of the physicalist language. The statement previously made . . . that the protocol languages of various persons are mutually exclusive, is still true in a certain definite sense: they are, respectively, non-overlapping sub-sections of the physicalist language."

Significant for the translatability of the protocol languages into the physicalist language is the fact that each agent can discover inferential connections between the physicalist language and his own protocol language. This relies on what Carnap calls a "contingent fact" that any given agent's protocols have certain ordinal properties that allow their qualitative determinations to be expressed as single-valued functions of physical quantity determinations. Of this contingent fact, Carnap writes (Unity, pp. 6of.):

Epistemology between logic and science

[An agent] can discover which physical determination (or class of physical determinations) corresponds to a definite qualitative determination of his protocol language . . . That the determinations of this kind are theoretically always possible is due to the fortunate circumstance (an empirical fact, not at all necessary in the logical sense) that the protocol has certain ordinal properties. This emerges in the fact of the successful construction of the physical language in such a fashion that qualitative determinations in the protocol language are single-valued functions of the numerical distribution of coefficients of physical states.

In other words, certain ordinal properties among protocol sentences provide the occasion for the construction of numerical quantities. The functional relations of those quantities allow the deduction of qualitative sentences of the protocol language. This is very much the view Carnap was putting forward as early as *Physikalische Begriffsbildung*. Carnap now stresses that it is simply a matter of fact about us that our protocol languages and the protocols we actually endorse have the right structure for this process to go forward.

This type of mapping from the physicalist language into a protocol language is, however, independent of the agent. That is, the ordinal properties of the protocol language necessary for the coordination of the physicalist language and the protocol language are identical for all of us. Carnap claims that this is also simply an empirical matter of fact (Unity, pp. 64f.):

The determined value of a physical magnitude in any concrete case is independent not only of the particular sensory field used but also the choice of the experimenter. In this we have again a fortunate but contingent fact, viz. the existence of a certain structural correspondence between the protocols of the various experimenters . . . Physical determinations are valid inter-subjectively.

This structural correspondence between the experience of various agents is what Carnap has been stressing throughout his work on the objectivity of science. What is new here again is the willingness to say without hesitation that this is simply an empirical matter of fact.

In *The Unity of Science,* Carnap draws the obvious conclusion from these considerations about the relation of the protocol languages to the physicalist language. There are two contingent psychological facts about human experience that ground the very possibility of intersubjective science (Unity, p. 65):

It may be noticed however that these facts, though of an empirical nature, are of far wider range than single empirical facts or even specific natural laws. We are concerned here with a perfectly general structural property of experience which is the basis of the possibility of Intersensory Physics and Intersubjective Physics.

But this is perilously close to nonsense. Carnap is now saying that two empirical facts ground the possibility of objective science. Consider the nature of this claim when I state it in the favored formal mode of speech: The possibility of science considered as a system of intersubjectively valid sentences in the physicalist language depends upon the contingent truth of two sentences stated in that language. These two facts count as candidates for factual status only by being statable in the physicalist language: To be factual is to be objectively expressible and true. It is hard to see how the very possibility of the physicalist language could depend on these two truths, therefore. The whole question as to their truth can arise only after they are couched in the language in question. But it is claimed that their truth is not exhibited by or deducible from the structure of the language itself. Carnap is claiming that the ultimate preconditions of the possibility of empirical truth in general are themselves simply empirical truths. This is not a defendable position, since it presupposes a perspective on empirical truth (i.e., that we can determine it for the very preconditions themselves) which it, in the same breath, sets forward as the topic of epistemological enquiry only after the preconditions have been granted. If the question of epistemology is "What are the preconditions of the possibility of objective, empirical truth?" then the answer cannot simply cite such truths.[8]

Once again Carnap's epistemology finds itself uneasily addressing three general fields. First, he continues to hold out the idea that epistemology is a discipline that is to answer the generally Kantian question about how objective empirical knowledge is possible. His answer continues to stress formal facts about experience, now considered as facts about the protocol languages. Second, epistemology is itself a logical discipline. This allows a place for a continuing epistemological project after the rejection of metaphysics. Third, the structure of experience is a structure that is empirically known only through psychological research.

The Kantian nature of Carnap's problem lends support to his claim that epistemology can be a formal discipline. If objectifying structure is logical structure, then presumably epistemology can fall in as a branch

---

8 I am not saying that naturalized epistemology is impossible. I am claiming that no naturalized epistemology can also claim to be answering Kantian questions about the preconditions of the possibility of objective experience.

of metalogic dealing with empirical languages. But his Kantian question cannot be given an empirical answer. Thus, the first and third aspects of the situation in *The Unity of Science* show continuing tensions. No answer to the general question about the possibility of empirical matters of fact can cite particular empirical matters of fact. Kantian epistemology simply cannot be naturalized in this way. If there is a genuine question being raised about the possibility of knowledge, the very question requires a perspective that abstracts from and investigates the possibility of empirical matters of fact. Again, Carnap's best hope is that formal logic provides this perspective.

Alternatively, if we can simply cite empirical matters of fact as answers to epistemological questions, then any and all motivation for Carnap's logical version of epistemology is lacking. If these questions allow empirical answers, they are empirical questions. One is tempted to say that in this case, Carnap's use of formal logic to "reconstruct" the sciences in a rational and rigorous fashion amounts to no more than make-believe. Why not, one wants to ask, simply settle for psychology?[9]

Carnap's talk of the logical structure of experience or the logical structure of the protocol languages can be seen, therefore, to have been ambiguous from the start. Throughout the work from the 1928 project to that of 1932, Carnap has been trying to combine the logical, the epistemological, and the psychological. The structure of experience is conceived of as a logical structure, and hence the philosopher can and must use the tools of modern logic. But this structure is also meant to provide the key to the answer to a general epistemological question about the possibility of objective knowledge. Thus, the structure of experience continues to play the role of the methodological *a priori* in neo-Kantianism. Finally, it is meant to be psychological structure and to be uncovered in the researches of psychology. Thus, we have a picture in which a simple matter of fact about the structure of human experience allows the formal reconstruction of all of science, which in turn exhibits the objectivity of that science. This is an intolerably ambiguous view of the relations among these disciplines.

Something must change from this view of the official project of epistemology if Carnap's philosophy of empirical knowledge is not to descend into a morass of confusion. What does change is the framing of the epistemological program itself. By 1934, Carnap no longer expresses the point of the business of epistemology as a movement from subjective

---

9 This question was, of course, asked by Quine (1969).

experience to objective knowledge. By 1935, Carnap urges that the project of epistemology be given up entirely and be replaced by a new project that he calls "the logical syntax of scientific language" or simply "the logic of science."

This movement is foreshadowed in *The Unity of Science* itself. Recall that Carnap's official view there is that the formal mode of speech is the only appropriate phraseology for scientific philosophy. If taken seriously, this view already has the consequence that the particular epistemological gloss of the movement from subjective experience to objective knowledge is not available to the scientific philosopher. Consider, for example, the following statement from *The Unity of Science*, the second half of which is a formal "translation" of the material claim given in the first (p. 45):

The simplest statements in the protocol-language refer to the given, and describe directly given experience or phenomena, i.e. the simplest states of which knowledge can be had.

The simplest statements in the protocol-language are the protocol sentences, i.e. statements needing no justification and serving as the foundation for all the remaining statements of science.

It is clear that reference to "the given," "experience," or "the phenomena" occurs only within the material mode of speech. These locutions disappear without remainder in the formal mode. This places the motivational epistemological distinction between objectivity and subjectivity firmly in the same camp as metaphysics generally. It is a misleading way of speaking about the purely logical connections of linguistic systems.

The difficulty must be taken with all seriousness. Carnap's attempt in *The Unity of Science* to speak in the material mode while warning against it indicates a desire on his part for the epistemological account of why we engage in formal reconstruction to take precedence. Just as in the *Aufbau*, Carnap does seek to motivate and explicate the project of the logic of knowledge through a prior epistemological vocabulary of objectivity and subjectivity. But this distinction was the very one that had found no comfortable home in the *Aufbau*. In *The Unity of Science*, he not only struggles with the conceptual confusions involved in the relations among epistemology, logic, and psychology; he also must motivate his view using a distinction that is officially unsayable.

The escape route is clear. If the epistemological story is unsayable, we should simply drop the desire to say it. The formal project for the reconstruction of science in logically precise languages can go forward, but we simply drop the epistemological motivation for the project. This requires that we stop reading claims like the formal mode claim quoted earlier (from Unity, p. 45) as true *by virtue of* the facts stated in the material mode claim. There is no notion of the facts in virtue of which such formal claims are true. Epistemology, or its residuum in the logic of science, is not a discipline dealing with the factual, certainly not with facts about the relation of facts in general to the intrinsically subjective.

After *The Unity of Science,* Carnap's general view is that the project of the reconstruction of the sciences in formal languages can and should go forward. This project will exhibit the meaning of scientific claims. It will, moreover, explicate how formalization works in the sciences and how formalization provides a tool for the acquisition of knowledge about the world. It will, finally, also bring precisely these virtues into philosophy itself, since this is now conceived as a wholly formal discipline. But this discipline is no longer understood as attempting to exhibit or discuss the movement from subjective experience to objective knowledge. There is no meaningful notion of the subjective for the epistemologist, any more than for any other scientist, that allows such a story to be told.

Throughout Carnap's early career, just such a story was the entire business of epistemology. Having decided that no such story could possibly make sense, by 1935 Carnap urges upon his fellow scientific philosophers that epistemology is an intrinsically confused discipline. In the end, he cannot succeed in finding a place for an epistemology separate from metaphysics, logic, and psychology. Metaphysics is rejected; psychology is left to the psychologists. What is left to the philosopher is the logic of science.[10]

---

10 This is urged, for example, in Carnap 1936, discussed in Chapter Nine of the present volume.

CHAPTER NINE

After objectivity: Logical empiricism as philosophy of science

I ENDED Chapter Eight with remarks about the development of Carnap's thought, especially his rejection of epistemology. I shall end our consideration of Carnap's early philosophy of empirical knowledge by examining more closely some of the major themes of this development as it occurred in the 1930s. This will indicate, I hope, that the interpretative framework within which we have been considering Carnap's early work can illuminate further developments as well. At the close, I shall indicate that from Carnap's point of view there can be no empiricism without dogmas, if we insist on using this term to characterize a view that claims methodological ineliminability of the analytic–synthetic distinction. To disagree with Carnap on this matter is to disagree with him about what empiricism is or could be.

FROM EPISTEMOLOGY TO THE LOGIC OF SCIENCE

In the mid-1930s Carnap rejected epistemology in no uncertain terms. This is most explicit in an address presented at the 1935 "Congress for the Unity of Science," in Paris, entitled "Von Erkenntnistheorie zur Wissenschaftslogik" (From epistemology to the logic of science; hereafter *VEW*). In this essay, Carnap invited his audience to view current developments as a move to a third stage of scientific philosophy. In the first stage, scientific philosophy had rejected metaphysics. This ushered in a "transition from speculative philosophy to epistemology" (VEW, p. 36). The second stage had involved the rejection of the synthetic *a priori* and the consequent adoption of empiricism in epistemology.[1] The third

---

1 It is important to note that for Carnap the rejection of metaphysics preceded the adoption of empiricism. This was true of his own philosophical development, as we have seen. His reconstruction of the history of scientific philosophy here, however, finds no space for the neutrality of the *Aufbau*.

stage is characterized as follows (p. 36): "The task of our current work appears to me to consist in the transition from epistemology to the logic of science. In this, epistemology is not, as were metaphysics and *a priorism* before, completely repudiated, but rather purified and decomposed into its constituent parts." These constituent parts are, on the one hand, psychological and, on the other, logical. Previous work in epistemology, including notably his own, is now taken by Carnap to have confusedly mixed these very different types of concern together. The logical empiricist philosophy of science – the new project that he called "the logical syntax of scientific language," or simply "the logic of science" – resolved these confusions by taking up only the logical questions and assigning the psychological questions to the empirical psychologists. Philosophy of science was best thought of, he argued, as an epistemology purified into the wholly analytic study of the logical relations of scientific language systems.

To understand Carnap's view here, we must search in two directions. First, we need to have a sense of the project of logical syntax in general. Second, we need to understand why the splitting of the logical and psychological questions means the end of epistemology. Nothing like an exhaustive account of the project of logical syntax is possible here.[2] We shall simply scout the main themes as they are relevant to the question of the logic of scientific language. On the second matter, not surprisingly, we shall find that the crucial issue is the impossibility of expressing the project of syntax within the interpretative framework of the movement from the subjective to the objective. With no such framework available, epistemology itself is no longer possible.

Carnap's project in *Die logische Syntax der Sprache* (The logical syntax of language; hereafter *Syntax*) is the fruition of his metalogical turn. In this book (1934, 1937) Carnap seeks to bring the clarity found in the object languages of formal logic into the metalanguages themselves. That is, Carnap sees formal logic as having brought clarity to the languages that it had studied; he seeks to bring that clarity to the languages in which such study is carried out. (An example of Carnap's concern here would be the suspicion that, whereas the language actually employed by Alfred North Whitehead and Bertrand Russell in *Principia*

---

2 Important recent work on the project of *Logical Syntax* includes Creath (1996), Friedman (1988, 1992b), Goldfarb (1996), Goldfarb and Ricketts (1992), Ricketts (1994), Sarkar (1992), and Devidi and Solomon (1995). My perspective on the issues raised by these essays was given a preliminary voice in Richardson (1994).

Mathematica was fairly precisely delimited in the definitions and proofs, the language in which they discussed and explicated that language was imprecise and misleading.) Thus, he presents the point of *Logical Syntax* as an effort (p. xiii) "to develop an exact method for the construction of ... sentences about sentences." A formal syntax language will provide a precise tool for defining important logical notions such as 'logical consequence' or 'analyticity' for the object languages under consideration. These definitions, in turn, will give us the wherewithal to separate those aspects of a given object language that belong to or follow from the rules of the language – the logical aspects of a linguistic framework – from the contentful claims that can be made after the adoption of that framework.

This procedure is crucial for understanding the rational structure of science. It first allows us to see which parts of a language for science present the logical framework that provides the meanings of the terms. Only subsequent to the adoption or construction of such a framework can we investigate the contentful sentences expressible in that framework to see which are in fact supported by the evidence. The evidence itself will be sentences expressed in the language. Thus, on Carnap's view, any question of the justification of (or the rationality of belief in) a sentence requires a linguistic system within which that sentence is couched and that provides the inferential relations requisite to make sense of claims about justification or confirmation. This project requires the project of logical syntax – the mathematics of language – within which the investigation of the logical structure of various object languages goes forward.

Throughout this brief sketch I have been talking about the various "object languages." In *Logical Syntax,* Carnap adopts the famous *principle of tolerance,* a principle that introduces a radical pluralism into logic. The official version of the tolerance principle is as follows (Syntax, p. 51): "It is not our business [in logic] to set up prohibitions, but to arrive at conventions." Although this version does go some distance toward expressing the idea that there is no checking the logic of a language for correctness by matching it against "the logic of the world," it is not very helpful. More to the point is Carnap's gloss on the principle a page later (Syntax, p. 52):

In logic, there are no morals. Everyone is at liberty to build up his own logic, i.e. his own form of language as he wishes. All that is required of him is that, if he wishes to discuss it, he must state his methods clearly, and give syntactical rules instead of philosophical arguments.

After objectivity

The meta-metalogical researches into the logico-mathematical resources of various formal languages and, thus, their suitability as formal syntax languages gives content to the final injunction. The standpoint of a formal syntax language is the standpoint from which the philosopher issues precise syntactical rules rather than philosophical arguments. As such, the standpoint of logical syntax provides an infinite variety of new projects in logic for Carnap's bold antimetaphysical and amoralist logicians (Syntax, p. xv):

> The first attempts to cast the ship of logic off from the *terra firma* of classical forms were certainly bold ones, considered from the historical point of view. But they were hampered by the striving after "correctness." Now, however, that impediment has been overcome, and before us lies the boundless ocean of unlimited possibilities.

There is no notion of correctness that accrues to the logical system of an object language. There is, however, a notion of correctness for the philosophical task of presenting a precise syntactic formulation of such a language. This notion depends on the formal strength of the syntax language within which the definitions are cast.

It should be noted that in this respect the project of logical syntax is stronger than our contemporary notion of syntax. It is stronger in that Carnap (in the mid-1930s) sees syntax as the locus of all the logically interesting notions. Thus, notions that today are viewed as quintessentially semantic, such as logical consequence and analyticity, are syntactic notions for Carnap. For languages of sufficient logical strength, they are *indefinite* syntactic notions and, therefore, not recursively specifiable. But this does not impugn their status as syntactic for Carnap. The crucial point is that in the project of logical syntax notions such as logical consequence are meant to be captured in terms of the rules of formation and transformation of the language (even if these are not recursively specifiable) rather than through more contemporary notions such as truth in a model.[3]

The pluralism implicit in the project of logical syntax finds its first important application in the change from the epistemology of *The Unity of Science* to the logic of scientific language of Carnap's (1932) essay "Über Protokolsätze" (On protocol sentences; hereafter *Protocol*). This is one essay in the internecine dispute among Vienna Circle members about the nature and structure of the sentences that form the observa-

---

3 I deliberately gloss over subtle and important interpretative issues in this paragraph. For discussion of them, see the literature cited in the preceding footnote.

tional basis of science, what they called "the protocol sentences." In this response to Otto Neurath's (1932) objections to the account in *The Unity of Science,* Carnap has finally dropped his attempt to express the motivating epistemological point of the relation between the protocol language and the language of science as showing the relation between the subjective and the objective. He severs any intrinsic connection between the structure of the protocol language and the "structure of experience." There are no facts about the structure of experience to which the protocol language is meant to be true. Thus, in Carnap's eyes, the protocol sentence debate is no longer a debate that involves any facts whatsoever. There is no fact about how the protocol language or the system language must look. Rather, it is a matter of proposals for formal languages within which to cast the findings of the sciences and thereby render the question of the confirmational status of scientific claims a genuine question. Thus, Carnap writes (Protocol, p. 457):

Neurath opposes certain features of the view about protocol sentences I advocated in my article on the physicalist language [Unity]. He wants to contrast it with another view according to which protocol sentences are in a different form and are manipulated according to other procedures. My opinion here is that this is a question, not of two mutually inconsistent views, but rather of *two different methods for structuring the language of science, both of which are possible and legitimate.*

There are no material investigations – say, those of a Gestalt psychological nature – that can constrain the possibilities for the structure of the protocol sentences. Carnap, in fact, is most attracted to a generally Popperian view that merely selects, for a given scientific enquiry, a class of sentences of the physicalist language that is to serve as the class of protocol sentences. Of this he writes:

Every concrete sentence of the physicalist language can serve under certain circumstances as a protocol sentence. (Protocol, p. 465)

With this procedure no sentence is an absolute endpoint for reduction. Sentences of all kinds can if necessary be reduced to others. Reduction proceeds at any given time until one arrives at sentences that one acknowledges by decision. Thereby everything takes place in the intersubjective, physicalist language. (Protocol, p. 467)

Since there are no facts to constrain the choice of a protocol language, Carnap's endorsement of this option is not of the form that this is the most correct understanding of the protocol language and its role in the justification of scientific claims. Rather, Carnap can only argue that there are pragmatic advantages to this view. One advantage is that there is no need to specify a separate language or syntactical structure to mark off the protocol sentences. Another is its evident simplicity compared to the baroque account given by Neurath.[4] The most important advantage, however, is the fashion in which it, as it were, exhibits the sense in which there are no facts to which it must be true. That is, Carnap's distinction between a protocol language and the language of science in *The Unity of Science* was meant to reflect the idea that a protocol language is private and subjective whereas the language of science is intersubjective. Since there is no longer any such distinction motivating Carnap's view, there is now nothing to stop the protocol language from simply being part of the language of science.[5]

Carnap expresses the sense in which the movement to the formal mode of speech liberates the philosopher from material considerations about the psychology of experience quite clearly in his Paris address. There he notes that the epistemologist's favored notion, 'the structure of experience,' is an inexpressible pseudoconcept (VEW, p. 39):

> It is not a matter of indifference how we formulate the question [of the theory of knowledge]. For the formulation in the formal mode of speech speaks of sentences and makes us thereby attentive to the circumstance that the question is still not complete, that is, that a statement of which language the question relates to is necessary . . . In contrast to this the contentful formulation, which speaks of "the form of the phenomena," can easily lead to the dangerous error that there is such a thing as an absolute, linguistic-form-independent, final given structure of the phenomena, which one need simply intuit and take up.

Carnap is attempting to make two points here. First, there is no sense to be made of an independent, uniquely philosophical access to a structure of experience that must be identical for all of us if science is to be possible. Thus, Carnap's own richly epistemological notion from the *Aufbau* is infected with the sort of meaninglessness that attaches to metaphysics generally. Second, the psychological structure to experience is simply a subject for science. The reconstructive task must be in place before any psychological theorizing can be fully understood and

---

[4] For a heroic attempt to find some coherence in Neurath's proposal for the structure of protocol sentences, see Uebel (1992b, chap. 11). That any story of the sort Uebel tries to tell is required to make sense of Neurath's proposal is one indication of why Carnap finds the whole attempt to fix a unique form for the protocol sentences misguided.

[5] For recent work on the protocol sentence debate, see Creath (1987), Lewis (1991), Turner (1996), Oberdan (1990, 1993, 1996), Zhai (1990), and, especially, Uebel's (1992b) blockbuster.

checked for justificatory status. Thus, that reconstructive task cannot possibly wait for and rely on an empirical account of the structure of human experience (or the nature of the primitive language we first learn). The independent epistemological notion of experiential structure is nonsense; the empirical notion is beside the point.

TOWARD A LOGICAL POINT OF VIEW

Almost immediately, Carnap's views on protocol sentences were attacked by other members of the Vienna Circle. Moritz Schlick (1934) and Edgar Zilsel (1932), in particular, felt that Carnap had sacrificed empiricism in his flight from absolutism and a "structure of experience." This is quite the reverse of Carnap's own view. Only with his adoption of the syntactic perspective does Carnap fully endorse "logical empiricism" as an appropriate moniker for his view. Internal to his own development, the move to the metalogical perspective severs the last important tie to neo-Kantianism: the epistemological perspective from which he and they explained their philosophical project.

Carnap's logical empiricism is one in which the notion of logic is preeminent, however. Certainly, the syntactic perspective is wider than strict empiricism. Syntactic researches into various languages can go forward independently of any concern with the observability or verifiability of any predicate or sentence of the language. Carnap engages in just such research in *Logical Syntax* itself. There he undertakes a detailed examination of two formal languages, termed "Language I" and "Language II," dealing only with the logico-mathematical resources of these languages. Only such resources are of particular interest to him there, since he is principally interested in these languages as candidates for *syntax languages*, and only mathematical richness matters for that.

But empiricism does not simply drop out of Carnap's picture. In "Testability and Meaning" (hereafter *TM*), published in 1936–7, Carnap argues that commitment to a program such as empiricism is not commitment to a thesis expressed in some language or other. Nor is it a universal constraint on the possibility of well-formed languages. It is, rather, a proposal to use certain languages as the languages into which to cast empirical science (TM, §27):

It seems to me that it is preferable to formulate the principle of empiricism not in the form of an assertion – "all knowledge is empirical" or "all synthetic sentences that we can know are based on (or connected with) experience" or the like – but rather in the form of a proposal or requirement. As empiricists, we

213

require that descriptive predicates are not to be admitted unless they have some connection with possible observations, a connection which has to be characterized in a suitable way.

In empiricist languages, the logical concepts with which logical syntax deals (such as logical consequence, analyticity, and reducibility) map onto and explicate the traditional epistemological notions of empiricism. They do this by standing in a "suitable" connection to experience. What can such a suitable connection look like for Carnap, though?

Carnap's formulation of the proposal or requirement for an empiricist language which I have just quoted is (as usual, in contexts where he talks about rather than implements his ideas) a pseudo–object sentence. A pseudo–object sentence is one that seems to speak of objects or processes in the world (in this case, "possible observations") but is translatable into a sentence in the formal mode of speech (in this case, as we shall see, into one involving "observable predicates"). Thus, the sentence is, strictly speaking, meaningless. The requirement amounts, in practice, to the requirement that the primitive predicates of the language be observable. Observability is, however, not a syntactical (or semantic) predicate; it is a notion taken from "psychology, . . . more precisely, the behavioristic theory of language" (TM, §11).[6] Carnap's rough formulation of this psychological notion is (TM, §11):

> A predicate "P" of a language L is called *observable* for an organism (e.g. a person) N, if, for suitable arguments, e.g. "b," N is able under suitable circumstances to come to a decision with the help of a few observations about a full sentence, say, "P(b)" or "-P(b)" of such a high degree that he will either accept or reject "P(b)" . . . This [psychological] explanation is necessarily vague. There is no sharp line between observable and non-observable predicates.

The notion of 'observable predicate' gives the starting point for confirmation – the basic sentences of these predicates are accepted independently of the acceptance of any other sentences. The concept of 'confirmation' in empiricist languages is, then, defined on the basis of observability. A sentence is "confirmable" if it stands in the relation of reducibility of confirmation to the class of observable predicates (TM,

---

6 "Testability and Meaning" was written during the period in which Carnap was moving from the syntactic to the semantic account of analyticity and linguistic frameworks. Thus, it is somewhat different from the earlier work, but not in ways that substantially modify my story. There are, of course, many issues around the movement to semantics that go beyond this brief sketch of Carnap's philosophy of science. See especially Coffa (1991), Creath (1991b), Oberdan (1993) and Ricketts (1996).

§11). Thus, the degree of confirmation of an observation sentence is simply assigned zero if it is rejected or one if it is accepted. In this manner, we are provided with a stock of basic observation predicates and a base clause for a recursive definition of degree of confirmation, and these feed into the general logical machinery of the language (as explicated in the syntax [or meta-] language). This allows procedures such as the introduction of new predicates on the basis of certain rules from the primitive ones and the assignment of confirmation values to higher-level sentences given the acceptance of particular observation sentences.

It may seem that this reveals a continuing mixing of the empirical and the psychological in Carnap's now officially austerely formal logic of science. The ability to recommend empiricist languages does require the availability of observable predicates. Epistemological vocabulary within empiricist languages is, moreover, defined on the basis of this psychological notion of observability. Does this not confute Carnap's strict division between the logical and the psychological? Does it not, in addition, take us beyond what can be said in Carnap's formal mode of speech?

To begin with the last question, it does take us beyond the formal mode of speech in a particular manner. 'Observability' is not a syntactical or logical notion; no research into the logic of a language reveals the observability of its predicates. It is, however, a linguistic notion that is true (or not) of predicates of a language but not of experience, physical objects, or any other thing in the world. This is just to repeat in different terms what was said before: Empiricism requires a way of culling the logically possible languages and recommending a certain subclass as the languages within which to reconstruct science. Empiricism does require an empirical, psychological component and does take us beyond the purely formal work that a pure logical syntax provides. But, Carnap's pragmatic recommendation of such empiricist languages is not a thesis of first philosophy. Nor is it an empirical or logical thesis. It is a pragmatic account of how one might do philosophy in an empiricist fashion. In this sense, it is a proposal for use of the term "empiricist" in a metalanguage for philosophy of science. Schlick asked how, specifically, one could be an empiricist on Carnap's view, and Carnap provided an answer: Find out from the psychologists which are the observable predicates, and base your language on these. (Do not, however, seek a philosophical explanation of how certain predicates achieve this status.) Moreover, the notion of observability seems very sensitive to local changes in expert knowledge, so "vacuum tube" may well be an observation predicate for a class of physicists. This means that we can reconstruct their language using this predicate as a primitive; for a larger class, the predicate must be defined. The constraints here are minimal and rely not on some general but private "structure of experience" but on empirical facts about speech communities.

Moveover, from the point of view of the logic of science, two things must be noted. First, the definition of 'confirmation' on the basis of observability requires that a structure for the system language be already in place. Psychology nominates a certain class of predicates as observable. These are slotted into a language within which logical relations are well defined. This allows the metalogical definition of the crucial notion of 'degree of confirmation.' But degree of confirmation is not defined on the basis of the concept of observability;[7] rather it is given a base clause that *refers to* the class of the observable predicates. These are the ones that yield primitive sentences that get either zero or one as degree of confirmation, depending on whether they are rejected or accepted. There is no epistemological story about how such acceptance or rejection occurs nor, therefore, any epistemological worry about the "incorrect" acceptance of such sentences.

Finally, although epistemology takes up this notion of 'observable predicate' for the empiricist, this is a far cry from Carnap's earlier reliance on a structure of experience. In particular, in the earlier epistemological story, the idea that knowledge depends on experience was understood entirely differently. On the account of the *Aufbau* it was understood as the claim that the epistemically primitive vocabulary was autopsychological, that is, was about private, subjective experience. Thus, we dealt at first with sentences such as "Otto perceives a red dot in the middle of his visual field" or even "Recollection of similarity holds between elementary experiences 4 and 27." The question was how to bootstrap out of such private languages into the intersubjective world of science. There is now no such concern. The basic sentences involving observable predicates are not subjective or private. Observation predicates simply form a subclass of the class of physicalist predicates of the common physicalist language. As Carnap puts it, observable predicates are not perception terms (TM, §11). From the point of view that sees the objective–subjective distinction as giving shape to epistemology, Carnap's new project is not epistemology at all. The logic of science begins on the objective side of the divide.

---

7 'Degree of confirmation' is the more general concept that is used in defining 'confirmation' for Carnap. Adding the base clause via observable predicates changes degree of confirmation into confirmation *simpliciter* in empiricist languages.

Carnap's account of empiricism as a practical recommendation of some from among the logically possible languages to serve as the languages for the reconstruction of science has a further consequence. It indicates that the project of logical syntax itself is not motivated by a preeminent philosophical commitment to empiricism. Some have claimed that Carnap's attempt to show that logico-mathematical structure is analytic, in *Logical Syntax,* is motivated by the desire to demonstrate that this structure is independent of empirical matters of fact. He does this, it is argued, by attempting to show that mathematical truths say nothing about the world. That is, without a commitment to empiricism, the whole project of demonstrating logic to be analytic is without motivation.[8]

That is not Carnap's view. For Carnap, every language, whether it is an empiricist language or not, has an analytic–synthetic distinction according to which the mathematical portions of the language are analytic. This is because there must be a structure inherent in any language that provides the framework within which that language can first express any matters of fact. Indeed, the whole notion of 'matter of fact' is internal to a logico-linguistic framework for Carnap. Thus, he is not motivated by the desire to show that logic is independent of "the facts," but rather to show that but for a prior specification of a logical structure the very notion of 'the facts' is without sense. Thus, for example, even a robustly Platonist metaphysical language requires a logical structure that delimits what can be said in that language and, hence, what counts as a potential fact from the point of view of that language.

ONE DOGMA OF THE LOGIC OF SCIENCE

If what has been said is correct, then in Carnap's hands the analytic–synthetic distinction is not a dogma of empiricism. If it is a dogma at all, it is a dogma of the logic of science. As such, the distinction acquires a degree of centrality to Carnap's general project that outstrips even what Quine claimed of it. A brief account of what I take to be Quine's ultimate misunderstanding of Carnap's philosophical project may, therefore, be useful. It will allow us to raise the final and most important question: What is the logic of science meant to show about science and about philosophy?

---

8 I take this to be the view of Isaacson (1992) and Putnam (1983). My response is largely derivative of Ricketts's (1994) meditation on Putnam's account.

Quine's attacks on the analytic–synthetic distinction, as presented in works such as "Two Dogmas of Empiricism" (1953/1961) and "Carnap and Logical Truth" (1963), are quite familiar, so we shall review them only briefly.[9] There are three principal strands to the argument. First, Quine argues that informal accounts of analyticity in terms of (for example) convention, definition, synonymy, and semantic rules are unexplanatory. Such accounts either trade in incoherencies (such as the notion of 'truth by convention') or give us no better understanding of what we are after than a primitive notion of 'analyticity' by itself. For example, 'synonymy' for terms is as obscure as 'analyticity' for sentences, so appeal to the former in explicating the later leaves explanation unbegun. Second, he argues that to give a technical definition of "analyticity-in-L" for some formal language L is pointless independently of some further grasp of what we are defining. In particular, such a definition may yield a list of sentences of L under the rubric "analytic sentences of L," but this tells us no more than that there is a definition that yields this list of sentences. Nothing about meaning or analyticity is elucidated by such metalogical techniques. Finally, he asks for the epistemological cash value of the notion of 'analyticity.' Carnap insists on this distinction in order to reconstruct and adjudicate epistemic disputes. But what are the means by which we can ascribe analyticity to particular utterances of the disputants, and what is gained in so doing? Quine argues that Carnap's technical work never provides a *criterion* of analyticity that we can apply to actual agents engaged in actual disputes about what to believe. The imposition of such a distinction upon such disputes seems, therefore, epistemologically useless. Carnap's vaunted distinction between change of language for pragmatic reasons and change of beliefs expressed within that language is a philosophical artifact that does no epistemological work. As epistemologists, it is better simply to see how in fact we get on without it.

Quine's criticisms of Carnap have been taken in many quarters to be devastating. Moreover, they have numerous important consequences. The rejection of the analytic–synthetic distinction leads to Quine's characteristically skeptical philosophy of language. This is not our major area of interest, however, so we shall leave that aside. More impor-

---

9 The secondary literature on the analytic–synthetic debate is too copious to cite; see the literature cited by Ricketts (1982) and Creath (1991a, introduction) for a start down the endless road. My interpretation of Quine has been guided mainly by Ricketts (1982), Solomon (1989), and Isaacson (1992). I have no reason to believe that any of them would endorse the claims of this section.

tant for thinking about Carnap is that for Quine the rejection of the analytic–synthetic distinction leads immediately to naturalism in philosophy of science and epistemology. For him, this is a very simple argumentative move. Quine takes it that synthetic *a priori* knowledge was rejected long ago. The rejection of analyticity is, therefore, the rejection of the last putative candidate for *a priori* knowledge. If there is no *a priori* knowledge, then all knowledge-producing fields are on the same footing as empirical science. Notably, these fields include mathematics and philosophy. From this it follows that philosophers have no methods distinct from those of empirical science, no theses that are more certain than those of empirical science, and therefore ought to have no scruples about using whatever material from empirical science may be relevant to their concerns. In the theory of knowledge, this means the importation of techniques and results from psychology and, perhaps, sociology.[10]

One philosopher who thought Quine's criticisms were less than absolutely compelling was Carnap himself. By the time of his response to Quine in "Replies and Systematic Expositions" (hereafter, *Replies*), 1963, Carnap goes beyond simply claiming that Quine had not refuted his views. In his response, Carnap claims that Quine basically relies on the analytic–synthetic distinction himself. Thus, in a rare instance of irony, Carnap responds in a tone of amused exasperation.

Consider this exchange from two of the essays. First, here are some relevant passages from Quine's essay "Carnap and Logical Truth" (1963, pp. 389–90):

> Now if we try to warp the linguistic doctrine of logical truth around into something like an experimental thesis, perhaps a first approximation will run thus: Deductively irresoluble disagreement as to a logical truth is evidence of deviation in usage (or meanings) of words. Already the obviousness (or potential obviousness) of elementary logic can be seen to present an insuperable obstacle to our assigning any experimental meaning to the linguistic doctrine of elementary logical truth ... For, that theory seems to imply nothing that is not already implied by the fact that elementary logic is obvious or can be resolved into obvious steps. I have been using the vaguely psychological word "obvious" non-technically, assigning it no explanatory value. My suggestion is merely that the linguistic doctrine of elementary logical truth likewise leaves explanation unbegun. I do not suggest that the linguistic doctrine is false and

---

10 Quine (1969) famously endorses the idea that naturalism leads to the view that epistemology is a branch of psychology. Those of a more social bent, such as Longino (1990) or Bloor (1974), have a more sociological view.

that some doctrine of ultimate and inexplicable insight into the obvious traits of reality is true, but only that there is no real difference between these two pseudo-doctrines.

Here is Carnap's answer to this argument (Replies, p. 922):

I believe that the distinction between analytic and synthetic statements, expressed in whatever terms, is indispensable for methodological and philosophical discussions. This is also indicated by the fact that the distinction is made by a large majority of philosophers, including some who do not explicitly acknowledge the distinction in these terms or even reject it. As an example, let me refer to a philosopher whose work I esteem highly, although I cannot agree in all points with his views. The philosopher once undertook to destroy a certain doctrine, propounded by some other philosophers. He did not mean to assert that the doctrine was false; presumably he regarded it as true. But his criticism concerned its particular kind of truth, namely that the truth of the doctrine was of the analytic kind. To be sure, he didn't use the word "analytic," which he did not seem to like very much. Instead, he used other expressions which, nonetheless, clearly seem to have essentially the same meaning as "analytic." What he showed was that various attempts to assign an experimental, empirical meaning to this doctrine remained without success. Finally he came to the conclusion that the doctrine, even though not false, is "empty" and "without experimental significance."

In passages such as this, Carnap goes a long way toward granting almost everything Quine says in his criticism of Carnap's views. The one thing he does not grant is the status of Quine's claims as *criticisms*. Here, for example, Carnap basically endorses the view that the claim that analytic sentences are true by virtue of the formal structure of the language in which they are analytic is unexplanatory. This account is itself an analytic sentence of the metalanguage and, as such, it does and must leave explanation unbegun. The linguistic doctrine of logical truth is not meant to explain that by virtue of which analytic truths are analytic; it is meant to gesture at how one goes about delimiting the range of analytic truths for a formal language in one's logical work.

There are other aspects to Carnap's puzzled response to Quine also. In his response to Quine's challenge to come up with a general criterion or definition of analyticity across languages, Carnap, especially in *Quine on Analyticity* (published posthumously in 1991; hereafter *QOA*) (pp. 430–1), divides the issue into two possibilities. On the one hand, Quine might be asking for a general definition of analyticity in L for an arbitrary *formal* language, L. Carnap's response is that this is an utterly unreasonable thing to ask him to do. No such definition is possible, and

One dogma of the logic of science

Quine knows that. The principal problem is that any definition of analyticity for a given formal language, L, must be cast in a metalanguage strong enough to contain a truth definition for L. But there is no language "strong enough" to contain the truth definitions for every formalized language, as the limitative results of Tarski and Gödel make clear. On the other hand, Quine may be asking for a general informal statement about what is being sought in a definition of analyticity. Here Carnap simply responds that the type of characterization that Quine rejects in "Two Dogmas" does nicely. His response to Quine's circularity worries is to claim that because such characterizations are, after all, informal, one should not expect them to bear any philosophical weight. Rather, they present a vague notion that is given an explicit meaning for a language in the formal definition of analyticity for that language.

This dialogue is frustrating. Quine asks Carnap for some help in understanding what he (Carnap) is up to. Carnap responds by making philosophical moves that are the very ones that Quine claims to find opaque. Quine wants something other than what Carnap can offer. However frustrating the dialogue may be for them and us, it does indicate a fundamental interpretative point, though. At the end of the day, Quine has an understanding of what Carnap can and must be doing that allows Quine to raise certain questions. Carnap, on the other hand, has a different understanding of what he can and must be doing, and from the Carnapian perspective Quine's questions quite literally make no sense. The two men have fundamental philosophical differences that cannot be overcome. In particular, they have deep differences over the relative priority of justificatory and logical questions in philosophy.

To see this we must investigate Quine's understanding of Carnap's project a bit more closely. For Quine, the linguistic doctrine of logical truth was presented in response to a pressing *epistemological* difficulty (Quine 1963, p. 386):

What now of the empiricist who would grant certainty to logic, and to the whole of mathematics, and yet would make a clean sweep of other non-empirical theories under the name metaphysics? The Viennese solution to this nice problem was predicated on language. Metaphysics was meaningless through misuse of language; logic was certain through tautologous use of language.

Thus Quine calls the linguistic doctrine of logical truth an "epistemological doctrine" and claims it was meant to answer the question "How is logical certainty possible?" As an epistemological doctrine, the linguistic doctrine of logical truth must answer to certain constraints that, for example, a model theoretic delimitation of the truths of first-order predicate calculus (which Quine accepts) does not. This latter specification of the class of logical truths (for a certain language) does not even raise, let alone pretend to answer, questions about our knowledge of logical truth or about logic's peculiar sort of certainty.

Thus, Quine's view is that Carnap's doctrine must discharge certain epistemological obligations. We must have some tie between the linguistic doctrine of logical truth and epistemological notions such as 'justification.' Fortunately, Quine sees just such a connection in the verifiability account of meaning, as presented in the work of Carnap and others. Thus, we can use the verification criterion in tandem with the linguistic doctrine of logical truth and get out the claim that analytic truths are those that are verified come what may. It is at this point that Duhem's underdetermination thesis gains its philosophical import. If any relatively high-level theoretical claim can be maintained "come what may," then the linguistic doctrine of logical truth has misfired; it has not captured the appropriate class of sentences for any empirical language.

It is important to note the terms in which Quine casts the point of the analytic–synthetic distinction. Analyticity is meant to answer an epistemological question and to confer certainty. This gets explicated via the connection between truth by virtue of meaning and confirmation come what may. For Quine, then, what is at stake is a matter of epistemology, and epistemology is concerned with confirmation, verification, or justification. Quine's point of view is summed up in a statement with which he began a recent essay (Quine 1993, p. 107): "The classical question of epistemology was handed down to us through a succession of British empiricists." As we have noted, Quine always considers Carnap as, philosophically, following in the tradition of the British empiricists.

But he was not. Whereas Quine thinks he is asking questions that Carnap must answer because they share a common empiricist philosophical framework, Carnap sees Quine as making incoherent philosophical demands. Quine takes as fundamental the very unexplicated epistemological vocabulary that Carnap seeks to do without. For example, we see Carnap objecting early on (Replies, p. 921): "I agree that 'any statement can be held true come what may.' But the concept of analytic statement that I take as an explicandum is not adequately characterized as 'held true come what may.'" This very notion of being held true come what may indicates that logical sentences are considered as subject to verification in just the same way as other sentences but differ only in doing maximally well in their degree of verification. This is not Carnap's view at all.

Throughout his entire career, Carnap never thought that any interesting epistemological questions could be asked about logic. To say that a particular sentence is "analytic" is not to say that it gets highest marks on an antecedently understandable question of confirmation; rather, it is to say that the sentence is one of the principles that first present the framework within which *all* questions, including epistemological ones, first make sense. Indeed, since the *Aufbau* itself, as we have seen, Carnap's major project was to cash out epistemological vocabulary, such as "objective" and "degree of confirmation," in purely logical terms. By the time he comes to announce the project of the logic of science, this means that epistemological questions are themselves relative to a logically precise language. Moreover, specification of the analytic sentences is part of thus logically specifying a language.

This privileged status for logic and the analytic should not be thought of in terms of the certainty of logical truth. This gloss reintroduces precisely what must be avoided – an exterior, epistemological flavor to the point. For Carnap, logic does not play this role in providing the framework for enquiry by virtue of being certain. Rather, the only epistemologically interesting thing to say about logic is simply that it does play this role. This is the ultimate way in which the neo-Kantian project of a logic of objective knowledge finds lasting expression in Carnap's thought.

The point for the analyticity debate is, then, this. For Carnap, there is no deeper level of description to which any definition of analyticity for a language must answer. There is no external, antecedent, language-transcendent epistemological perspective from which the point of the analytic–synthetic distinction can or must be understood. The logical description of a linguistic system is just the deepest level of description available, and the definition of analyticity is part of such a description.

We can illustrate this by considering the verification theory of meaning. Quine seems to be on firm ground here, since he seems to share with Carnap a commitment to verificationism. In fact, however, this impression is wholly misleading. Carnap does not seek to explicate analyticity in terms of meaning, and meaning in terms of verification; he has no epistemic theory of meaning or logic. Rather, Carnap subscribes to a logical theory of meaning and a logical theory of verification. Consider this statement from his "Überwindung der Metaphysik durch logische Analyse der Sprache" (Elimination of metaphysics through the logical analysis of language; hereafter *Elimination*) (§1):

> In what, then, does the *meaning of a word* consist? . . . First, the *syntax* of the word must be fixed, i.e. the mode of its occurrence in the simplest sentence in which it is capable of occurring; we call this sentence form its *elementary sentence* . . . Second, for an elementary sentence [S] containing the word an answer must be given to the following question, which can be formulated various ways:
>
> (1) What sentences is S *deducible* from, and what sentences are deducible from S?
> (2) Under what circumstances is S supposed to be true, and under what conditions false?
> (3) How is S to be *verified*?
> (4) What is the *meaning* of S?
>
> (1) is the correct [metalogical] formulation; (2) accords with the phraseology of logic; (3) with the phraseology of the theory of knowledge; (4) with that of philosophy (phenomenology).

If we take Carnap at his word here, we can see that no antecedent epistemological vocabulary is imported into his account of logical deducibility and, hence, meaning relations. He may be a verificationist in the weak sense that he is happy to analyze both meaning and verification in terms of the same logical relations, but this is a symmetric relation, and logical deducibility does all the philosophical work.

We can now see clearly what Carnap finds so misleading about talk such as "confirmed come what may" in an account of analyticity. On Carnap's view, a confirmation theory is given only subsequent to and relative to a linguistic framework. Given a linguistic framework, we can define a confirmation theory for it. But the specification of the linguistic framework and, thus, of the analytic sentences must come first. After this is done, the confirmation theory can be defined, and it is a constraint on such a theory that the logical and analytic sentences get the highest values of confirmation. So, internal to a complete framework and confirmation theory, the analytic sentences are indeed "confirmed come what may," but the specification of the analytic sentences precedes the confirmation theory entirely.[11]

---

11 Indeed, we have already noted that "the facts" are dependent on the linguistic framework for Carnap. Thus, 'what may come' is not a universal or antecedently understandable notion for him, but only one with a determinate meaning within a linguistic framework.

THE POINT OF THE LOGIC OF SCIENCE

What, then, is the point of the analytic–synthetic distinction for Carnap? Carnap's phrase, in his reply to Quine that I quoted in the preceding section of the present chapter, "indispensable for methodological and philosophical discussions," provides the key to this issue. The project from which Carnap takes his perspective – the generally neo-Kantian and conventionalist project – trains its eyes on methodological issues in the exact sciences as the locus of the most significant lessons for reflection on the nature and scope of knowledge. Moreover, this project connects such methodological issues to questions of logical form.

Carnap's methodological concerns induce him to insist on a sharp distinction among several types of questions. We may, for example, ask after the confirmational status of a theory such as the special theory of relativity. We may ask, moreover, after the logical relation of certain terms, such as "mass" and "force," within a given theory. We may also ask after the logical relations that obtain between two theories. Questions of confirmation deal with the connections between the theoretical language of the theory and the protocol language (which may contain quite a bit of the theoretical language). The other questions have to do with the logical structures of the theoretical languages themselves. Carnap insists that any philosophy of knowledge that cannot make a distinction between narrowly confirmational and more widely construed logical questions simply does not illuminate the structure of science. Any philosophy of science that can make such a distinction has implicit in it some notion that does the work of the notion of analyticity.[12] Moreover, this distinction between confirmational questions and prior and more fundamental conceptual or logical questions and, indeed, the whole notion of conceptual clarification through formalization is a project Carnap sees as wholly internal to science.

In a sense, Carnap is asking us to take the history of the sciences *more* seriously than is Quine. He is trying to provide a general framework for reflecting on and illuminating the very process of mathematization that drove fundamental changes in physical methodology in the period during which he was trained. This is a process internal to science that also intersected with certain formalistic tendencies coming out of a Kantian

---

12 I am not endorsing this controversial claim; I am simply indicating that, given his general philosophical framework, Carnap sees no way to make out any such distinctions without a commitment to formulating an analytic–synthetic distinction.

tradition that tied methodological issues to logical ones, via the notion of transcendental logic. The neo-Kantians felt they had the philosophical stance that rendered this methodological movement intelligible. Carnap took over and then radically revised this philosophical framework. Eventually, he enfolded it back into itself by turning the transcendental logic of objective knowledge into the formal project of the logical syntax of scientific language.

This movement within Carnap's thought arose, as we have stressed, from the inability of neo-Kantianism and his own earliest projects adequately to explicate its vocabulary of the objective and subjective, which provided the antecedent epistemological point of the project. Once Carnap sees how to get around this distinction, therefore, he could safely set aside any and all prior epistemological vocabularies and let logic have the central focus on its own. Carnap can, in this fashion, import the formal techniques of concept clarification from the exact sciences into philosophy itself. The project of logical syntax is thus a version of working from within the sciences: The sciences provide a repertoire of conceptual techniques that can be employed in logical syntax, and logical syntax in its turn can provide the general framework for the understanding of such techniques.

In this manner, also, he can finesse rather than engage in the foundational disputes in mathematics in the project of *Logical Syntax.* Carnap sees no philosophical question about mathematics antecedent to the specification of logical languages for various versions of mathematics. Mathematics is crucial, not as a locus of epistemological dispute, but as providing the most general frameworks from which to engage in concept clarification, whether in empirical science or in philosophy itself.[13]

This leaves us with one more important issue. Quine's naturalism derives from his rejection of the analytic–synthetic distinction. His understanding of the point of that distinction leads him to consider logical empiricism as the last best hope for a first philosophy above the sciences. This stance has been taken by many other naturalists since Quine, most explicitly and notably by Ronald Giere (1986, 1988) and Philip Kitcher (1991). Here is how Kitcher puts the point in his survey article on naturalism, "The Naturalists Return" (1991, pp. 54ff.):

Pre-Fregean philosophy was distinguished not only by its emphasis on problems of knowledge, but also by its willingness to draw on the ideas of the

---

13   Here I take a stand on a vexed issue of Carnap interpretation. For more along these lines, see Richardson (1994).

emerging sciences . . . There are many kinds of naturalism. But all share an opposition to the Frege–Wittgenstein conception of a pure philosophy above (or below?) the special disciplines . . . Frege's philosophical heirs may well find contemporary versions of naturalism in epistemology as shallow, scientistic, unphilosophical, and wrong-headed as Frege did. By the same token, naturalists might see the movement Frege inaugurated as an odd blip in the history of philosophy, a desertion of philosophy's proper tasks and proper roots.

I suggest a different response. Kitcher sees the dispute over naturalism as one over what counts as "philosophical." This is surely right; what is wrong is that the terms in which he casts the dispute are taken from within one of the camps. However much philosophy might be "pure" in the hands of someone such as Carnap, this does not mean that this philosophy, in the eyes of its practitioners, is more certain, enshrined "above the special sciences," or is some species of "first philosophy" in any historically recognizable sense of that term. Carnap is quite explicit about this at the end of *Logical Syntax* (p. 332):

He who wishes to investigate the questions of the logic of science must, therefore, renounce the proud claims of a philosophy that sits enthroned above the special sciences, and must realize that he is working in exactly the same field as the scientific specialist, only with a somewhat different emphasis.

Carnap is, of course, no naturalist. He is, however, a scientific philosopher who seeks a seamless whole consisting of science and a scientifically responsible philosophy. He offers no vision of a philosophy differing from science in the security of its foundations, the fixity of its theses, or the way in which it can be known. His vision is not any form of first philosophy. It is a vision that differs from Quine's not by enshrining philosophy *above* the sciences but in its description of how philosophy fits *within* the sciences. Carnap sees an important *a priori* role for mathematics in science in the methodological sense of the *a priori*. He also sees mathematics as comprising frameworks rich enough to express any genuinely philosophical question.

Analytic sentences of formal languages take over the role of the methodological synthetic *a priori* for Kant and the neo-Kantians: They present formal principles that give the conditions for the possibility of judgment for those languages. In adopting logical pluralism, Carnap finds the conceptual space within which he can fully explore the relativized synthetic *a priori*. Quine's holism seems at once to agree with Carnap's view that judgments cannot be justified individually – for Carnap, justification is both relative to the linguistic framework and holistic within it – but to disagree about whether there are particular types of principles that provide the identity conditions of the linguistic frameworks and thus the conditions for the justification of any such empirical judgment. To Carnap's mind, that falsifies the practice of formalization in science and, thus, it is a condition of any adequate philosophy of science that something like an analytic–synthetic distinction be found.

In this final section, I have argued that Carnap need not find Quine's rejection of the analytic–synthetic distinction compelling; Quine's notion of what is at stake in this distinction is fundamentally different from Carnap's. I have also argued that some of the ways that naturalism has been motivated against the background of the rejection of logical empiricism have misrepresented the point of departure of Carnap's work. In making these claims, I am not asserting that Carnap wins the analyticity debate or that naturalism is fundamentally misguided. The point I wish to make is at a farther remove from the two sides of the debate than that. What is of lasting importance in the analyticity debate and in the naturalist–formalist divide in analytic philosophy of science is this: These aspects of the history of analytic philosophy show how deeply visions of the "proper roots and proper tasks" of philosophy differ. A common interest in science, mathematics, and logic and a common desire to see philosophy participate in scientific methods can blind practitioners of different kinds of philosophical projects to their underlying philosophical differences.

Thus, telling the history of Carnap's early thought is, to my mind, less a "Back to Carnap!" or "Back to logical empiricism!" story than an opportunity to take stock of where we are and where we might be in contemporary analytic philosophy of science. Owing to renewed connections between philosophy of science and both the sciences and other humanistic approaches to the understanding of science (such as history and sociology of science), this is a period of great ferment and excitement. It is, in addition and correlatively, however, a period of considerable methodological confusion. Precisely what it is to have a philosophical perspective on science or what the nature of the epistemological question about science is is once again in doubt. A story of the origins of the "received view" of philosophy of science, of logical empiricism, is therefore a help for stocktaking here and now. It can illuminate various aspects of, in our case, Carnap's thinking that we no longer share and also some that we do share, if in altered or attenuated form. It can provide clues to paths taken and not taken. It can remind us of what

The point of the logic of science

was genuinely new and exciting in the technical projects, as well as of what was taken over from established philosophical traditions.

Thus, for example, it is not the case that the issues around the mathematization of science and philosophy have been fully played out and lead inevitably to naturalism. Similarly, the various connections that were or could be made among various conventionalisms (logical, methodological, metrical, semantic, social) remain topics of interest in post-Kuhnian philosophy of science and can be usefully considered from a historical point of view. I myself am less interested in how such issues are resolved – still less in their being resolved favorably to the perspective I have argued was Carnap's – than I am in making sure that we do not lose sight of them as *issues*.

Carnap urged his fellow philosophers to take up the project of the logic of science with these words (Syntax, p. 332):

Our thesis that the logic of science is syntax must therefore not be misunderstood to mean that the task of the logic of science could be carried out independently of empirical science and without regard to its empirical results ... All work in the logic of science, all philosophical work, is bound to be unproductive if it is not done in close co-operation with the special sciences.

This is a valuable lesson for philosophers of science, one urged with renewed vigor today. To it I should only like to add this final comment: The interpretation of all work in philosophy of science is bound to be unilluminating if it is not done with careful regard for the reason why its practitioners take it to be *philosophical* work. This holds for our own work as well as for that of others.

Bibliography

Allison, Henry. 1990. *Kant's Theory of Freedom*. Cambridge: Cambridge University Press.
Asprey, William and Kitcher, Philip (eds.). 1988. *Essays in History and Philosophy of Modern Mathematics*. Minneapolis: University of Minnesota Press.
Bauch, Bruno. 1911. *Studien zur Philosophie der exakten Wissenschaften*. Heidelberg: Carl Winter Verlag.
    1914. "Über den Begriff des Naturgesetzes." *Kant-Studien* 19: 303–37.
    1915. "Idealismus und Realismus in der Sphäre des philosophischen Kritizismus." *Kant-Studien* 20: 97–116.
    1917. *Immanuel Kant*. Berlin: G. J. Göschen'sche Verlagshandlung.
Beck, Lewis White. 1960. *A Commentary on Kant's "Critique of Practical Reason."* Chicago: University of Chicago Press.
Bell, David and Vossenkuhl, Wilhelm (eds.). 1992. *Science and Subjectivity*. Berlin: Akademie Verlag.
Bloor, David. 1974. "Popper's Mystification of Objective Knowledge." *Science Studies* 4: 65–76.
Buchdahl, Gerd. 1992. *Kant and the Dynamics of Reason*. Oxford: Blackwell.
Butts, Robert (ed.). 1986. *Kant's Philosophy of Physical Science*. Dordrecht: Reidel.
Carnap, Rudolf. 1922. *Der Raum. Ein Beitrag zur Wissenschaftslehre*. *Kant-Studien* Ergänzungsheft 56. Berlin: Reuther und Reichard. Translated by Michael Friedman and Peter Heath as "Space. A Contribution to the Theory of Science," unpublished.
    1923. "Über die Aufgabe der Physik und die Anwendung des Grundsatzes der Einfachstheit." *Kant-Studien* 28: 90–107.
    1924. "Dreidimensionalität des Raumes und Kausalität." *Annalen der Philosophie und philosophische Kritik* 4: 105–30.
    1925. "Über die Abhängigkeit der Eigenschaften des Raumes von denen der Zeit." *Kant-Studien* 30: 331–45.
    1926. *Physikalische Begriffsbildung*. Karlsruhe: Braun.
    1927 "Eigentliche und uneigentliche Begriffe." *Symposion* 1: 355–74.

Bibliography

1928a. *Der logische Aufbau der Welt*. Berlin: Weltkreis. 2nd ed. Hamburg: Felix Meiner Verlag, 1961. Translated by Rolf George as *The Logical Structure of the World*. Berkeley and Los Angeles: University of California Press, 1967.

1928b. *Scheinprobleme in der Philosophie*. Berlin: Weltkreis. Translated by Rolf George as *Pseudoproblems in Philosophy*. Berkeley and Los Angeles: University of California Press, 1967.

1929. *Abriss der Logistik*. Vienna: Springer Verlag.

1932a. "Überwindung der Metaphysik durch logische Analyse der Sprache." *Erkenntnis* 2: 219–41. Translated by Arthur Pap as "The Elimination of Metaphysics through Logical Analysis of Language." In A. J. Ayer (ed.), *Logical Positivism*. New York: Free Press, 1959, 60–81.

1932b. "Die physikalische Sprache als Universalsprache der Wissenschaft." *Erkenntnis* 2: 432–65. Rev. ed. translated by Max Black as *The Unity of Science*. London: Kegan, Paul, Trench Teubner, 1934.

1932c. "Erwiderung auf die vorstehenden Aufsätze von E. Zilsel und K. Duncker." *Erkenntnis* 3: 177–88.

1932d. "Über Protokollsätze." *Erkenntnis* 3: 215–28. Translated by Richard Creath and Richard Nollan as "On Protocol Sentences." *Noûs* 21 (1987): 457–70.

1934a. *Die logische Syntax der Sprache*. Vienna: Springer Verlag, 1934. Rev. ed. translated by Amethe Smeaton as *The Logical Syntax of Language*. London: Kegan, Paul, Trench Teubner, 1937.

1934b. *Die Aufgabe der Wissenschaftslogik*. Vienna: Gerold. Translated by H. Kraal as "The Task of the Logic of Science." In Brian McGuinness (ed.), *The Unity of Science*. Dordrecht: Reidel, 1987, 46–66.

1936. "Von Erkenntnistheorie zur Wissenschaftslogik." *Actes du 8e Congrès International de Philosophie Scientifique*, vol. 1. Paris: Hermann, 1936, 36–41.

1936–7. "Testability and Meaning." *Philosophy of Science* 3: 419–71; 4: 1–40.

1963a. "Intellectual Autobiography." In P. Schilpp (1963), 3–84.

1963b. "Replies and Systematic Expositions." In P. Schilpp (1963), 859–1016.

1991. ["Quine on Analyticity."] In R. Creath (ed.), 1991a, 427–32.

Cartwright, Nancy and Cat, Jordi. 1996. "Neurath against Method." In R. Giere and A. Richardson (eds.), 1996, 80–90.

Cassirer, Ernst. 1907. "Kant und die moderne Mathematik." *Kant-Studien* 12: 1–49.

1910. *Substanzbegriff und Funktionsbegriff*. Berlin: B. Cassirer. 2nd unrevised German ed., 1923. Translated by W. C. Swabey and M. C. Swabey as *Substance and Function*. New York: Dover, 1953.

1921. *Zur einstein'schen Relativitätstheorie*. Berlin: B. Cassirer. Translated by W. C. Swabey and M. C. Swabey as *On Einstein's Theory of Relativity*. New York: Dover, 1953.

Coffa, J. Alberto. 1991. *The Semantic Tradition from Kant to Carnap*. Cambridge: Cambridge University Press.

Creath, Richard. 1987. "Some Remarks on 'Protocol Sentences.'" *Noûs* 21: 471–5.
  1991a. *Dear Carnap, Dear Van: The Quine–Carnap Correspondence and Related Work.* Berkeley and Los Angeles: University of California Press.
  1991b. "The Unimportance of Semantics." In A. Fine, M. Forbes, and L. Wessels (eds.), *Proceedings of the Philosophy of Science Association Meetings 1990,* vol. 2. East Lansing, MI: Philosophy of Science Association, 405–16.
  1996. "Languages without Logic." In R. Giere and A. Richardson (eds.), 1996, 251–65.
Daston, Lorraine. 1992. "Objectivity and the Escape from Perspective." *Social Studies of Science* 22: 597–618.
Daston, Lorraine and Galison, Peter. 1992. "The Image of Objectivity." *Representations* 40: 81–128.
Dear, Peter. 1992. "From Truth to Disinterestedness in the Seventeenth Century." *Social Studies of Science* 22: 619–31.
Demopoulos, William. 1995. "Frege and the Rigorization of Analysis." In W. Demopoulos (ed.), *Frege's Philosophy of Mathematics.* Cambridge, MA: Harvard University Press, 68–88.
Devidi, David and Solomon, Graham. 1995. "Tolerance and Metalanguages in Carnap's *Logical Syntax of Language.*" *Synthese* 103: 123–39.
Flach, Werner and Ollig, Hans-Ludwig (eds.). 1979–80. *Erkenntnistheorie und Logik in Neukantianismus.* Hildesheim: Gerstenberg.
Folina, Janet. 1992. *Poincaré's Philosophy of Mathematics.* Stirling, UK: MacMillan.
  1995. "Poincaré on Mathematics, Intuition and the Foundations of Science." In D. Hull, M. Forbes, and R. Burian (eds.), *Proceedings of the Philosophy of Science Association Meetings 1994,* vol. 2. East Lansing, MI: Philosophy of Science Association, 217–26.
Frege, Gottlob. 1977 [1918]. "The Thought." English translation by Peter Geach, in P. Geach (ed.), *Frege: Logical Investigations.* New Haven: Yale University Press.
Friedman, Michael. 1983a. *Foundations of Space-Time Theories.* Princeton: Princeton University Press.
  1983b. "Critical Notice: Moritz Schlick, *Philosophical Papers.*" *Philosophy of Science* 50: 498–514.
  1987. "Carnap's *Aufbau* Reconsidered." *Noûs* 21: 521–45.
  1988. "Logical Truth and Analyticity in *Logical Syntax of Language.*" In W. Asprey and P. Kitcher (eds.), 1988, 82–94.
  1991. "The Re-Appraisal of Logical Empiricism." *Journal of Philosophy* 88: 505–19.
  1992a. "Epistemology in the *Aufbau.*" *Synthese* 93: 15–57.
  1992b. "Carnap and A Priori Truth." In D. Bell and W. Vossenkuhl (eds.), 1992, 47–60.
  1993. *Kant and the Exact Sciences.* Cambridge, MA: Harvard University Press.

1994. "Geometry, Convention, and the Relativized A Priori." In W. Salmon and G. Wolters (1994), 21–34.

1995. "Poincaré's Conventionalism and the Logical Positivists." In J-L. Greffe, G. Heinzmann, and Kuno Lorentz (eds.), *Henri Poincaré: Science and Philosophy*. Berlin: Akademie Verlag.

1996. "Overcoming Metaphysics: Carnap and Heidegger." In R. Giere and A. Richardson (eds.), 1996, 45–79.

Galison, Peter. 1990. "Aufbau/Bauhaus: Logical Positivism and Architectural Modernism." *Critical Inquiry* 16: 709–52.

1996. "Constructing Modernism: The Cultural Location of *Aufbau*." In R. Giere and A. Richardson (eds.), 1996, 17–44.

Giere, Ronald. 1986. "Philosophy of Science Naturalized." *Philosophy of Science* 52: 331–56.

1988. *Explaining Science*. Chicago: University of Chicago Press.

Giere, Ronald and Richardson, Alan (eds.). 1996. *Origins of Logical Empiricism*. Minneapolis: University of Minnesota Press.

Goldfarb, Warren. 1988. "Poincaré against the Logicists." In W. Asprey and P. Kitcher (eds.), 1988, 61–81.

1996. "The Philosophy of Mathematics in Early Positivism." In R. Giere and A. Richardson (eds.), 1996, 213–30.

Goldfarb, Warren and Ricketts, Thomas. 1992. "Carnap and the Philosophy of Mathematics." In D. Bell and W. Vossenkuhl (eds.), 1992, 61–78.

Goodman, Nelson. 1953. *The Structure of Appearance*. Cambridge, MA: Harvard University Press. 3rd ed. Dordrecht: Reidel, 1978.

1963. "The Significance of *Der logische Aufbau der Welt*." In P. Schilpp (1963), 545–58.

Griffin, Nicholas. 1991. *Russell's Idealist Apprenticeship*. Oxford: Oxford University Press.

Haack, Susan. 1977. "Carnap's *Aufbau*: Some Kantian Reflexions." *Ratio* 19: 170–6.

Haller, Rudolf (ed.). 1982. *Schlick und Neurath – ein Symposion. Grazer Philosophische Studien* 16–17.

Haller, Rudolf and Stadler, Friedrich (eds.). 1993. *Wien–Berlin–Prag: Der Aufstieg der wissenschaftlichen Philosophie*. Vienna: Hölder–Pichler–Tempsky Verlag.

Hamilton, Andy. 1990. "Ernst Mach and the Elimination of Subjectivity." *Ratio*, n.s. 3: 117–35.

1992. "Carnap's *Aufbau* and the Legacy of Neutral Monism." In D. Bell and W. Vossenkuhl (eds.), 1992, 131–52.

Hart, W. D. 1992. "Frege and Carnap on Structure, Logic and Objectivity." In D. Bell and W. Vossenkuhl (eds.), 1992, 169–84.

Hilbert, David. [1899] 1971. *Grundlagen der Geometrie*. Tenth edition, translated by Leo Unger as *Foundations of Geometry*. LaSalle, IL: Open Court.

Bibliography

Howard, Don. 1994. "Einstein, Kant, and the Origins of Logical Empiricism." In W. Salmon and G. Wolters (1994), 45–105.

　　1996. "Relativity, *Eindeutigkeit*, and Monomorphism: Rudolf Carnap and the Development of the Categoricity Concept in Formal Semantics." In R. Giere and A. Richardson (eds.), 1996, 115–64.

Hudson, Rob. 1994. "Empirical Constraints in the *Aufbau*." *History of Philosophy Quarterly* 11: 237–51.

Husserl, Edmund. 1976 [1913]. *Ideen zu einer reinen Phänomenologie und phänomenologischen Philosophie. Husserliana*, vol. 3. Edited by Walter Biemel. The Hague: Martinus Nijhoff.

　　1954. *Die Krisis der europäischen Wissenschaften und die transzendentale Phänomenologie. Husserliana*, vol. 6. Edited by Walter Biemel. The Hague: Martinus Nijhoff.

Hylton, Peter. 1990. *Russell, Idealism and the Emergence of Analytic Philosophy*. Oxford: Oxford University Press.

Isaacson, Daniel. 1992. "Carnap, Quine and Logical Truth." In D. Bell and W. Vossenkuhl (eds.), 1992, 100–30.

Kant, Immanuel. 1965 [1781/1787]. *Critique of Pure Reason*. Translation by W. Kemp Smith. New York: St. Martin's.

　　1985 [1786]. *Metaphysical Foundations of Natural Science*. Translation by J. Ellington. In *Kant: Philosophy of Material Nature*. Indianapolis: Hackett.

Kitcher, Philip. 1986. "Projecting the Order of Nature." In R. Butts (1986), 201–35.

　　1991. "The Naturalists Return." *Philosophical Review* 100: 53–114.

Kleinknecht, Reinhard. 1980. "Quasianalyse und Qualitätsklassen." *Grazer Philosophische Studien* 11: 23–43.

Köhnke, Klaus. 1986. *Entstehung und Aufstieg der Neukantianismus*. Frankfurt: Suhrkamp Verlag. Translated by R. J. Hollingdale as *The Rise of Neo-Kantianism*. Cambridge: Cambridge University Press, 1989.

Lewis, David. 1969. "Policing the *Aufbau*." *Philosophical Studies* 20: 13–7.

Lewis, Joia. 1991. "Hidden Agendas: Knowledge and Verification." In A. Fine, M. Forbes, and L. Wessels (eds.), *Proceedings of the Philosophy of Science Association Meetings 1990*, vol. 2. East Lansing, MI: Philosophy of Science Association, 159–68.

Longino, Helen. 1990. *Science as Social Knowledge*. Princeton: Princeton University Press.

Mayer, Verena. 1992. "Carnap und Husserl." In D. Bell and W. Vossenkuhl (eds.), 1992, 185–201.

Mormann, Thomas. 1994. "A Representational Reconstruction of Carnap's Quasianalysis." In D. Hull, M. Forbes, and R. Burian (eds.), *Proceedings of the Philosophy of Science Association Meetings 1994*, vol. 1. East Lansing, MI: Philosophy of Science Association, 96–104.

Moulines, C. Ulises. 1985. "Hintergründe der Erkenntnistheorie des frühen Carnap." *Grazer Philosophische Studien* 23: 1–18.

1991. "Making Sense of Carnap's *Aufbau.*" *Erkenntnis* 35: 263–86.
Nagel, Thomas. 1979. "Objective and Subjective." In his *View from Nowhere.* Oxford: Oxford University Press.
Natorp, Paul. 1910a. *Die logischen Grundlagen der exakten Wissenschaften.* Leipzig: Teubner.
  1910b. *Logik in Leitsätzen zu akad. Vorlesungen.* 2nd ed. Marburg: Elwert.
Neurath, Otto. 1932. "Protokollsätze." *Erkenntnis* 3: 204–14.
Neurath, Otto, Hans Hahn, and Rudolf Carnap. 1929. *Wissenschaftliche Weltauffassung: Der Wiener Kreis.* Vienna: Wolf.
Oberdan, Thomas. 1990. "Positivism and the Theory of Observation." In A. Fine, M. Forbes, and L. Wessels (eds.), *Proceedings of the Philosophy of Science Association Meetings 1990,* vol. 1. East Lansing, MI: Philosophy of Science Association, 25–37.
  1993. *Protocols, Truth, Convention.* Amsterdam: Rodopi.
  1996. "Postscript to Protocols: Reflections on Empiricism." In R. Giere and A. Richardson (eds.), 1996, 269–91.
Ollig, Hans-Ludwig (ed.). 1982. *Neukantianismus. Texte der Marburger und die südwestdeutschen Schule, ihrer Vorläufer und Kritiker.* Stuttgart: Reclam.
  1987. *Materialien zur Neukantianismus-Diskussion.* Darmstadt: Wissenschaftliche Buchgesellschaft.
Poincaré, Henri. 1952 [1902]. *Science et Hypothese.* Translated by W. J. Greenstreet as *Science and Hypothesis.* New York: Dover.
Popper, Karl. 1972. *Objective Knowledge.* Oxford: Oxford University Press.
Porter, Theodore. 1992. "Quantification and the Accounting Ideal in Science." *Social Studies of Science* 22: 633–52.
Proust, Joelle. 1989 [1986]. *Questione de Forme.* Translated by A. A. Brenner as *Questions of Form: Logic and the Analytic Proposition from Kant to Carnap.* Minneapolis: University of Minnesota Press.
Putnam, Hilary. 1981. *Reason, Truth and History.* Cambridge: Cambridge University Press.
  1983. "Philosophy and Human Understanding." In his *Philosophical Papers,* vol. 3. Cambridge: Cambridge University Press, 184–204.
  1990. "Objectivity and the Science/Ethics Distinction." In his *Realism with a Human Face.* Cambridge, MA: Harvard University Press, 163–78.
Quine, Willard van Orman. 1961 [1953]. "Two Dogmas of Empiricism." In his *From a Logical Point of View.* Cambridge, MA: Harvard University Press, 20–46.
  1963. "Carnap and Logical Truth." In Schilpp (1963), 385–406.
  1969. "Epistemology Naturalized." In his *Ontological Relativity and Other Essays.* New York: Columbia University Press, 69–90.
  1976. "Homage to Carnap." In his *Ways of Paradox.* 2nd, enlarged ed. Cambridge, MA: Harvard University Press, 40–3.
  1981. "Five Milestones of Empiricism." In his *Theories and Things.* Cambridge, MA: Harvard University Press, 67–72.

Bibliography

1993. "In Praise of Observation Sentences." *Journal of Philosophy* 90: 107–16.
Reichenbach, Hans. 1920. *Die Relativitätstheorie und Erkenntnis A Priori.* Berlin: Springer Verlag.
    1928. *Die Philosophie der Raum-Zeit-Lehre.* Berlin: Springer Verlag.
Rescher, Nicholas (ed.). 1985. *The Heritage of Logical Positivism.* Lanham, MD: University Press of America.
Richardson, Alan. 1990. "How not to Russell Carnap's *Aufbau.*" In A. Fine, M. Forbes, and L. Wessels (eds.), *Proceedings of the Philosophy of Science Association Meetings 1990,* vol. 1. East Lansing, MI: Philosophy of Science Association, 3–14.
    1992a. "Logical Idealism and Carnap's Construction of the World." *Synthese* 93: 59–92.
    1992b. "Metaphysics and Idealism in the *Aufbau.*" *Grazer Philosophische Studien* 43: 45–72.
    1994. "The Limits of Tolerance: Carnap's Logico-Philosophical Project in *Logical Syntax of Language.*" *Proceedings of the Aristotelian Society,* supplementary volume, 67–82.
    1996. "From Epistemology to the Logic of Science: Carnap's Philosophy of Empirical Knowledge in the 1930s." In R. Giere and A. Richardson (eds.), 1996, 309–32.
Rickert, Hans. 1986 [1929]. *Die Grenzen der naturwissenschaftlichen Begriffsbildung.* 5th, rev. ed. Edited and translated by Guy Oakes as *The Limits of Concept Formation in Natural Science.* Cambridge: Cambridge University Press.
Ricketts, Thomas. 1982. "Rationality, Translation, and Epistemology Naturalized." *Journal of Philosophy* 79: 117–36.
    1985. "Frege, the *Tractatus,* and the Logocentric Predicament." *Noûs* 19: 3–15.
    1986. "Objectivity and Objecthood: Frege's Metaphysics of Judgment." In L. Haaparanta and J. Hintikka (eds.), *Frege Synthesized.* Dordrecht: Reidel, 65–95.
    1994. "Carnap's Principle of Tolerance, Empiricism and Conventionalism." In P. Clark and B. Hale (eds.), *Reading Putnam.* Oxford: Blackwell, 176–200.
    1996. "Carnap: From Logical Syntax to Semantics." In R. Giere and A. Richardson (eds.), 1996, 231–50.
Runggaldier, Edmund. 1984. *Carnap's Early Conventionalism: An Inquiry into the Background of the Vienna Circle.* Amsterdam: Rodopi.
Russell, Bertrand. 1900. *Leibniz.* London: Allen and Unwin.
    1903. *The Principles of Mathematics.* Cambridge: Cambridge University Press.
    1914. *Our Knowledge of the External World.* London: Allen and Unwin.
    1919. *Introduction to Mathematical Philosophy.* London: Allen and Unwin.
    1959 [1912]. *Problems of Philosophy.* Oxford: Oxford University Press.
    1973 [1905]. "On Denoting." In D. Lackey (ed.), *Essays in Analysis.* New York: Braziller, 103–19.

1981a [1917]. *Mysticism and Logic.* Totowa, NJ: Barnes and Noble Books.
1981b [1911]. "Knowledge by Acquaintance and Knowledge by Description." In Russell (1981a), 152–67.
1981c [1901]. "Mathematics and the Metaphysicians." In Russell (1981a), 59–74.
1981d [1914]. "On Scientific Method in Philosophy." In Russell (1981a), 75–93.
1981e [1914]. "The Relation of Sense-Data to Physics." In Russell (1981a), 108–31.
1981f [1915]. "The Ultimate Constituents of Matter." In Russell (1981a), 94–107.
1984 [1913]. *The Theory of Knowledge.* Vol. 7 of *The Collected Papers of Bertrand Russell.* London: Allen and Unwin.
Ryckman, Thomas A. 1991. "*Conditio sine qua non?* Zuordnungen in the Early Epistemologies of Cassirer and Schlick." *Synthese* 88: 57–95.
  1992. "P(oint)-C(oincidence) Thinking: The Ironical Attachment of Logical Empiricism to General Relativity and Some Lingering Consequences." *Studies in the History and Philosophy of Science* 23: 471–93.
  1996. "The Einstein *Agonists:* Weyl and Reichenbach on Geometry and GTR." In R. Giere and A. Richardson (eds.), 1996, 165–209.
Salmon, Wesley and Wolters, Gereon. 1994. *Logic, Language, and the Structure of Scientific Theories.* Pittsburgh: University of Pittsburgh Press.
Sarkar, Sahotra. 1992. "'The Boundless Ocean of Unlimited Possibilities': Logic in Carnap's *Logical Syntax of Language.*" *Synthese* 93: 191–237.
Sauer, Werner. 1985. "Carnap's *Aufbau* in kantianischer Sicht." *Grazer Philosophische Studien* 23: 19–35.
  1989. "On the Kantian Background of Neopositivism." *Topoi* 8: 111–19.
  1993. "Über das Verhältnis des *Aufbau* zu Russells Aussenwelt-Programm." In R. Haller and F. Stadler (eds.), 1993, 98–119.
Schilpp, Paul A. 1963. *The Philosophy of Rudolf Carnap.* LaSalle, IL: Open Court.
Schlick, Moritz. 1920. *Raum und Zeit in der gegenwärtigen Physik.* 3rd ed. Berlin: Springer Verlag.
  1925. *Allgemeine Erkenntnislehre.* 2nd, rev ed. Berlin: Springer Verlag. Translated by A. Blumberg as *General Theory of Knowledge.* LaSalle, IL: Open Court, 1974.
  1934. "Über das Fundament der Erkenntnis." *Erkenntnis* 4: 79–99.
Schnädelbach, Herbert. 1983. *Philosophie in Deutschland, 1831–1933.* Frankfurt: Suhrkamp. Translated by Eric Matthews as *Philosophy in Germany, 1831–1933.* Cambridge: Cambridge University Press, 1984.
Sklar, Lawrence. 1973. *Space, Time, and Space-Time.* Berkeley and Los Angeles: University of California Press.
Solomon, Miriam. 1989. "Quine's Point of View." *Journal of Philosophy* 86: 113–36.
Stadler, Friedrich (ed.). 1993. *Scientific Philosophy: Origins and Developments.* Dordrecht: Kluwer.

Turner, Joia Lewis. 1996. "Conceptual Knowledge and Intuitive Experience: Schlick's Dilemma." In R. Giere and A. Richardson (eds.), 1996, 292–308.
Uebel, Thomas. 1992a. "Neurath vs. Carnap: Naturalism vs. Rational Reconstructionism before Quine." *History of Philosophy Quarterly* 9: 445–470.
  1992b. *Overcoming Logical Positivism from Within*. Amsterdam: Rodopi.
  1992c. "Rational Reconstruction as Elucidation? Carnap in the Early Protocol Sentence Debate." *Synthese* 93: 107–40.
  1996. "Conventions in the *Aufbau*." *British Journal for the History of Philosophy* 4: 381–97.
Uebel, Thomas (ed.). 1991. *Rediscovering the Forgotten Vienna Circle*. Dordrecht: Kluwer.
Ward, James. 1927 [1890]. "The Progress of Philosophy" In his *Essays in Philosophy*. Cambridge: Cambridge University Press, 112–40.
Whitehead, Alfred North and Russell, Bertrand. 1910. *Principia Mathematica*. Cambridge: Cambridge University Press. 2nd rev. ed. 1925.
Williams, Bernard. 1985. *Ethics and the Limits of Philosophy*. Cambridge: Cambridge University Press.
Wittgenstein, Ludwig. 1961 [1921]. *Tractatus Logico-Philosophicus*. Translated by D. F. Pears and B. F. McGuinness. London: Routledge and Kegan Paul.
Wood, Allen. 1970. *Kant's Moral Religion*. Ithaca, NY: Cornell University Press.
Zeller, Eduard. 1862. "Über Bedeutung und Aufgabe der Erkenntniss-Theorie." Heidelberg: K. Groos.
Zhai, Zang. 1990. "The Problem of Protocol Statements and Schlick's Concept of '*Konstatierungen*.'" In A. Fine, M. Forbes, and L. Wessels. (eds.), *Proceedings of the Philosophy of Science Association Meetings 1990*, vol. 1. East Lansing, MI: Philosophy of Science Association, 15–23.
Zilsel, Edgar. 1932. "Bemerkungen zur Wissenschaftslogik." *Erkenntnis* 3: 143–161.

Index

Allison, Henry, 97
analyticity
   Carnap–Quine dispute, 218–24
   need for, in Carnap's epistemology, 194, 225
   relations to methodological sense of the synthetic *a priori*, 143, 196, 225–8
antireductionism
   in Carnap's pre-*Aufbau* writings, 161, 163–4, 172, 180–1
   in constitution of the world of physics, 74–6, 89–90
autopsychological realm, 9, 34, 65–70, 187, 189
Avenarius, Richard, 22

Bauch, Bruno, 116–17, 123, 137
Beck, Lewis White, 97
Bloor, David, 4, 219
Buchdahl, Gerd, 96, 97

Cantor, Georg, 119
Cassirer, Ernst, 2, 4, 38–40, 90, 142, 147–8, 152, 170, 173–4, 186
   functional account of concepts, 117–19, 174
   logic of objective knowledge, 120–1, 124, 147
   rejection of logicism, 119–21, 144
   see also logic as essence of philosophy; neo-Kantianism
Clark, Peter, 194
Coffa, J. Alberto, 28, 108, 117, 132, 214
Cohen, Hermann, 2, 117
concepts
   formal and empirical, 43, 46
   proper and improper, 43–7
   see also definition; intuition
confirmation, 214, 216, 224
   see also verification
constitution, 6

constitutional analogy, 83–4
constitutional system, 6–10
   empirical and analytic theorems, 66
   with physical basis, 24, 173
convention, 229
   and axiom of simplicity, 151–2, 160, 164–6
   in constitution of the world of physics, 75–6
   and geometry, 106, 124–7, 145–52
   in introduction of quantitative concepts, 175–80
   and neo-Kantianism, 127–34
   see also logical truth
Couturat, Louis, 119
Creath, Richard, 208, 212, 214, 218

Daston, Lorraine, 4, 31
Dear, Peter, 31
Dedekind, Richard, 118–19
definition
   constitutional, 7, 40–7, 72–3, 182
   implicit, 7, 40–7, 144–5
Demopoulos, William, 112
determinism, 162, 164, 171
Dingler, Hugo, 116, 151, 159–60, 165
Driesch, Hans, 22, 117
Dubislav, Walter, 22

Einstein, Albert, 125, 131
empiricism, 20, 180–1, 207
   Carnap's account of in 1930s, 213–17
   and geometry, 99–100, 129
   as received view of the *Aufbau*, 10–3, 22–4, 28
epistemology
   in the *Aufbau*, 9, 22–4, 180–2
   Carnap's rejection of, 204–5, 207–8
   naturalized, 203, 219, 226–8
   relations to logic, 20, 181–2, 191–6, 203–4, 208–13, 221–4
   relations to psychology, 35, 187–92,

Index

201, 204, 212–13, 215–16
experience
  first- and second-level, 167–72
  matters of fact, 114, 132–3, 135–6, 146, 149–51, 217
  structure of, 204–5, 212–13
  subjectivity of, 32–5, 187–91
expression relation, 76–9

Folina, Janet, 105
form
  necessary and optional, 136, 146–53, 160–4, 167, 175
  relation to mind, 136–8, 180–1
  topological and metrical, 136–7, 177–80
  see also logic; objectivity
formal and material modes of speech, 198–9, 204
Frege, Gottlob, 14, 18, 78, 120, 136, 193–4, 195
Friedman, Michael, 2, 6, 47, 88, 94, 96, 97, 103, 106, 117, 124, 125, 126, 132, 137, 208

Galison, Peter, 4, 31
geometry, 124–9
  Euclidean, 93, 95–7, 102–3, 110–11, 151
  metrical, 141, 145–52, 154–5
  non-Euclidean, 97–8, 99, 110–11
  topological, 141, 143, 146, 173–5
George, Rolf, 6, 65
Giere, Ronald, 226
Gödel, Kurt, 221
Goldfarb, Warren, 15, 16, 105, 208
Goodman, Nelson, 5, 51, 65, 69
  objections to quasi analysis, 59–64
Griffin, Nicholas, 14

Haack, Susan, 2
Hahn, Hans, 10
Hamilton, Sir Andy, 34
Hart, W. D., 88
Hegelian philosophy, 99
Heidegger, Martin, 4
Hellman, Geoffrey, 137
heteropsychological realm, 9, 23, 76–82, 83
Hilbert, David, 40–1, 144, 177
  see also definition
Hönigswald, Richard, 117
Howard, Don, 126
Hudson, Rob, 2–3
Hume, David, 94
Husserl, Edmund, 4, 105, 117, 153–4, 170
Hylton, Peter, 14, 15, 16, 18, 20

intersubjective correspondence, 84–6
intersubjective world, constitution of, 76–86, 185–6, 187–92
intersubjectivity, 29–30, 89, 186–7, 202–3
intuition
  and concepts in Kant, 94, 103
  and geometry, 102–3, 111–12
  rejection by neo-Kantians, 118–21
  roles in Carnap's *Der Raum*, 141, 153–7, 170–1, 179–80
Isaacson, Daniel, 217, 218

Kant, Immanuel
  refutation of idealism, 94, 110, 133, 134–5
  transcendental philosophy, 93–7, 105, 108
  see also intuition; logic; neo-Kantianism; synthetic *a priori* judgments
Kitcher, Philip, 94, 226–7
Kleinknecht, Reinhard, 51
Köhnke, Klaus, 2

Lewis, David, 5, 51
Liebmann, Otto, 117
logic
  Aristotelian, 38, 94, 102–3, 119
  modern, 14–17, 102–3, 112, 119, 173–5
  transcendental, 117, 121, 137–8, 147
  see also form; objectivity
logic as essence of philosophy
  in Carnap, 24–8, 138, 191–6, 220, 223
  in Cassirer, 122–3, 137
  in Russell, 16
logic of science, 205–6, 225–8
  see also logical empiricism; logical syntax
logical empiricism, 28, 197–8, 208–17
logical syntax, 208–10
  see also metalogic
logical truth, 7, 174–5, 193–6
  and convention, 7, 184–5, 193, 196
  see also analyticity
logicism, 14–6, 36–7, 43, 51–2, 140, 143–5
  and physical world, 166, 176, 179–80
Longino, Helen, 4, 219

Mach, Ernst, 22, 117, 126–7
metalogic, 194–8
metaphysics
  elimination of, 8, 26–8, 166–7, 181, 191–2, 200–1
  see also ontology
methodological solipsism, 33–4
Moore, G. E., 13
Mormann, Thomas, 51, 59

240

Index

"my body"
 as intersubjective object, 84–5, 189
 as visual(-tactile) object, 73

Nagel, Thomas, 4, 31
Natorp, Paul, 2, 116–17, 121–2, 132, 137, 142
neo-Kantianism, 22, 29, 37, 90, 92, 110–11, 141–2, 144, 168–70, 180–1
 disagreement with empiricism, 40, 132–3
 and transcendental philosophy, 134
Neurath, Otto, 4, 5, 10, 211–12

Oberdan, Thomas, 40, 212, 214
object, 6, 38
objectivity
 and communicability, 85, 186–7
 for neo-Kantians, 123
 as structure, 22–4, 29–30, 32, 114–15
 see also form; intersubjectivity; logic; physics
ontology
 relation to logic, 122
 relation to reduction, 19–20, 25–6

Peano, Giuseppe, 14
Petzoldt, Josef, 117
phenomenology, 140, 155–6, 170
 see also Husserl; intuition
physicalist language, 199
 relations to protocol language, 200–3
physics
 constitution of the world of, 70–6, 79, 82
 Newtonian, 93–7, 98, 100, 106–8, 113
 as preeminently objective science, 35–6, 76, 167–72, 176–81
 quantitative concepts in, 161, 175–80
 relativistic, 98, 111–12, 116, 125–6, 131
 role in constitution of intersubjective world, 85–6
Poincaré, Henri, 105–6, 124–7, 129, 131, 133, 135, 151, 159–60, 165
 see also convention; geometry
Popper, Sir Karl, 4
Porter, Theodore, 31
principle of tolerance, 209–10
protocol language, 199, 210–12
 as subjective, 200
Proust, Joëlle, 51, 59
psychology
 Gestalt, 9, 34–5, 63, 188, 201
 relations to logic, 122
 see also epistemology; experience

purely structural definite descriptions, 29–30, 47–51, 87–90, 181–2
Putnam, Hillary, 4, 5, 13, 31, 217

quasi analysis
 and analysis, 51–3
 on basis of part identity relation, 53–7
 on basis of part similarity relation, 57–9
 and synthesis, 53
 use in constitutional system, 66–7
 see also Goodman
Quine, W. V., 5, 10–13, 19, 21, 72–3, 91, 204, 218–28
 see also analyticity

recollection of similarity (Rs), 9, 32–3, 65–6, 70, 190
 elimination of, 87–9, 193–4
Rehmke, Johannes, 168
Reichenbach, Hans, 131–2, 152
Richardson, Alan, 28, 192, 226
Rickert, Heinrich, 2, 37–41, 90, 117, 137
Ricketts, Thomas, 78, 195, 208, 214, 217, 218
Riehl, Alois, 117
Riemann, Bernhard, 119
Runggaldier, Edmund, 139, 185
Russell, Bertrand, 120–1, 128–9, 136, 159, 193–4
 acquaintance, principle of, 18–21
 external world program, 11, 71
 formal and philosophical logic, 14–16
 Principia Mathematica, 7, 11–12, 15, 43, 140, 143, 193–5, 208–9
 theory of descriptions, 17–19
Ryckman, Thomas, 126

Sarkar, Sahotra, 208
Sauer, Werner, 2, 121
Schlick, Moritz, 40–3, 132, 213
Schnädelbach, Herbert, 2
sign production, 77–82
Sklar, Lawrence, 124
Solomon, Graham, 208
Solomon, Miriam, 218
space
 formal, 140–5
 intuitive, 140–2, 153–8
 physical, 140–1, 145–53
 see also geometry; physics; space-time
space-time
 as logico-mathematical object, 71, 74
 as physical manifold, 71–4
subjectivity, *see* experience; objectivity; protocol language

Index

synthetic *a priori* judgments
  account of, in Carnap's *Der Raum*, 141–3, 148
  extent and role within Kantian philosophy, 93–7
  methodological role of, 100, 106–8, 108–10, 112–14, 120, 162, 204, 227 (*see also* analyticity)
  nominal definition of, 101–3, 108–10, 110–12
  relativized, 114–15, 130–8, 152–3, 157, 159, 162, 196
  semantic account of, 104, 108–10, 112 (*see also* concepts; intuition)
  universal, 114–15, 130–8, 147–8, 157

Tarski, Alfred, 221
Turner, Joia Lewis, 40, 212

Uebel, Thomas, 3, 212
unity of science, 8, 183–7

Vaihinger, Hans, 117, 167
verification, 199–200, 223–4
  see also confirmation
visual sense
  constitution of, 68
  five dimensionality of, 67, 87

Ward, James, 99
Whitehead, Alfred North, 13–14
  see also Russell
Williams, Bernard, 4
Windelband, Wilhelm, 2
Wittgenstein, Ludwig, 7, 195
Wood, Allen, 97

Zeller, Eduard, 99
Zhai, Zang, 212
Ziehen, Theodor, 22, 117, 168
Zilsel, Edgar, 213